Reclaiming Klytemnestra

Reclaiming Klytemnestra

Revenge or Reconciliation

KATHLEEN L. KOMAR

University of Illinois Press

URBANA AND CHICAGO

© 2003 by the Board of Trustees
of the University of Illinois
All rights reserved
Manufactured in the United States of America
C 5 4 3 2 1

∞ This book is printed on acid-free paper.

Library of Congress Cataloging-in-Publication Data
Komar, Kathleen L.
Reclaiming Klytemnestra : revenge or reconciliation /
Kathleen L. Komar.
p.   cm.
Includes bibliographical references (p.) and index.
ISBN 0-252-02811-2 (cloth : alk. paper)
1. Clytemnestra (Greek mythology) in literature.
2. Literature, Modern—20th century—History and
criticism. 3. Literature—Women authors—History
and criticism. 4. Women murderers in literature.
5. Adultery in literature. 6. Revenge in literature.
I. Title.
PN57.C57K66   2003
809'.93351—dc21   2002011211

To Ross
and the many other feminists
who encouraged me to complete this project

Contents

Preface

Mother and mariticide, Klytemnestra is an irresistibly fascinating character whose actions haunt the founding of Western culture. This study began, however, with my work in German literature and Christa Wolf's *Kassandra*. I had long been interested in the relationship between classical texts and modern women's writing exemplified in books such as Wolf's. After team-teaching a course on archetypal patterns with Katherine Callen King, a scholar of classics and comparative literature, I was inspired to look more deeply into contemporary women and their revisions of classical figures.

During my research, Kassandra largely disappeared from my study in favor of Klytemnestra. My curiosity increased as I discovered the large number of revisions American and European women writers have produced of the classical Klytemnestra—particularly in the 1980s. I was also intrigued by Klytemnestra's displacement in the 1990s by her daughters, Electra and Iphigenia. My attempts to trace Klytemnestra's fate at the end of the millennium led me from literary texts to contemporary performance pieces and finally to cyberspace. I was more than a little surprised to find myself tracking the women of the House of Atreus on the Internet.

Two major issues interest me in late-twentieth-century women's revisions of Klytemnestra. First, why would contemporary women writers want to reconstruct an adulterous woman notoriously blamed for horrific violence? Second, what happens to this violence in the modern texts and pieces of popular culture? In an era when humankind has faced atomic destruction and the Holocaust and has grown increasingly aware of domestic brutality and incest, how do women writers conceptualize the violence that is inextricably woven into the story of Klytemnestra? My study focuses on these central problems.

In comparing texts by women writers, one always walks the many tight-ropes familiar to feminist scholars as well as those who work in ethnic and multicultural studies. How do we mark commonalities among texts by women without seeming essentialist? How do we analyze such texts without flattening them under a universalizing grid that we in the West have been taught to impose as the necessary prerequisite to rational analysis? How do we retain enough critical distance to analyze while gaining enough intimacy with the texts to recognize cultural difference? How do we reveal similarities without occluding local details?

In this study, I deal with texts by European and North American women in the last quarter of the twentieth century. They have in common a compelling interest in reexamining the story of Klytemnestra as one of the founding myths of Western culture. I discuss a number of texts in detail to reveal their local characteristics, but I also risk broader generalizations in order to evaluate their common characteristics.

I hope to contribute to current discussions of literature as well as cultural studies in two different ways: first, by adding detailed analysis of specific texts to the growing body of women's literary history; second, by contributing to the ongoing formulation of theory in both the feminist and the nonfeminist arenas. To accomplish this goal, I examine the dialogic and the intertextual as well as the intracultural aspects of the texts in order to trace the restructuring of supposedly "timeless" archetypes as the social and historical foundations of these types of change.

The contemporary women writers in my study draw heavily for their background materials on classical Greek texts. I am not, however, approaching these classical texts so much in their own historical context as in that of the revisionist writers who take them up in the late twentieth century. Many of the writers I analyze do not themselves know Greek. Several years ago, I participated in intensive seminars with the renowned translator and scholar Robert Fagles, who examined in detail a range of classical texts—including the most critical for my study here, Aeschylus's *Oresteia.* In those cases where a Greek word or phrase was crucial, I relied on the help and advice of classicist colleagues who read my drafts and were very forthcoming. In dealing with the classical materials, I establish a foundation that outlines the figure of Klytemnestra and those features that characterize her. I then build on that base to analyze the contemporary women's rewriting and rethinking of Klytemnestra's tale. All translations of contemporary materials are my own unless otherwise specified.

Acknowledgments

This project developed over several years with the input and advice of many friends and associates. Numerous generous colleagues and students encouraged me in this research, ferreted out new materials, and assisted me in revisions of this book. I would especially like to thank my UCLA compatriots Ross Shideler, for his tireless support and advice; Arnold Band and Katherine King, for their counsel on Greek materials; Albert R. Braunmuller, for his insightful editorial suggestions; Françoise Lionnet, for her comments on French translations; and Lucia Re, for introducing me to Dacia Maraini's work. Ralph Freedman, Margaret Higonnet, Joan Templeton, Anca Vlasopolos, and Theodore Ziolkowski read the manuscript and offered sage advice for bettering it. Robert Fagles encouraged me to delve into classical materials, even though I am not a classicist. Many former and current graduate and undergraduate students helped with both research and honest discussion of the manuscript, but I would like especially to thank Dr. Amy Morris, Dr. Joyce Boss, Dr. Craig Kinosian, Christina Bogdanou, Joanna Nizynska, Nikki Halpern, Lori Lantz, Susan Bausch, Carole Viers, Valerie Keller, Brent Wilner, and Alison Bahr. Bill Phelan read the manuscript early on and helped enormously with editing comments. Willis G. Regier, director of the University of Illinois Press, made invaluable suggestions for improvements, and his superb staff at the University of Illinois was a joy to work with.

I would like to thank the Academic Senate of the University of California, Los Angeles, for providing research grants to support the writing of this book and the *Germanic Review* and *Thamyris* for their permission to reprint parts of articles that first appeared in those journals. And finally, my warm appreciation goes to those colleagues who gave me much needed feedback at meetings of the American Comparative Literature Association, the International Comparative Literature Association, and the Modern Language Association, at which I presented papers related to this project.

Reclaiming Klytemnestra

Introduction: Foundations of Western Culture—Re-collecting Klytemnestra

Klytemnestra: Cynosure of Violence

In the literature and myth depicting the establishment of the Greek polis and the patriarchal system of law that underpins the Western tradition, few female figures can claim a more central role than Klytemnestra. Her hand rocked the cradle of noble children but also wielded the axe that brought down her husband and king. Slain by her own son in retribution, she paid for her deed with her life. The trial of Orestes for his mother's murder precipitated the founding of the law court of Athens and the beginnings of Western democracy. This ancient female figure of such power and promise, who is so crucial to the establishment of Western culture's sense of law, democracy, and patriarchy, fascinates women writers at the end of the last millennium. This book explores the meaning of that phenomenon.

An irrepressible will to act, steeped in extreme violence, marks Klytemnestra's story. Violence is a founding feature of the Western tradition: heroes gain immortality through it; nations are founded upon it; families entrenched in it destroy themselves. But violence seems especially disturbing when it concentrates around women in the classical tradition—particularly the famous sisters Helen and Klytemnestra. This vibrant sororal pair is embroiled in some of the West's most famous and sustained eruptions of violence— the Trojan War and the exploits of the House of Atreus. Helen and Klytemnestra hold the dubious distinction of being cited as either the causes of or the direct perpetrators of military, political, domestic, and personal violence.

The classical male evaluation of Klytemnestra and her sister is often harsh (although Helen usually arouses more sympathy). Homer's Odysseus assigns a good deal of the blame for the Trojan War and the fall of the House of Atreus to the sisters. The gods wreak their vengeance on men through women like these:

> "How Terrible!
> Zeus from the very start, the thunder king
> has hated the race of Atreus with a vengeance—
> his trustiest weapon women's twisted wiles.
> What armies of us died for the sake of Helen . . .
> Clytemnestra schemed your [Agamemnon's] death while you were
>   worlds away!"
> (Homer, *The Odyssey,* Book 11, ll. 435–39 [ll. 493–98 in Fagles's
> numbering]).[1]

It is telling that the ancient world does not more often see the sisters as victims of violence. Helen suffers rape, abduction, and physical imprisonment, while Klytemnestra loses two children and a previous husband to Agamemnon's violence.[2] The sisters could as easily be depicted as trauma survivors as the root cause of violence.

Klytemnestra and the violence that engulfs her become the focus of a number of women writers in the last quarter of the twentieth century. These authors present a wide range of re-creations and a broad spectrum of ways of conceptualizing the violence inherent in the stories surrounding Klytemnestra. This book focuses on how women of the late twentieth century and the end of the last millennium rethink Klytemnestra, why they are committed to doing so, and how they deal with the violence enacted both upon and by women in Klytemnestra's story.

This interdisciplinary journey will take us from ancient Greece through novels, dramas, poems, dance, and performance in the 1980s and 1990s to the Internet of 1999. Klytemnestra serves as our guiding star in tracing this constellation of violence and female roles in the West. But in order to chart the movements of this constellation, we must examine the issues involved in revisions of classical female archetypes.

In Search of Female Voices

Revising classical figures was not, of course, invented by women writers— or by the twentieth century. It is an ancient technique reinvoked in the twentieth century by a wide range of writers. In 1923, in "*Ulysses,* Order and Myth," T. S. Eliot announced that James Joyce's *Ulysses* helped to "make the modern world possible for art," because by using past myths to shape contemporary anarchy, its "mythic method" made literature viable again in the culturally alienated twentieth century. But for women, this renaissance based on myth is problematic. Women looking back to the classical roots of the Western tradition too often see themselves missing or disenfranchised. The women of antiquity tend to be sacrifices or prizes or objects of history rather than its subjects—they are seldom poets (with the crucial exception of Sappho), and if they are seers, they are not believed. But women have not remained content with this historical and aesthetic elision. To make their own modern world possible for art and for themselves, contemporary women writers question and reconceptualize the underlying classical and biblical myths themselves.

In many ways, creating a revisionary text is akin to teaching a foreign language. Not until we learn another language does it occur to us that our own is not really a transparent window on the world, a god-given and accurate medium for understanding our surroundings. We are forced to become aware of the culturally constructed nature of our own signifying system. Revisionary texts function as a new language system; they destabilize and therefore revitalize our thinking and judgment about the founding cultural myths of the West.

The act of revision has become a familiar concept among feminist as well as ethnic theorists. When Adrienne Rich spoke of "Writing as Re-Vision" thirty years ago, she lent a new spark to the project already underway of seeing old texts, the sacred canon of Western literature, through new, specifically female, eyes. As Rich famously puts it (alluding in her title to Ibsen's turn-of-the-century drama):

> Re-vision—the act of looking back, of seeing with fresh eyes, of entering an old text from a new critical direction—is for women more than a chapter in cultural history: it is an act of survival. . . . A radical critique of literature, feminist in its impulse, would take the work first of all as a clue to . . . how we have been led to imagine ourselves, how our language has trapped as well as liberated us, how the very act of naming has been till now a male prerogative, and how we can begin to see and name—and therefore live—afresh. . . . We need to know the writing of the past, and know it differently than we have ever known it; not to pass on a tradition but to break its hold over us. ("When We Dead Awaken," 35)[3]

The women writers I examine take Rich's admonition seriously; they look back to the very inception of the Western tradition of law, democracy, and patriarchy and to the alembic in which many of the female role models of these Western practices are distilled. These women authors scrutinize the

Trojan War, the House of Atreus, and the founding of Western culture in order to analyze roles and identities assigned to women at the beginnings of Western civilization and to question those identities. They are engaged in what Sigrid Weigel, writing a dozen years after Rich, describes as wiping away those images of women painted by the male hand on the cultural mirror in which women examine themselves:

> Woman in the male order has learnt to see herself as inferior, inauthentic and incomplete. As the cultural order is ruled by men but women still belong to it, women also use the norms of which they themselves are the object. [Woman] sees the world through male spectacles. . . . She is fixated on self-observation refracted in the critical gaze of man. . . . Thus her self-portrait originates in the distorting patriarchal mirror. In order to find her own image she must liberate the mirror from the *images of woman* painted on it by a male hand. ("Double Focus," 61. Emphasis in the original.)[4]

The writers examined in this book are busy wiping the mirror clean so that new images of a female self can be reflected in it.

Some cultural surfaces are more easily cleansed than others. The very complexity of the figure of Klytemnestra makes her problematic; she is a prickly character whose edges cannot be dulled without doing her a different kind of violence. Entangled in maternity and mariticide as well as slaying another woman (Kassandra), Klytemnestra is not easily reclaimed as a feminist model. In addition, many women writers find that the very act of revision threatens to make them complicit in perpetuating other, often vexed depictions of men and women and their roles.

Female authors are faced with a very complex view of the cultural foundations of the West and the ways in which gender roles are embedded in them. They rewrite and unwrite a good deal of cultural and literary tradition in their late-twentieth-century texts. They become what Judith Fetterley terms "resisting readers" and resisting writers.[5] Long trained to identify with the image on Weigel's mirror and repress any internally generated self-image, these women writers come to understand their position as female readers and reconstruct it as female writers. As Fetterley explains, "the female reader is co-opted into participation in an experience from which she is explicitly excluded: she is asked to identify with a selfhood that defines itself in opposition to her; she is required to identify against herself" (xii).

No longer willing to "identify against themselves," these contemporary women writers seek to reestablish genuine female voices, unmediated by the male bard or scribe, at the beginnings of Western culture. This leads them to change the perspective from which Western myths are narrated and to provide a more articulated psychology for the female characters constituted in those myths. These writers engage in naming, or rather renaming, of an acutely critical variety and in deconstructing versions of the past in order to reconstruct a more viable present. They also attempt to re-create the missing female subjects of ancient history who have been turned by violence into objects—of desire, or barter or sacrifice or conquest. In the process, these authors also redefine their own selves and their function as writers within Western culture at the close of the last millennium.

Surveying the Textual Territory

A surprising number of late-twentieth-century women authors provide texts on the central female characters from the Trojan War. Of the women's revisions of the Trojan War that I examined from the second half of the twentieth century, only a few predate 1960.[6] Martha Graham's fascinating 1958 ballet, *Clytemnestra*—revived in the 1980s—was the only 1950s "text" I could find.[7] The impulse to rewrite classical female role models from Troy grew stronger along with the women's rights movements of the 1960s, 1970s, and 1980s. H. D.'s (Hilda Doolittle's) series of poems *Helen in Egypt* appeared in 1961 and Oriana Fallaci's *Penelope alla guerra* in 1962. In addition, the following texts are among the many that deal with this problem: Stevie Smith's 1966 poem "I had a dream . . ."; Margarita Karapanou's 1974 *He Kassandra Kai Ho Lykos* (trans. *Kassandra and the Wolf,* 1976); Marie Mactoux's 1975 *Penelope: Légènde et mythe;* Christa Reinig's 1976 *Entmannung;* Alice Sampaio's 1977 *Penelope, a infanta;* Pamela White Hadas's 1979 poem "A Penny for Her Thoughts"; Gwendolyn MacEwen's 1979 drama *The Trojan Women;* Ursule Molinaro's 1979 *The Autobiography of Cassandra, Princess and Prophetess of Troy;* Miranda Seymour's 1979 *The Goddess;* Nancy Bogen's 1980 *Klytaimnestra Who Stayed at Home;* Dacia Maraini's 1981 play *I sogni di Clitennestra;* Judy Grahn's 1982 Helen poems *The Queen of Wands;* Christine Brückner's 1983 *Wenn du geredet hättest, Desdemona,* which contains a Klytemnestra monologue entitled "Bist du nun glücklich, toter Agamemnon"; Marie Cardinal's 1983 *Le passé empiété;* Christa Wolf's 1983 *Kassandra;* Christine Brooke-Rose's 1984 "novel" *Amalgamemnon;* Séverine Auffret's 1984 "narrative essay" *Nous, Clytemnestre;* Magaly Alabau's 1986 poems *Electra, Clitemnestra;* Marion Zimmer Bradley's 1987 novel *The Firebrand;* Judy Grahn's 1987 Helen play *The Queen of Swords;* Inge Merkel's 1987 novel *Eine ganz gewöhnliche Ehe: Odysseus und Penelope;* Maria-Josep Ragué i Arias's 1987 play *Clitemnestra;* Alki Zie's 1987 *Achilles Fiancée;* Judy Hogan's 1988 poems *Cassandra Speaking;* Judith Piper and Nancy Tuana's 1988 collaborative performance piece,

The Fabulous Furies reVue; Linda Cargill's 1991 *To Follow the Goddess;* Laura Kennelly's 1993 poem "Clytemnestra Junior in Detroit"; Rosita Copioli's 1994 *Elena;* Oksana Zabuzhko's 1994 poem "Clytemnestra"; Ellen McLaughlin's 1995 *Iphigenia and Other Daughters;* Ruth Margraff's 1997 opera (revised as a play in 1999) *The Elektra Fugues,* and Diana M. Concannon's 1998 novel *Helen's Passage.* In addition to these printed texts, we find Judy Malloy's 1992 hypertext novel, *Its Name Was Penelope,* as well as late-1990s Web sites including <http://www.Iphigenia.com> and <http://www.Electra.com>.

From this list, it is evident that the Klytemnestra texts are concentrated in the last two decades of the twentieth century. (Only Martha Graham's ballet [1958, but revived in the 1980s] and Christa Reinig's novel [1976] predate the 1980s.) I became fascinated with questions of why Klytemnestra haunts the last decades of the millennium and how women recast her as the century came to an end. Her narrative and those of her daughters, Electra and Iphigenia, move from novels to the contemporary stage and from the printed page to cyberspace in the 1980s and 1990s.

In chapters 2 and 3, I select a cross-national group of texts from Martha Graham's 1958 ballet through the end of the 1980s. I suggest why the 1980s might be such fertile territory for revisions of Klytemnestra and explicate what marks those reconceptualizations. In addition to examining local contexts, comparing the major modern texts allows me to suggest that a consistent problematics of revision runs through these culturally and linguistically diverse texts.

Chapter 4 examines Klytemnestra's displacement in the 1990s by her daughters. In the 1990s, I follow Klytemnestra's journey beyond national boundaries by expanding my intermedia investigations to include the World Wide Web as well as a recent photograph. Finally, my conclusion returns to the theoretical concepts of the dialogic, female voice, and issues of gender and how they play out in women's revisions of Klytemnestra.

Re-membering Myths

Klytemnestra as depicted in the literature of antiquity represents several major roles traditionally assigned to women. She can figure the demonic and vengeful woman, the adulterous wife, or the avenging mother. I read the contemporary revisions of Klytemnestra by using several classical texts in which these female roles are established as a template. Chapter 1 locates the classical Klytemnestra in the texts (particularly those of Aeschylus, Sophocles, and Euripides) that define the competing versions of her story. This classical foundation makes clear how much is at stake in Klytemnestra's story as a pivotal moment in the creation of Western legal, democratic, patriarchal culture. The Greek tragedies also reveal those characteristics that make Klytemnestra an irresistible (if problematic) female figure who inspires revisions at the end of the twentieth century. This base allows me to analyze how contemporary female authors re-collect the classical tradition that formed such a crucial part of Western culture and deconstruct earlier myths of the female types in order to construct their own versions of female existence and the roles of women in social and political orders.

Several feminist literary critics display similar concerns. For example, Alicia Ostriker, in "The Thieves of Language: Women Poets and Revisionist Mythmaking," examines American women poets from the 1960s onward who rewrite the myths that have determined man's view of woman. Often deflating and satiric, the revised myths attempt to put women back into the literary and mythic landscape from which they have been excluded and to make cultural change possible. Julia Kristeva's investigation of the cult of the Virgin Mary and its effect on views of motherhood in her essay "Hérethique de l'amour" is a related project. And Judith Butler's *Antigone's Claim* reinterprets Antigone and the kinship and legal relationships that her story represents in order to rethink the mythic origins of the West so as to redefine our present social and cultural conditions.

Texts in a variety of fields participate in the revisions of early myths. The volumes range from psychology to popular culture and from archaeology to literary criticism. The amount of traditional scholarship in these texts varies. While some of their findings are hotly disputed by experts, they all attest to the interest among late-twentieth-century women in revisions of the West's mythic foundations.[8]

Hélène Cixous's essay "Sorties" also provides a prominent example of a modern woman rethinking the cultural myths of the West. Cixous's is a very personal appropriation of myth. She recalls being a child envisioning herself as Achilles, passionate in war and in love—until she realized that she was a woman; there were no female models that captured her image of herself. She examines Medea, Ariadne, and Dido and finds them all victims. But Cixous does identify with one woman from classical literature; she identifies with Helen, with the Helen objectified and turned into an image by men, with the Helen used as an excuse in the history from which she is so carefully excluded (*Newly Born Woman*, 69–70).

Given frustrating personal experiences such as Cixous's, one might well ask why women would bother to appropriate myths or texts that so aggressively seek to exclude them, vilify them, or relegate them to inferior positions, or even superior—that is, idealized—but always passive positions such as "vessel of the Holy Spirit."⁹ One answer is provided by Cixous's intense searching among the women of antiquity for a woman with whom she can identify. She seeks a reflection of the selves she might become among the famous women of the past. Unfortunately, Cixous learns that women quickly bump up against the patriarchal mirror about which Sigrid Weigel warns.

European women are not alone in feeling this elision from history; the contemporary American writer Ellen McLaughlin expresses this exclusionary feeling in notes for her play *Iphigenia and Other Daughters*:

> I believe that most women feel, deep down, that they are not part of the real history of mankind, the important stuff, the heroic stuff, the stuff that matters. And we are in fact correct—the his/story of man/kind is precisely that. So we are left to make up our own. . . . But there is always a certain self-loathing that one keeps at bay, . . . the sense that one would like to be able to identify oneself with something more substantial, more vivid, more, well, powerful. But power in the hands of women has nearly always been perceived as monstrous in terms of his/story—hence characters like Clytemnestra—or merely sexual—hence, oh, you name it. So one ends up identifying oneself with men. . . . Literature, politics, virtually everything that was part of my education involved my identification with the male.¹⁰

Like Cixous, McLaughlin finds women excluded from the official versions of history, from participation in "the important stuff." She finds women relegated to domestic rather than public spaces, to powerlessness or demonization. If women want to imagine themselves as part of the "stuff that matters," they are forced to identify with men and thus to betray their gendered selves. The powerful myths that underpin Western culture do not easily provide a viable space for women to develop a sense of self that can be central to that culture. Women rapidly find, as did Cixous and McLaughlin, that we cannot fully be Achilles, and that the passionate female warriors and lovers are suppressed or distorted by cultural tradition into victims (like Dido) or villainesses (like Klytemnestra) or objects and images (like Helen) or supports for patriarchy (like Athena).

Athena is a prime example of a problematic female figure in ancient tradition: known for wisdom and valor, she is totally appropriated by patriarchy. Athena's mother, Metis, (whose name means counsel or wisdom and who is famed for her intellectual acuity) was swallowed by her husband, Zeus, who feared she would give birth to a mighty child who would rule the universe. Having swallowed Metis, Zeus had her always with him and thus automatically enjoyed the advantage of her counsel. With her mother out of sight and subsumed (or consumed) by the male, Athena is born from her father's mind and seems entirely her father's child. She utters the final damning judgment that chooses Father Right over Mother Right in the *Eumenides,* in which she declares herself to be her father's offspring:

> No mother gave me birth.
> I honor the male, in all things but marriage.
> Yes, with all my heart I am my Father's child.
> I cannot set more store by the woman's death—
> she [Klytemnestra] killed her husband, guardian of their house.
> Even if the vote is equal, Orestes wins.
> (Aeschylus, *The Oresteia,* 292. *The Eumenides,* ll. 751–56)

Not entirely eradicated by Athena's judgment, the older female order is literally driven underground as the *Eumenides* closes.[11]

As the female deity essential to the founding of Athens and to quelling the rebellion of the female furies loosed by Klytemnestra's death, Athena occupies a special place in the story we will trace. Nicole Loraux analyzes Athena's role in the imaginary of Athens in her study *The Children of Athena.* Loraux points out that Athena is *parthenos* (a young female virgin), a virgin goddess who is motherless, a female who refuses marriage and maternity, and a female who oversees the autochthonous birth of the first (male) Athenian, Erichthonios, as well as the creation of the first female, Pandora—the clearly negative beginning not of humanity but of the "race of women." Athena sidelines women and protects the institutions of men. As Loraux puts it, Athena's dual role

> represents security itself for the *andres* [collectivity of men as males, citizens, and fighters]: the security of the hero, whose exploits Athena attends, the security of the [male] citizen, whose *polis* she protects, the security of the male, comforted in his fantasy of a world without women by the idea that his goddess at least was not born from a woman's body—she who "was not nourished in the darkness of the womb." She represents the security of the male for all time; he knows he can continue to dream on without anxiety, since, in the active reality of civic cult, the Warrior Goddess keeps watch over the fertility of Athens. (11)

The quotation within a quotation here is from Aeschylus's *Eumenides,* in which Athena upholds the civic, male order against female, blood rights.

By having Athena as their protectress, however, the male Athenians are still forced to contemplate the role of women in their society. According to one myth recounted by Loraux, Athena seems at least indirectly responsible for women losing their civic rights.[12] As the myth goes, the gods were dividing

honors; Athena and Poseidon argue over the city of Kekrops.[13] In this mythic time, women could still vote, and they vote for Athena while the men vote
for Poseidon. Since women outnumber the men by one, Athena wins, and
Athens is named for her. But in order to compensate Poseidon, the women
"lose all participation in power, and the authority to name their own children, and even the title of Athenian, which they had just invented" (Loraux,
Experiences, 187). Women are punished for using their power and for defeating men. But they also have been tricked into supporting precisely the male
order in voting for Athena, who will side with the male in everything but bed.
The male order can only be ensured by getting women to act against themselves, to be complicit in establishing male, Western culture.

As Loraux stresses, however, the Athenian civic imagination does not finally "succeed in separating the goddess from the women of Athens" (*Children
of Athena,* 11). Women haunt Athenian art and tragedy. To claim an autochthonous birth for the first (and metaphorically for all) Athenian (male) citizens does not really dispense with the reality of motherhood—and the threat
that its ardent defenders, such as Klytemnestra, present to the civic order of
an Athenian democracy. Shield of the male order, Athena, whose statue towers
over Athens, nonetheless by her very presence as dominant image makes the
idea of the female an inescapable problem that the fifth-century B.C. Athenian tragedians would be forced to face.

Contemporary women's readings of Athena might be exemplified in the
American poet Amy Clampitt's "Athena," in which she sees the goddess as the

> Force of reason, who shut up the shrill
> foul Furies in the dungeon of the Parthenon,
> led whimpering to the cave they live in still,
> beneath the rock your city foundered on. (27)

This goddess tames the female Furies but only to create the conditions for
future cultural conflict. Clampitt's Athena has reason (usually attributed in
classical culture to the male) but not as a wholly positive characteristic, with
a "mind that can make a scheme of anything." (Euripides might well agree
here.) Clampitt's figure is the "uncompromising / mediatrix, virgin married
to the welfare / of the body politic." In Athena, the roles normally given to
the female in classical tradition, nurturing mother and wife, are transformed
into a wise warrior whose nurturing goes not to the domestic, the personal
child, but rather to the public, the polis itself. The female is co-opted for what
were male purposes in the classical world. Clampitt's goddess/female is a living oxymoron with a female form but male characteristics; she carries the
olive branch and founds the law court but wears battle armor. She is the fe-

male who subdues the female principles and blood rights. Clampitt also acknowledges that "we have invented all you stand for, / though we despise the artifice—." The "we" here is Western culture as a whole, which creates the figure and the meaning of Athena and in which contemporary women as well as the goddess are inextricably entangled. But the "we" is also women themselves, who understand that they are always gazing into Weigel's patriarchal mirror. The women I examine in this volume set about reinventing that cultural narrative to create an artifice they and we could despise less.

Most frequently, women figures and writers have little voice of their own in the classical tradition—particularly in democratic Athens.[14] While the aristocratic or predemocratic period in Greece might have allowed women more freedom—as is the case with Sappho (who is also from the island of Lesbos rather than Athens, thus representing a geographical as well as chronological counterexample)[15]—their voices have barely survived compared to those of their male counterparts. Women's views are most often mediated by the male scribe or teller. When women do speak, as Aeschylus has Athena do, they tend to be made supports of patriarchy (like Athena) or its scapegoat (like Helen or, in the Christian tradition, Eve). Ousted from the primary position of blood-centered and mother-centered culture by a male-voiced woman,[16] women must restate their cases—this time in an unmediated female voice—to regain a place of equality in cultural and literary tradition.

The classical myths and the texts that convey them belong to an elevated cultural realm that has been sanctioned and sanctified by the spiritual and intellectual establishment. As Roland Barthes points out in *Mythologies,* myths have the seductive capacity to conceal their own historical contingency so that they appear to be eternal, unchangeable truths with enormous cultural significance (142–43); myths, according to Barthes, "transform history into nature" (129). This alchemy gives myths the glint of cultural gold. They are part of high culture and carry with them the authoritative voice that alone commands enough respect to question its own foundations. By using this authoritative voice against itself, contemporary women writers produce revisions that become clearly subversive acts with enough weight and authority to precipitate genuine cultural rethinking.

As the Italian writer Dacia Maraini articulated when asked why she wrote a Klytemnestra text, "These women figures are too symbolically important in our culture. They *must* be rewritten."[17] Maraini argues, "Mythology . . . deals with women's life and thus offers many insights into what has happened in the past," thus women in the present can "make use of mythology symbolically, meaningfully" (Sumeli Weinberg, 69). Echoing Rich's comments on "re-vision," Maraini notes, "The myths we carry around with us from childhood on are the male ones, and so I'm interested in delving into them, as into a wood that keeps me prisoner . . . that doesn't belong to me but that I'm inside of. The only way out is to . . . try to understand" (Anderlini, 158). The American playwright Ellen McLaughlin voices a similar feeling: "Clytemnestra transcends the tininess of modern-day psychology. She and her daughters are archetypes. They embody roles. Their scale is much greater than individual psychology."[18]

Late-twentieth-century women revise not for nostalgia's sake but for gender issues and politically related ends. They demonstrate that the present is often very much—*too* much—like the past already. The weight of tradition and authority that supports the texts being revised allows the women writers to add a larger cultural dimension to texts that are often marked by a personal voice. The women thus escape being relegated to the category of *Trivialliteratur,* or "low" or "minor" genres, in which women writers are often hidden away and that some critics declare "too personal and private" to mount a serious challenge to the literary tradition itself. By its own rules, the patriarchal literary establishment must take seriously a challenge to its supposed origins that uses the texts that form that origin. Women writers thus subvert the rules of the game to their own advantage to create a platform from which they hope to alter the game itself. By forcing those critics who insist on a hierarchy of genres to confront their own assumptions, these women writers subvert the underpinnings of both genre and hierarchy.

In the essays preceding *Kassandra,* Christa Wolf ponders how human life would change if women were allowed to participate fully in Western culture, to act, even violently, in a crucial way: "Shouldn't an experiment be made to see what would happen if the great male heroes of world literature were replaced by women? Achilles, Hercules, Odysseus, Oedipus, Agamemnon, Jesus, King Lear, Faust, Julien Sorel, Wilhelm Meister. Women as active, violent, as knowers? They drop through the lens of literature. People call that 'realism.' The entire past existence of women has been unrealistic" (*Cassandra: A Novel and Four Essays,* 260). Monique Wittig, in *Les guérillères,* suggests the same idea in a fictional guise as she changes Oedipus to Oedipa, Sigismund to Sigismunda, Faust to Fausta, and so on, thus feminizing all the great roles of history and literature. In Wittig's view, this move reverses the gendered power structure of Western civilization; but in mounting this challenge, Wittig retains something of the binary opposition that underpins the Western hierarchy. Wolf argues that women's active participation would change our very vision of what is significant.

Wolf then goes on to project a new women's writing, a "living word" that would "no longer produce stories of heroes, or of antiheroes, either. Instead, it would be inconspicuous and would seek to name the inconspicuous, the precious everyday, the concrete. Perhaps it would greet with a smile the wrath of Achilles, the conflict of Hamlet, the false alternatives of Faust. It would have to work its way up to its material, in every sense, 'from below,' and if that material were viewed through a different lens than in the past, it might reveal hitherto unrecognized possibilities" (*Cassandra*, 270–71).[19] Wolf envisions a revised literature and culture not dependent on the binary oppositions and hierarchy necessary to patriarchy. She foresees a culture without the heroic ethic that determines so much of Western thought. It would be a very different culture.

In "Sorties," Cixous shares Wolf's view of the radical transformation that would take place if women began to effect culture:

> If some fine day it suddenly came out that the logocentric plan had always, inadmissibly, been to create a foundation for (to found and fund) phallocentrism, to guarantee the masculine order a rationale equal to history itself.
>
> So all the history, all the stories would be there to retell differently; the future would be incalculable; the historic forces would and will change hands and change body . . . will transform the functioning of all society. We are living in an age where the conceptual foundation of an ancient culture is in the process of being undermined by millions of species of mole (Topoi, ground mines) never known before.
>
> When they wake up from among the dead, from among words, from among laws.
>
> . . . Most women who have awakened remember having slept, *having been put to sleep.* (*Newly Born Woman*, 65–66)

The women revisionists do, indeed, remember having been put to sleep by thousands of years of cultural and literary history. When these dead awaken, they do so, as Cixous describes, to challenge the foundations of the culture that has abased or ignored them. And they are particularly focused on the role of violence against and by women in that culture.

The late-twentieth-century women who rewrite Troy and its aftermath challenge customary images of gender roles; they question the Western, heroic tradition and the ways in which violence helps to found that tradition and define female archetypes; they explore the notion of female voice in literature and history; they seek to unearth a female subjectivity from the centuries of objectification that women have experienced. These thematic transformations frequently engender structural transformations as well.

Many of these texts are formally innovative. They challenge generic boundaries, refusing to pay tribute to the careful hierarchical arrangement of forms that the literary tradition has dictated. Wolf, for example, mixes narrative, diary, travel journal, work notes, and essay in her *Kassandra* texts; Auffret mingles personal and scholarly commentary with dramatic fragments in *Nous, Clytemnestre*. Piper and Tuana's *The Fabulous Furies reVue* appropriates pieces of earlier texts (from both low and high culture) to produce a postmodern collage. These formal innovations buttress the thematic, political, and philosophical challenges mounted in the various women's texts.

The Dialogic

The texts that I examine offer a particularly vibrant case of Bakhtin's well-known concept, the dialogic. The notion of inter- and intratextual dialogue, of multiple interacting voices, traditions, and cultural assumptions, is especially suited to my subject. As Michael Holquist and Caryl Emerson explain in their translation of Bakhtin's work, "A word, discourse, language or culture undergoes 'dialogization' when it becomes relativized, de-privileged, aware of competing definitions for the same things" (427). This relativizing and questioning are precisely what the women revisionists generate. They strive to make competing voices and interpretations of cultural foundations evident and inescapable. They enter into both diachronic and synchronic dialogues—and debates—with ancient texts as well as with texts by other contemporary male and female writers who are also reexamining Western culture by rethinking some of its founding documents. This relativizing by women revisionists makes conspicuous the heteroglot nature of the founding myths. This, in turn, makes those ancient myths available for reinscription in a new context that can provide them with new meanings and a different cultural charge. Thus, the women's rewritings of Klytemnestra necessarily enter into a dialogue not only with the classical texts but also with the entire patriarchal tradition of which those classical texts are the foundation. The women writers launch, if you will, an attack on the very assumption of an origin.

The realization that origin is illusion became a critical commonplace in the age of deconstructive theory. But that theoretical realization does not necessarily eradicate the cultural power of those texts that have an aura of origin. The women writers in this study refract that aura. They realign literary tradition by decentering the texts that form its "origin" and by claiming a more central position for female literary voices. They also broaden visions of a female self. This attempt to complicate views of the female self corresponds to what Weigel calls "der schielende Blick" or a "double vision." Modern women must constantly scrutinize the dominant patriarchal images that set the patterns of their existence with one eye while seeking with the other eye a broader vision of the new selves they are attempting to create

("Double Focus," 71). To do this, they must engage those texts that form the roots of the tradition that excludes them.

The widespread occurrence of this type of cultural revision indicates that these particular women writers are not so intent on establishing a separate countertradition as they are on salvaging part of the Western human tradition that could allow them a place of equal status. Despite her vilification in the literary tradition, Klytemnestra represents a woman of strength and importance. Even the classical materials present competing definitions of her character and role. That men feel compelled to fear and condemn her only adds to her significance. Getting at precisely what defines that significance requires peeling away the layers of cultural insulation that keep this female figure safely isolated from the men she threatens.

The literary and cultural dialogue in which the revisionary texts engage thus represents a revolutionary act. The concept of the dialogic, therefore, seems particularly suited to (in fact, inescapable for) these texts. Women writers must necessarily enter into a dialogue not just with earlier texts (by men and women) but also with the male literary tradition itself. Their texts trigger the realization that traditional cultural assumptions have indeed become "relativized" and "de-privileged"; they make us unavoidably "aware of competing definitions for the same things," as Holquist and Emerson suggest the dialogic does. Their writing must inherently come to grips with a language in which the universal is male and they themselves are forever a special (inferior) subset. Women writers, therefore, cannot avoid presenting voices that question the tradition that has held them in check (and often in silence) for so long. The dialogic quality of their texts thus goes beyond the intertextual to a more essential and problematizing structure.

Functioning on many levels, the notion of the dialogic helps to elucidate numerous issues at stake in women's revisionary texts. In "Feminist Criticism and Bakhtin's Dialogic Principles," Friederike Eigler argues that "the Bakhtinian notion of the dialogic includes tension or struggle between antagonistic 'voices' and thus also accounts for those voices that either refuse to enter into any kind of dialogue or that are excluded from discourse" (197). Eigler notes that the notion of tension and struggle among voices makes Bakhtin's concept particularly appropriate to feminist criticism. Not until recently (roughly the mid-1980s), however, have critics used the concept to study texts by women.[20] Patricia Yaeger, Elaine Showalter, and Patrocinio P. Schweickart all employ it, but Anne Herrmann produces the most ambitious attempt to define and engage a female dialogic in *The Dialogic and Difference: "An/Other Woman" in Virginia Woolf and Christa Wolf.*

Herrmann redefines the dialogic as an attempt to reappropriate not just the male text but also the female subject. With Wolf's work in mind, Hermann argues that other dialogic readings "leave out the inscription of the other not just as the hegemonic male text but as the reappropriation of the 'other' woman, that is, in the reappropriation of conventionally female literary forms, in the construction of female characters, and in the very act of saying 'I'" (21). This opening up of the dialogic to include other women as well as the female self as such is an important addition for the purposes of this study.

In addition to Bakhtin's comments on the dialogic, my analysis is informed by Kristeva's reading of Bakhtin's seminal books, *Rabelais and His World*[21] and *Problems of Dostoevsky's Poetics,* in her essay "Word, Dialogue, and Novel." Kristeva's reading of Bakhtin extends his concept of the carnivalesque to include such modernist authors as Joyce, Kafka, and Proust; she emphasizes the ambivalent nature of the carnivalesque in addition to its cynical, bawdy, and scatological characteristics (as represented more obviously in Rabelais and Swift). While remaining close to Bakhtin's tenets and concerns, Kristeva extends his theories toward the later poststructural era.

Following Bakhtin, Kristeva defines the "literary word" ("le mot littéraire") as "an *intersection of textual surfaces* rather than a *point* (a fixed meaning), as a dialogue among several writings: that of the writer, the addressee (or the character) and the contemporary or earlier cultural context" ("Word, Dialogue, and Novel," 65, emphasis in the original)—or in the case of this study, both the contemporary and earlier cultural contexts. Kristeva goes on to explain:

> By introducing the *status of the word* as a minimal structural unit, Bakhtin situates the text within history and society, which are then seen as texts read by the writer, and into which he inserts himself by rewriting them. Diachrony is transformed into synchrony, and . . . *linear* history appears as abstraction. The only way a writer can participate in history is by transgressing this abstraction through a process of reading-writing; . . . The poetic word, polyvalent and multi-determined . . . fully comes into being only in the margins of recognized culture. . . . Carnivalesque discourse breaks through the laws of language. . . . and, at the same time, is a social and political protest. ("Word, Dialogue, and Novel," 65, emphasis in the original)

Women revisionists share Kristeva's and Bakhtin's view of the text as always in opposition to an earlier structure, as existing on the margins of recognized culture but with the power to break through earlier laws of language in order to mount a social and political protest. The writers in this volume consciously take up the charge inherent in all dialogic literature by making their engagement with earlier texts and cultural forms an open debate.

Kristeva also examines the epic as a particularly monologic form in which "the narrator's absolute point of view" coincides "with the wholeness of a god or community" ("Word, Dialogue, and Novel," 77). The epic of Homer, for example, rests on a coherent and highly articulated system of gods (temperamental and cruelly whimsical though they may be) and community. This leads epic logic to "pursue the general through the specific; it thus assumes a hierarchy within the structure of substance. Epic logic is therefore causal, that is, theological; it is *a belief* in the literal sense of the word" ("Word, Dialogue, and Novel," 78). But for Maraini, Wolf, Reinig, Auffret, and other authors I will examine, this coherent and articulated system of order beyond the individual is either illusory or oppressive and must be destroyed and replaced by a dialogue of competing new potential orders or disorders that cannot be resolved within the ambivalent dialogic world of their texts. The women's revision of the epic system is thus a look at the real chaos beyond the apparent patriarchal and heroic order.

The revisions of these contemporary women writers also employ the devices that Kristeva sees as germane to carnivalesque language, such as repetition and the use of nonexclusive opposition. By disputing the laws of language based on what Kristeva calls the 0–1 interval (in which monologic discourse, such as the epic, subordinates the code to 1, to God), "the carnival challenges God, authority and social law; in so far as it is dialogical, it is rebellious" ("Word, Dialogue, and Novel," 79). The challenge to God, patriarchal authority, and social law (which also embodies gender roles) is exactly what is at stake for female revisionists. As Kristeva suggests, "The epic and the carnivalesque are the two currents that formed European narrative, one taking precedence over the other according to the times and the writer" ("Word, Dialogue, and Novel," 80). My study of women revisionists looks at the collision of the two forms, the point at which the carnivalesque—in the sense of multivalent, antirational, antitheological—challenges the epic (and monologic). In this case, it is also a challenge by female writers to the patriarchal tradition that supports masculine dominance.

Formulating a Female Self

A second type of dialogic in these texts is not discussed by Bakhtin. The woman writer and her female center of consciousness must always be aware of themselves as subjects in their own discourse and as "other" in the dominant discourse. This awareness produces a dialogue with one's self as other, which comes close to the visual image of "double focus" that Weigel suggests. In many texts that I examine, the female self comes to incorporate other women without reducing them to inferior or fragmented status. The women's texts keep the dialogue alive as a discourse among equal subjects rather than resolving a "debate" by creating a hierarchy of patriarchal logic.

Women's texts also contain a dialogue among the various selves of a single individual that eventually coalesce (but do not ossify) into a new female self that is plural or multiple, a "we" rather than an "I." In many cases, this new self remains open, in question, unresolved. This internal dialogue of female voices reflects another major challenge for female revisionists: the challenge to present a female self as subject in literature, to make a space for those female voices that have so long been only reflections in a male projection of the female.

The impulse to create a new female subject comes from many sources—including what Weigel describes as the "latent schizophrenia" of the female subject, which "consists in the fact that those elements of the model of femininity which earn [woman] *moral* respect (for example, motherliness, understanding, sociability) are also the basis for her social subordination" ("Double Focus," 80). In Klytemnestra's case, motherliness will become a particularly vexed issue that precipitates her violent expulsion from society. Women thus find themselves forever at odds with the definitions imposed on them by the society in which they live. They find themselves constantly demeaned, their own needs and desires repressed in favor of those of the dominant (male) culture. Klytemnestra's love of her daughter Iphigenia and Iphigenia's own desire to live leap to mind.

Some of the women revisionists fiercely defend aspects of femininity that they value. Often the murder of Agamemnon by Klytemnestra forms the center of that defense. For other women writers, however, gender itself becomes a problematic issue in seeking to understand new possibilities for female identity. Reinig and Cardinal, in particular, question whether a female self must be gendered as exclusively feminine or envision the world only from a woman's perspective. Reinig explores the literal performance of the "other" gender in her text, while Cardinal has her bodily female narrator occupy male consciousness and experience male sexuality. These authors ask whether other gender positions can be imagined that do not reduce male and female to relentless binary oppositions. And if so, what effect does this gender fluidity have on Klytemnestra's story and on the male-female battle it encompasses? Butler's work on performativity, gender, and identity in *Gender Trouble* suggests ways in which to investigate these questions. Her work in *Antigone's Claim* also provides a model for rethinking issues of kinship and gender as they are inscribed in classical texts.

The women revisionist writers depict characters who often come to realize that their selves are split and multiple, that their difficulty in saying "I" arises partly from subordination, partly from conflicting allegiances, and partly from an uncertainty about their own "meaning" and value. They often discover that a unified self need not be singular and finished. They develop selves that are constantly changing and merging with the other to create newly communal senses of the subject that cannot be painted into an archetype. They are, to a greater or lesser degree, what Kristeva calls "questionable subjects-in-process" ("en procès")[22] since at this point in history they exist only in and through the poetic text. Not finally singularly and definitively defined, the female "questionable subject-in-process" is outlined against the knowledge and meaning of the traditional patriarchal world. This new female subject reaches back to a maternal, semiotic level of heterogeneity and relation that resists the repressively fixed meaning imposed by the patriarchal symbolic system. The revisionist women writers in this study release such new female subjects from the patriarchal role assignments in which they have so long been held prisoners. This release does not, however, often issue into any kind of utopia or even a state of happiness. The self-in-process can sometimes explode into violence or be defined as "abnormal" and recaptured by the system it seeks to escape.

Notes

1. Fagles provides the line count for the Greek in parentheses at the top of each page. I quote from Fagles's line count since my readers will be following his translation in my discussion.

2. A less well-known facet of Klytemnestra's story is that in order to win Klytemnestra as his wife, Agamemnon kills her first husband, Tantalus, as well as the couple's child. I will discuss this in more detail below.

3. For discussions of "re-vision" by a number of leading feminist critics in addition to Rich, see Kolodny; Miller; Schor; and Showalter, among others. See also Miller, "Arachnologies"; Froula; Kolodny, "A Map for Rereading"; and Homans, among many others.

Neely worries that "re-vision" assumes the priority of the original patriarchal model, and "that re-vision has not brought and cannot bring about" (82) the innovations in the academy that feminism promises. While I share her concerns, I believe that we already exist within a cultural and linguistic tradition even if it has sometimes excluded the active participation of women. As Jehlen puts it, "Feminist thinking is really *re*thinking, an examination of the way certain assumptions about women and the female character enter into the fundamental assumptions that organize all our thinking" (69). Our innovations, therefore, must be revisionary.

4. Jehlen comes to a very similar conclusion (76).

5. See Fetterley. On the issue of becoming "resisting readers," see also Kolodny, "A Map for Rereading" and "Dancing through the Minefield"; Jacobus; and Schweickart. On some

of the prejudices that traditionally have been used to devalue women's writing, see Miller, "Emphasis Added," and Winnett.

6. There are a few earlier examples. Ilse Langner's tragedy *Klytämnestra* was written during the war but not published until 1947. Marshall explores this play in "Ilse Langner's *Klytämnestra*." Langner also wrote in 1948 *Iphigenie kehrt Heim,* a dramatic poem. Marguerite Yourcenar presents an even earlier lyrical prose Klytemnestra monologue in her 1936 collection, *Feux,* which was translated into English in 1981. Laura Riding's novel *A Trojan Ending* from 1937 also regained prominence in the 1980s with its reissuance in 1984.

7. Poets such as Anne Sexton and Sylvia Plath were writing revisionist texts in the 1950s and 1960s but were not focusing on the women of the Trojan War. On the relationship of female poets to myth as well as to fairy tale and other forms of tradition, see Montefiore.

8. I cite only a few examples here. See Lauter and Rupprecht for a broad investigation of female archetypes from a revised Jungian perspective. Stone's two volumes on female myth attempt to rediscover the prepatriarchal myths that centered on women figures. Stone's attempts to uncover female rites that she believes long predate the male rituals is not a popular enterprise (despite their closeness to Bachofen's nineteenth-century attempt to argue along the same lines in *Das Mutterrecht* [1861] and Briffault's similar analysis in *The Mothers* [1927]). Her work has met with criticism in the scholarly establishment. Whether we accept her work as "accurate" in a scholarly sense, her studies contribute to the impulse of contemporary female authors to rethink the foundations of Western culture from a gender-conscious perspective.

Gimbutas works in a similar vein in *The Language of the Goddess* and *Goddesses and Gods of Old Europe.* More recent work in this area from the 1990s includes Dexter and Orenstein. In her two volumes, Pomeroy seeks to revise common images of women in antiquity, as do Keuls, Cameron and Kuhrt, Foley, and Peradotto and Sullivan. Rabinowitz and Richlin's *Feminist Theory and the Classics* contains a very thought-provoking critique by Shelby Brown on the work of earlier feminist archeologists, including Gimbutas.

Works by several classical scholars inform my study. These scholars include Page DuBois, Froma Zeitlin, Katherine Callen King, and Nicole Loraux; the work of these scholars will be discussed in my text. Glenn's *Rhetoric Retold* and Jarratt's *Rereading the Sophists* have also been quite helpful.

9. The debate over myth has gone on in feminist circles for some time. Beauvoir argues against myth in *The Second Sex,* 157–223. Stone's two volumes demand that we recognize a level of female myth and ritual that precedes patriarchal myths. Gubar argues that some myths can be useful to women writers. Kristeva's discussion of the repercussions of the loss of the myth of the Virgin Mary is also relevant here.

10. McLaughlin's notes on *Iphigenia and Other Daughters,* 1. The notes, which were used in the playbill when the piece premiered in 1995, were sent to me by the author in February 1999. I am most grateful to have access to them.

11. Many scholars argue the replacement of an older female-centered religious and social order by later patriarchal systems. In addition to Stone, see, among many others, the Jungian psychologist Neumann; Graves; Whitmont; Gimbutas; Dexter; and Orenstein.

12. *Experiences of Tiresias,* 187. Loraux's footnote cites Varro, in Saint Augustine, *City of God* 18.9.

13. Kekrops is a fascinating figure. According to Loraux, he is "the primordial autoch-thon, with a hybrid body . . . , half-man, half-snake. King of Athens before Athens comes into existence, Kekrops accomplishes the transition from savagery to civilization by col-lecting men together into a city (*asty*) and by introducing marriage, which puts an end to promiscuity. A very ancient hero, on Athenian vases he quite naturally attends the birth of Erichthonios in his capacity as an autochthon" (*Children of Athena*, 25).

14. Keuls points out that women were deprived not only of a voice but also of a name. She describes the practice of referring to women by their husband's or father's name (a practice that survives into our own day) as well as the total lack of female individual names in legal proceedings and even in many literary texts from classical Athens (86–93). She argues that depriving women of names was "a device for diminishing women's sense of identity which was probably superbly effective" (88). Keuls maintains that women in the phallocracy of classical Athens were meant to be invisible, silent, and without name.

15. DuBois has written extensively on Sappho and her special status.

16. Keuls says of Athena, "By the mid-fifth century, the image of Athena was stripped of any vestige of femininity. . . . The Athena Parthenos (the Virgin) was, as a late Roman author put it, a 'virago,' a sexless man-woman who can defend her position in a male world, but only at the expense of her own sexual role" (38). Loraux's reading in *Children of Athena* is more nuanced but also recognizes the gender problems.

17. Maraini made this point when I interviewed her (in English) at the University of Southern California on February 13, 1990. The interview followed her talk entitled "My Mothers: Some Italian Women Writers of the Twentieth Century." See also Cavallaro's discussion of Maraini and myth (35–40).

18. Phone interview, February 12, 1999.

19. I am indebted to my colleague Anca Vlasopolos for pointing out the similarity be-tween Wolf's description and Auerbach's analysis of Virginia Woolf's *To the Lighthouse*. It was gratifying to see a male, German critic from the 1940s so clearly anticipate Wolf's point about women's writing.

20. Yaeger sees a dialogic conflict between "feminocentric" and dominant ideologies. Showalter, in "Feminist Criticism in the Wilderness," proposes a similar view when she discusses women's writing as "'double-voiced discourse' that always embodies the social, literary, and cultural heritages of both the muted and the dominant" (263), thus produc-ing the competing definitions and relativized view crucial to the dialogic. And Schweick-art attempts to use a dialogic paradigm to define a new feminist model of reading.

21. Also useful in this context is Bakhtin's *Esthétique et théorie du roman*.

22. For a discussion of the "questionable subject-in-process," see Kristeva, "D'une iden-tité l'autre," translated as "From One Identity to an Other," in *Desire in Language*. In his introduction (17), Roudiez points out that "en procès" implies both in process (i.e., un-settled, questionable) and on trial (in a legal sense).

1. The Classical Klytemnestra

Klytemnestra—Matriarch or Mariticide: Whose Blood in the Bath?

The enraged woman, wielding a double-headed axe,[1] rushes forward—to murder her husband, to defend her lover from her own son, or to kill a rival captive woman? Terrifying and haunting, this image is immortalized in archaic and early classical art depicting Klytemnestra[2] as the adulterous, jealous, and murderous wife.[3] Clearly a threat to husbands and sons, the *labrys*-wielding Klytemnestra is also a menace to other women, since her one undisputed murder is of the Trojan prophetess Kassandra. This figure of the violently active woman fascinates Western culture. Authors from antiquity to the present scrutinize Klytemnestra to analyze the complex woman beneath the axe.

Although Aeschylus would probably have used the word *pelekus* to describe the axe (if indeed that was what his Klytemnestra wielded) rather than *labrys*, I have chosen the word *labrys* because it has become an important symbol for various women's concerns and is used directly by authors such as Christa Wolf. Barbara G. Walker explains that the *labrys* was used as a scepter by the ancient Amazonian goddess Gaea (or Rhea, Demeter, or Artemis). Eventually, according to Walker, when a male priesthood took over the goddess's shrine at Delphi, which had been founded by Cretan Amazons, they adopted the *labrys* as their own symbol, and so the double-bladed axe moved from the female to the male realm of iconography. In anthropological studies, Marija Gimbutas connects the *labrys* to the shape of the butterfly (and the bee), which figured the female capacity for (re)generation (*Goddesses and*

The Dokimasia Painter, *Bowl for mixing wine and water (Calyx krater)*, side B: "Orestes' Revenge," about 460 B.C. Side A of the same piece depicts "The Death of Agamemnon." (William Francis Warden Fund, Courtesy, Museum of Fine Arts, Boston. Reproduced with permission. ©2000 Museum of Fine Arts, Boston. All rights reserved.)

Gods of Old Europe, 181–90). Even if one questions the scholarship behind these assertions, a number of contemporary women use this version of the *labrys* for feminist ends. In modern times, some lesbian groups, for example, have reappropriated the *labrys* as a symbol of "the all-female community of Lesbos and its founding mothers who worshipped only the Goddess in nature and in each other" (Walker, 523).

Wolf explores the symbolism of the *labrys* in one of the essays that precedes her *Kassandra* narrative:

> The labrys . . . is said to be a token of the Cretan Zeus. . . . We . . . see it . . . in the . . . representations of the goddesses cult on the little Minoan seals in the Heraklion museum. Never . . . has the Minoan double ax been found in the hand of a male deity. The ax . . . is believed to owe its sacred character to the fact that it was originally used to fell trees—in primitive societies a labor performed by women. Then it became identified with the lightning that attracts rain, and the Cretan mother goddess Eileithyia was gradually transferred into the male-dominated Olympian pantheon, with Zeus at the summit beside Hera, his wife. Via this long-drawn-out route marked by struggles, conflicts, and defeats, the double ax comes into the hands of Zeus—and when they retraced its route back to its origin, the American feminists took it as a symbol. (*Cassandra,* 194–95)

Wolf expresses some skepticism regarding the enthusiasm of the American feminists she meets on her journey to Greece, but they also move Wolf to consider the desperate need of contemporary women to find a cultural origin that has the female at its center. Whatever reading we use of the history of the *labrys,* Klytemnestra's identification with this ceremonial weapon by contemporary women writers marks both her connection to earlier female deities and her violent resistance to having her female rule displaced by patriarchy.

To recapitulate Klytemnestra's story briefly (I will later explore it in detail), she is the daughter of Leda and Tyndareos, sister of Helen and the Dioskuri (her brothers, Kastor and Polydeukes), and wife of Agamemnon. She is infamous for her slaying (with the help of her lover, Aegisthus) of her husband Agamemnon upon his return from the Trojan War. She also slew his captured prize of war, the Trojan princess and seer, Kassandra. Some classical authors attribute Klytemnestra's actions to political ambition, desire for her lover, Aegisthus, and jealousy of Kassandra; others see her mariticide as revenge for Agamemnon's sacrifice of his and Klytemnestra's daughter Iphigenia to gain success in the war. Still other writers indicate that Agamemnon killed Klytemnestra's first husband and child in addition to Iphigenia, thus increasing her motive for revenge.[4] To avenge Agamemnon's death, Klytemnestra's son, Orestes, with the help of his sister Electra, slays his mother. Klytemnestra's history before her marriage to Agamemnon is often down-played or overlooked in reference works—particularly those in English.[5] In *Iphigenia in Aulis,* Euripides indicates that Klytemnestra is taken by Agamem-non from her first husband, Tantalus, whom Agamemnon killed along with the couple's baby.[6] Without this early history, readers form an entirely dif-ferent image of Klytemnestra's motivations.

Klytemnestra displays an individual strength and violence usually denied to women (with the notable exceptions of figures such as Medea, whose sto-ry also provides material for revisions at the end of the twentieth century). She is the perfect embodiment of female frustration. When seen from a fem-inist perspective, she personifies the psychologically (and in contemporary revisions, physically and sexually) abused victim. But Klytemnestra also sig-nals the female capacity to fight *back* against violence visited upon women (upon her daughter Iphigenia as well as a previous child and husband). Si-lenced and suppressed by patriarchy that demands her daughter's death, Klytemnestra becomes a heroine who finally takes the knife (or the axe) to the chief symbol of patriarchal repression.

Klytemnestra represents the feminist cause par excellence. Her story is really *the* story of the struggle of female, blood right against the founding of male, rational law and the establishment of patriarchy.[7] Much is at stake, therefore, in how one sees Klytemnestra and her killing of Agamemnon. Is she a murdering adulteress who is not willing to relinquish power when her husband returns? Or is she the avenging mother who executes the murderer of her daughter? Does Mother Right hold up against Father Right?[8] These questions generated by the classical authors are reexamined by late-twenti-eth-century female authors in their revisions of Klytemnestra.

At issue is the crucial subject of the cultural construction of violence. Why is very brutal male violence in war not only sanctioned but lauded in the classical texts, while female violence represents terrifying sacrilege? Part of the answer, of course, is that whereas quarrels among men only cause a shift in leadership within patriarchy, the violence of the female against a male threatens the stability of patriarchy itself. But Klytemnestra represents a par-ticularly crucial case of female violence because, in the mythic realm, she mounts the last major challenge to the founding of patriarchy itself as rep-resented in Athens and the rule of law inscribed in Western culture in Aes-chylus's *Oresteia.*[9]

In his trilogy (*Agamemnon, Choephoroe, Eumenides*), Aeschylus records the movement from kinship-based social and political organization, which priv-ileges blood rights connected with the female, to democracy, patriarchal priv-ilege, and the rule of law as figured in the founding of the law court of Athens. The primacy of Mother Right and connections of kin and blood, which Klytemnestra represents, must be replaced by the dominance of Father Right and legal connections. When Klytemnestra's son, Orestes, is acquitted of her murder in the *Eumenides,* both patriarchal dominance and male-centered law become the foundation of Athenian democracy and Western culture.

Klytemnestra's capacities and attributes (having or wanting power and control, willingness to use violence against the male, insistence on freedom to choose a sexual partner, being aligned more closely with the child [Iphigenia] than with the husband, and thus threatening patriarchal control) also make her the perfect scapegoat for carrying the sins of feminism itself. One of Wolf's acquaintances in the travel journal that precedes her *Kassandra* labels Klytemnestra "the first feminist" for precisely these characteristics. All of these attributes make Klytemnestra a terrifying embodiment of the ancient fear that females are out of control—or, more frightening, that they seek to be *in* control—thus threatening all of civilization. Aeschylus makes this powerful argument in his *Oresteia* in 458 B.C.[10]

The remainder of this chapter seeks to establish Klytemnestra's characteristics in the ancient texts and to sketch the outline of the archetype she embodies in classical materials. Comprehending what issues of gender and violence are inherent in the classical story is necessary to analyzing why modern women respond to Klytemnestra so passionately. Understanding which details the women use and which they delete, as well as which classical authors they draw upon, is vital to analyzing the modern texts.

Klytemnestra in Antiquity

A woman whose name used as a common noun came to mean "adulteress" or "murderess,"[11] Klytemnestra is much more reviled in the classical tradition than her sister, Helen. Klytemnestra's actions are not in dispute: she kills her husband Agamemnon along with his captive, Kassandra, upon his return from the Trojan War. What remains in question are the reasons behind Klytemnestra's actions.

The daughter of Leda and Tyndareos and sister of Helen and the Dioskuri, Klytemnestra inherits a mortal status, while Helen eventually gains immortality through her father, Zeus. The events leading to Klytemnestra's slaying of Agamemnon begin with his murder of her first husband and child and his taking her as wife and queen in Mycenae. Her story will end, however, not with her death in Mycenae but with the acquittal of her son, Orestes, in Athens. This migration is crucial because of the nature of the origins of Athenian citizenship and Athens's critical role as the founding model of Western democratic culture. As Nicole Loraux points out, Athens is a city in which citizenship demands being male, in which the myth of civic origin depicts Athenian males as autochthonous—in short, it is a city in which women are excluded. Athens has a male-generated, female deity, Athena, as its protectress, thus fulfilling the patriarchal dream of a female operating entirely in the service of *andreia* (manly courage) (*Children of Athena,* 18).

But as Loraux also indicates, Athenians must have dealt with the ineluctable fact of birth from two and the Periclean law of bilateral parentage for citizenship. Women, then, are a continuous problematic presence for Athens and its male dream of autochthonous birth. Athens is thus the perfect setting in which to play out the power struggle between the sexes, a struggle with Klytemnestra at its center. In order to inscribe a male-ordered political system, Athens must reconcile the contradictory elements of its own origin and create a narrative that acknowledges but at the same time suppresses the female and blood rights, that paradoxically allows the eternal virgin Athena to become protectress of childbirth. Aeschylus's *Eumenides* provides precisely this narrative. But in order to enact it, Aeschylus must not just remove Klytemnestra—the aggressive mother who trespasses into the (male) political arena, who values female child above husband and king, *oikos* (house or home) above polis—he must discredit her. Klytemnestra and her maternal fury must be made to appear so unnatural that Orestes' matricide can be forgiven for the good of the patriarchal state.

Nonetheless, Klytemnestra's identity remains ambiguous, which is revealed in the various spellings of her name in ancient texts and vase paintings—either Klyte*mn*estra (etymologically "praiseworthy or famous wooing" or even "renowned for suitors") or Klyte*m*estra ("famous cunning").[12] It seems ironic that Klytemnestra should be cited for suitors and wooing when she is not wooed but violently won by Agamemnon and ultimately by Aegisthus.[13] This irony is intensified by Klytemnestra's having the famously wooed Helen as a sister[14] and the persistently wooed Penelope as a foil.[15] Patricia A. Marquardt suggests the reading "wooed for her fame,"[16] which raises the politically probable notion that Klytemnestra would be pursued for her station. Taking her gives one the kingdom. This status vests more political power in Klytemnestra but also makes her prone to violent conquest. The second version of the name, Klyte*m*estra ("famous cunning"), imbues Klytemnestra with more intelligence and self-determination; it thereby also makes her more guilty in Agamemnon's slaying. Unlike the wiliness of Odysseus or his wife, Penelope, which helps to reestablish home, husband, and patriarchal rule, Klytemnestra's cunning serves matriarchal political power and maternal vengeance.

For some scholars, the letters *mne* of Klytemnestra call to mind *mnēnē*, that is, memory or the recurrent effect of past experience.[17] Thus her name would suggest "famous for memory" or "famous for the recurrent effects of past experience." This interpretation supports reading Klytemnestra as a mother who remembers offenses long past—and acts to avenge them. As someone obsessed with the past, Klytemnestra becomes a foil to her rival and victim, Kassandra, who is obsessed with the future. Unfortunately for her, Klytemnestra passes on her obsession with past wrongs to her daughter Electra.

Homer and Stesichorus

Homer's[18] Nestor depicts Klytemnestra as a basically good, initially faithful woman seduced by Aegisthus. Nestor explains that Orestes eventually buried his "hated mother, craven Aegisthus too" (*Odyssey,* Fagles translation, 117, 3.350) in retribution for their murder of Agamemnon. Not surprisingly, Homer's Agamemnon has a damning view of Klytemnestra when he speaks to Odysseus from Erebos. He describes Klytemnestra's cruelty in slaying Kassandra, as well as her bestial and treacherous behavior in slaying him. Agamemnon depicts a Klytemnestra akin to Eve in the Christian tradition when he argues that she "bathes in shame not only herself but the whole breed of womankind, even the honest ones to come, forever down the years!" (Fagles, 263, 2.490–92). Odysseus grants Agamemnon that the sons of Atreus have certainly been tormented by unruly women.

In attributing guilt, the lyric poet Stesichorus (c. 632–629 B.C. to c. 556–553 B.C.) partly blames Aphrodite for making Tyndareos's daughters unfaithful because their father forgot his sacrifice to her: "And she in anger . . . made them twice married and three times married / and brides who deserted their husbands" (Lattimore, 23. From Stesichorus's *Helen and Klytaimestra*). However, explaining both Helen's and Klytemnestra's behavior as caused by a forgetful father (whose sins are visited upon his daughters rather than sons) and the gods does not alleviate their personal culpability. Classical Greek authors frequently attribute mortals' mistakes and misdeeds to the gods without negating their individual human responsibility.[19]

Aeschylus

While Klytemnestra plays only a minor role in Homer's recounting of the Trojan War, she rises to disturbing grandeur in Aeschylus's *Oresteia* (458 B.C.). This trilogy represents the crucial document for our understanding of Klytemnestra's complicated role in the founding of Western culture and in the shift from Mother Right to patriarchal laws.

The *Oresteia*'s appeal rests on several facts. First, the trilogy has powerful and determined female characters—particularly Klytemnestra. Aeschylus not only gives Klytemnestra a voice, he also endows her with a capacity to manipulate language in order to persuade and entrap her husband and to transform her slaying of him into a sacrifice in retribution for her daughter's murder. This Klytemnestra is intelligent and articulate—much more so than the men who surround her. Aeschylus does not make his task of defeating her and the powers she embodies an easy one.

Second, Aeschylus's *Oresteia* is a crucial document in the evolution of Western civilization and its attitudes toward women.[20] As Robert Fagles and W. B. Stanford explain, the trilogy marks the transition from "the savagery of past wars and feuds" to "a new harmony—religious, political, and personal" (3). Aeschylus depicts the moment when endless vengeance and bloodletting give way to law and civilized society. He holds out the hope that "Perhaps Athens would achieve what public-spirited men and women have always longed for, a peaceful, lawful community, a city of benevolent gods and beneficent men" (3). In Aeschylus's vision, we move from the savagery of the tribe represented by the self-devouring House of Atreus to the polis, the city of Athens and its system of law and democracy.[21] Man learns "to suffer into knowledge" (*pathe mathos*), to turn his inherited guilt and ethical conflicts into a better world.

Troubling, however, is the fact that it is so determinedly *man* who suffers into knowledge in Aeschylus's trilogy. Women tend to suffer into oblivion, repression, or benevolent subservience. The female is linked to ancient blood rights and to the irrational—all of which must give way to found a patriarchal system in which legal inheritance by the male can be assured. Klytemnestra must be removed to produce progress; the female principles embodied in the Furies must be tamed and led to the depths from which they can function benevolently. Ironically, this is accomplished largely by another female character, Athena, who is indeed her father's daughter and is co-opted by the male order. Linking the subjugation of the female to the male order to produce Western civilization and culture is at the heart of the trilogy and of Klytemnestra's importance to women even today. The *Oresteia* investigates cultural evolution and how it is tied in Western thinking to a very crucial battle of the sexes in which women come out quite literally on the bottom.

Even the title of the trilogy favors the male. Why should Orestes get the eponymous billing? He does not even appear in the *Agamemnon*. The eponym should really belong to Klytemnestra. She is the one who initiates the action, who is both violent and abused, whose retaliation pits female "irrational" principles against male reason and law. But Klytemnestra remains an irritant in Western culture; she and the principles she represents must be repressed and forgotten. As far as we know, no classical tragedy is named for her—a fact that bespeaks the need to bury her name under the rational, male tradition. Aeschylus, however, realizes the difficulty and complexity of suppressing the mother and denying motherhood to women. His Klytemnestra is a woman of power and passion, an unforgettable presence who persists long after her death.

Before we examine Aeschylus's *Oresteia*, we should recall the history of the family into which Klytemnestra marries, the House of Atreus. The founder of the family was Tantalus of Lydia, who offended the gods by serving them his son, Pelops, as a meal. The gods sentenced Tantalus to starve in Hades, surrounded by food just out of his reach. The gods restore Pelops, who journeys to Greece, where he marries Hippodameia after causing her father's death in a chariot race. Pelops produces two sons, Atreus and Thyestes. Thyestes seduces Atreus's wife and attempts to claim the throne. Atreus banishes Thyestes but later invites him back for a reconciliation feast at which he emulates his grandfather in serving Thyestes his own children as a meal. Thyestes curses Atreus and his house, then flees with his remaining son, Aegisthus. Atreus produces two sons, Agamemnon and Menelaus, who marry Tyndareos's daughters, Klytemnestra and Helen. Agamemnon leads a fleet to Troy to avenge the abduction of Helen by Paris. Aeschylus takes up the family saga when Agamemnon returns from Troy. The curse that Thyestes settles on Atreus and his descendants in revenge for having been served the flesh of his own children is that Atreus's house will be "self-devouring." Agamemnon's sacrifice of his daughter, Klytemnestra's slaying of her husband (with the help of Thyestes' son, Aegisthus), and Orestes' murder of his mother are all actions seen as part of this curse. (See the appendix for a genealogy of the descendants of Tantalus as well as the genealogy of Klytemnestra.)

Before we meet Klytemnestra in the *Agamemnon,* we hear of her daughter's slaughter by Agamemnon. We (along with the classical Greek audience raised on these myths) know what will drive Klytemnestra's vengeance. Iphigenia, lured to her death under the pretense of her marriage to Achilles, must be sacrificed in order to allow the Greeks to avenge the violated marriage of Helen and Menelaus. The divine Helen's female child is spared; her mortal sister's daughter must pay the price. The chorus introduces the Fury that drives the Greeks to avenge Helen (ll. 65–78, 107 Bantam edition), but the audience surely thinks of the Furies that Klytemnestra's ghost will loose later. Klytemnestra's first words call up the dark female principles and the mother's womb, "Let the morning shine, as the proverb says, / glorious from the womb of Mother Night" (ll. 264–65). The mother's womb and Mother

Right will drive her vengeance and avenge her death. Klytemnestra is a queen of power who controls her land and "maneuvers like a man" (l. 13).

Violence figures prominently in the trilogy's first play. The chorus dwells on the violence of war in Troy. But we also see the violence done by Agamemnon to his daughter, a violence enacted against the female, mother and daughter. That violence will breed; Klytemnestra nurtures it into her vengeance. The heroic violence of war transmutes into domestic violence that must be eliminated in order to protect patriarchy. Both the sons of the House of Atreus, Menelaus and Agamemnon, and Leda's daughters, Helen and Klytemnestra, are caught in a whirlpool of violence.

But Klytemnestra also reveals her intelligence and ironic wit as she greets her returning husband. She laments that their child is not there. Agamemnon can only think of the female, Iphigenia, but Klytemnestra claims to mean the son, Orestes, whom she claims to have sent away for his protection. But when she utters the lines, "Our child is gone. That is my self-defense / and it is true" (ll. 876–77), both she and her audience have Iphigenia in mind. Klytemnestra is thus able to speak relatively openly, if ironically, about her motivations. When she invites Agamemnon to walk on the tapestries she lays down for him (which in itself constitutes a blasphemy since these were fabrics sacred to the gods and treading on them adds to Agamemnon's guilt),[22] she adds, "Let the red stream flow and bear him home / to the home he never hoped to see— Justice, / lead him in" (ll. 902–4). Implied to be a sign of his victory, "the red stream" is also Agamemnon's blood, which is about to flow and take him to the underworld. Clearly, Klytemnestra feels justified in the execution she will carry out. Justice will lead Agamemnon to his death. Klytemnestra's motivation and intentions are announced and defended before she even glimpses Kassandra, the Trojan princess who accompanies Agamemnon. Vengeance for the slain daughter far outweighs any jealousy over a new concubine.

In the *Agamemnon*, Klytemnestra is the master of double entendre as she declares that she "would have sworn to tread on legacies of robes . . . suffer the worst to bring that dear life back" (ll. 964–66). The now flattered Agamemnon thinks his to be the life for which Klytemnestra would do the worst, but it is Iphigenia we envision. When Klytemnestra compares Agamemnon to Zeus, who "tramples the bitter virgin grape for new wine" (l. 972), we think again of the sacrificed virgin, Iphigenia, as Agamemnon envisions himself as a god. One might label Klytemnestra duplicitous, but she cannot be seen as lacking the courage of her convictions. She declares her feeling in metaphor, but only an arrogant Agamemnon could miss all the implications of her speech. In a moment of dramatic irony, the audience and the chorus surmise her double meanings and are terrified.

Clytemnestra tempts Agamemnon to tread upon the sacred tapestries of the house. In Martha Graham's *Clytemnestra*, with Graham dancing Clytemnestra. (Photo by Martha Swope. Martha Swope/Timepix)

Klytemnestra's multivalent statements mark her ability both to do violence to language and to announce violence through language. Hers is an intellectual as well as a physical violence. She has the ability to wrest meanings from language that are hidden by its surface declarations. Her detractors might say that she misuses words, exerts a deforming control over them and subverts their referential function. Such capacities make her a danger to society, which must rely on a transparent use of language to sustain social intercourse.[23] Klytemnestra's subversion of normal communication undermines the exchange of ideas through language, just as her adultery undermines the kinship-based exchange of value through the exchange of women in marriage. Klytemnestra is a woman who follows her personal inclinations in sexuality and her personal meanings in language. Both subversions are dangerous to a society that must depend on successful exchanges of women and words.

Klytemnestra's linguistic dexterity allows her to lure her victim to his fate,[24] but it also permits her to account for her physical violence by explicating her intentions before she slays and by demonstrating Agamemnon's guilt. Her words tempt Agamemnon to greater acts of hubris (such as walking on the tapestries of the house) that help to justify his death. Like Odysseus, the hero of many intellectual twists and turns, Klytemnestra is a thinking actor. Her vengeance and violence are cerebral as well as corporeal. She is a clever weaver of plots, but she can also wield a sword (or an axe)—like a man. Klytemnestra's usurping of both gender positions provides another threat to her society.

Klytemnestra's ability to act like a man is underlined by Kassandra's vision of her mariticide. She envisions Agamemnon as a great bull dragged from its mate—by the woman, who gores him through. Klytemnestra does the goring; she has the power to penetrate and to kill. In Aeschylus's version of the killing, Klytemnestra takes the male role while Aegisthus hides and assumes the passive, female role. In her visions, Kassandra also sees the Furies dancing atop the roofs of the House of Atreus; these spirits avenge blood-related killings, of which the House of Atreus is only too full. Klytemnestra serves their cause when she murders her husband in revenge for her daughter, a nonblood killing to right a blood slaying. This relationship to the Furies impels Kassandra to see Klytemnestra as a "detestable hellhound" (l. 1237), "the monster of Greece" (l. 1242), a "viper," and a "sea-witch" (l. 1243); she is "the raging mother of death" (l. 1245). The violent mother, the woman who slays the man, the female as raging lioness to replace the raging lion Achilles at Troy, is a terrifying figure to Kassandra as well as to her Greek listeners. Kassandra foretells that Klytemnestra's own child Orestes will kill her in turn to avenge his father.

After slaying Agamemnon, Klytemnestra emerges carrying the sword and glorying in her deed. She describes entangling Agamemnon in a net, snaring him like an animal or a fish—dehumanizing him—and then stabbing him three times. Far from attempting to mitigate her violence, she boasts that she "did it all" (l. 1400) and that her deed is a "masterpiece of Justice" (l. 1430). Aeschylus thus paints a strong, proud queen who is sure of the justice of her cause. Aegisthus, nowhere to be seen, has not yet emerged from hiding; this is Klytemnestra's revenge, and she takes full credit for it. In later centuries, male dramatists would paint a weak woman seduced by an evil lover, and, in modern times, even many women writers depict a woman abused and powerless. Aeschylus, however, presents a complex and powerful figure. She rebukes the chorus for not having banished Agamemnon when he sacrificed his own daughter. A blood killing should have exiled him. Klytemnestra, in contrast, claims the justice of her own act—which is not a blood slaying since she is not related to Agamemnon by blood—swearing by "the child's Rights I brought to birth, / by Ruin, by Fury—the three gods to whom / I sacrificed this man" (ll. 1459–61). Hers is a maternal vengeance, sanctioned by the Furies and by blood rights. Part of the long history of the self-devouring House of Atreus, Klytemnestra's action carries forward a prolonged tradition of family slayings.

Aegisthus appears in the last few pages of the play to recount the kin murders, cannibalism, and betrayal of Atreus visited upon Aegisthus's father, Thyestes. While his recounting of the curses helps to justify the murder of Agamemnon, Aegisthus himself is a despicable figure who would silence old men's criticism with a sword. Klytemnestra stops him, and the two return to the palace to begin their joint rule of Argos.

In *The Libation Bearers,* Klytemnestra is displaced in favor of her daughter Electra and her son, Orestes, who meet after several years at Agamemnon's grave. Orestes has returned from exile to avenge his father. Electra turns all her hopes for revenge to Orestes, whom she addresses as father, mother, sister, and brother. He has become her whole family and world; his actions will give her peace. Electra is unable to complete her own fate without him. Orestes asserts that he has been sent by Apollo to slay his mother. Apollo instructs Orestes to "Gore them [Klytemnestra and Aegisthus] like a bull" (l. 280), and thus to replace Klytemnestra's act of goring in the first play. Orestes must replicate his mother's action in order to avenge his father. But unlike Klytemnestra's execution of Agamemnon, Orestes' murder of his mother is a blood slaying (at least we believe so until Apollo's rhetorical denial of motherhood in the *Eumenides*). Ironically, Apollo threatens Orestes with pursuit by his father's Furies if he does not carry out the killing. But it will be his mother's Furies who pursue him after the deed.

Orestes' own motivation is a threefold mixture that includes self-interest and duty. First he cites the god's command, second sorrow for his father, and third the loss of his own inheritance to the usurper Aegisthus. He and Electra invoke both Zeus and Mother Earth to give them the rage necessary for revenge. Orestes learns that his father was mutilated and buried unsung. Electra adds her tale of woe and abuse to fuel his hate and determination. Theirs is a world in which murder breeds murder; violence nurtures violence. This endless cycle must be halted if the self-devouring House of Atreus is ever to escape its curse—and if civilization is to have a chance to form lasting societies not based on feud. The cycle of violence is not destined to be halted in this play, however; the violence must be played out. The violent woman must meet a violent end at her son's hands.

In order to accomplish their goal, Electra and Orestes pray to their dead father. Electra replaces her sacrificed sister, Iphigenia, by asserting that she too will "pour [her] birthright out to you [Agamemnon]—the wine of the fathers' house, my bridal wine" (ll. 473–74). Like Iphigenia, Electra is willing to sacrifice her future and marriage in order to support the patriarchal order by avenging her father. Like Athena, she is her father's daughter. Ironically, Electra also invokes Persephone, who personifies the strength rather of the mother-daughter bond and who, like Iphigenia, is taken from her mother in order to be married to death. This complex series of competing invocations keeps the rival claims of Mother Right and Father Right alive in the audience's mind.

Klytemnestra has a premonition of her impending death; she dreams of giving birth to a snake that feeds at her breast and draws blood. To calm herself, she has a long row of torches lit, recalling the torches that opened the first play and announced both Agamemnon's return and his death. Her own death seems illuminated by this new fire. And Orestes sees himself figured in the snake that will kill his mother. The chorus compares Klytemnestra to all manner of violent women who slay men, including Althaia, who murdered her son; Scylla, who murdered her father, King Nisos; and the women of Lemnos, who murdered the males of their island in retribution for their mistreatment. The list is meant to highlight Klytemnestra's violence and violation of the patriarchal order as well as to horrify the audience.

The disguised Orestes sets his plan to kill Aegisthus and Klytemnestra in motion by appearing at the palace to announce his own death. Klytemnestra answers the door. As in the first play, her speech is still marked by double meanings, but she no longer seems to be in control of the implications of her words. She announces that in her house, "the eyes of Justice look on all we do" (l. 653), but the audience is meant to understand that Justice has shifted from Klytemnestra's camp to Orestes'. Her words become ominous for her and Aegisthus. The chorus encourages Orestes to be only his father's son and to reject his mother's pleas. When Klytemnestra reminds Orestes that he suckled at her breast (ll. 883–85), we are also reminded of the snake dream that foretold her death.

In murdering his mother, Orestes reenacts Klytemnestra's own actions from the *Agamemnon*. He appears standing over the bodies of Klytemnestra and Aegisthus, as Klytemnestra stood over Agamemnon and Kassandra in the first play. Orestes takes from the bodies of his mother and her lover the robes that entangled them as they had earlier netted Agamemnon; Orestes displays them as his mother had done at the first murders. He insists publicly that his matricide is just, that the mother he once loved must now be loathed as a viper who killed her mate. The shroud that wound Agamemnon now also encompasses his murderers. The coil of fate has formed another loop in the self-devouring House of Atreus. Orestes recognizes that his victory over his mother is also his curse and his guilt. Orestes must now return as a suppliant to Apollo at Delphi, who demanded this murder. Orestes knows that he cannot escape the blood that is his own, and he is immediately beset by the Furies of his mother's vengeance. The curse of the house continues to consume it.

The final play of the trilogy, the *Eumenides,* must reconcile the competing claims of Mother Right and Father Right, female and male orders; it must decide if Orestes' slaying of his mother (a blood-related killing) or Klytemnestra's slaying of her husband (a nonblood-related killing) is the greater crime. In order to do this, Aeschylus must find a way to deny the maternity of the woman, to allow Orestes to claim that Klytemnestra is not his mother. Aeschylus has Apollo argue that the woman is not really mother but only vessel to the child, contributing matter but not soul. In an antilogical turn that seems all but preposterous to a twenty-first-century audience, Aeschylus denies already disenfranchised women their claim to motherhood itself. Nonetheless, later Greek authorities, such as Aristotle,[25] agree with this argument, and the single-parent concept persists into the Middle Ages with the notion of the whole fetus contained entirely within the male sperm and using the female egg only for nourishment.[26] Apollo's denial of motherhood to women allows Orestes' murder of Klytemnestra to be seen as a nonblood killing—a literally infuriating claim that necessitates appeasing and repressing the female Furies, who are outraged at the eventual acquittal of Orestes.

The *Eumenides* begins with Apollo's priestess, the Pythia, offering prayers. She begins by praying to Mother Earth as the first of the ancient gods; she ends by invoking the newest, Olympian gods headed by "Father Zeus." The trajectory of Aeschylus's trilogy as a whole makes the same movement from ancient Mother Right to the newly founded patriarchal order of emerging Athens. Athena is also invoked as we embark on a trial in which she will figure centrally. When the Pythia emerges from her cave, she is terror-struck by Orestes—dripping blood, surrounded by hideous Furies, and asking Apollo to purge him. Apollo detests the disgusting female Furies. Ironically, he refers to them as "eternal virgins," a phrase that recalls Athena, who will tame the Furies, as well as Iphigenia, whose sacrifice began the bloody cycle. As virgins, the female principles are relegated early on to a nonmaternal role.

As Orestes, accompanied by Hermes, goes off to Athens and Athena's judgment, Klytemnestra returns as a ghost to goad the Furies back to action. This is Klytemnestra's only appearance in the final play. Her principles are carried on by the Furies, whose special province is avenging murderers of blood kin. They are therefore closely aligned with female blood rights and are staunch defenders of motherhood. The Furies complain of Apollo's tricks and of the new gods who have no respect for ancient goddesses (ll. 144–75). The two sides begin the argument that is the pivot of the play. The Furies claim vengeance for a matricide, the killing of a blood relation. Apollo claims vengeance for the murder of a husband—not a blood killing. He argues that the bond of marriage is sacred, "the source of mankind's nearest, dearest ties. Marriage of man and wife is Fate itself, stronger than oaths, and Justice guards its life" (ll. 214–16). The crucial contest between blood rights and legal social arrangements is set.

Orestes reaches Athens and seeks a trial before Athena. The Furies demand blood for a blood slaying. Justice is vengeance for them, not legal process.[27] Encircled by the Furies, Orestes, who has "suffered into knowledge" as the first play indicates human beings must, now understands the price of his matricide, but he also seeks to be pardoned. The Furies invoke Mother Night and assert their power, "spun . . . by the Fates" (l. 335), to punish kin murderers. To break the impasse, Athena appears armed for combat with her aegis and her spear. Athena, however, shows the Furies respect and fairness; in return, they give her judgment over Orestes' fate. Athena, shrewd as always, understands that she is in a double bind. If she acquits Orestes, the Furies will plague her land; if she condemns him, Apollo and her human citizens will be angered. The problem calls for Athena's wisdom. Her answer is to appoint the ten best men of Athens as judges, thus founding the law court of Athens and the legal system that underpins Western civilization.

At Orestes' trial, the Furies point out the dangers of letting children murder their parents with impunity. To defend Orestes, Apollo argues that women are not really mothers or parents at all and that the father is the real creative force:

The woman you call the mother of the child
is not the parent, just a nurse to the seed,
the new-sown seed that grows and swells inside her.
The *man* is the source of life—the one who mounts.
She, like a stranger for a stranger, keeps
the shoot alive unless god hurts the root.
(*Oresteia*, 288, *Eumenides*, ll. 666–71)

Demonstrating a clear case of legal casuistry (or womb envy), men usurp the female contribution to birth and deny woman their most irrefutable function. At this moment in cultural history, the ancient traditions of Mother Right based on blood relationships give way to a new order founded on legal relationships and on the subjugation of women.

. Froma Zeitlin explores the implications of this shift as represented in the *Eumenides* when she points out the central importance of creating from the male-female dichotomies and conflicts a hierarchical order with the male on top. The newly inscribed order would curb the violence associated with the constant conflict between opposing forces. As she puts it, "the basic issue in the trilogy is the establishment in the face of female resistance of the binding nature of patriarchal marriage where wife's subordination and patrilineal succession are reaffirmed" (149).[28] Creating social order is necessary to found Western civilization; for the Greeks, that order depends on the subservience of women to higher social goals. The *Oresteia* creates a new myth to legitimize this order within cultural tradition. This new myth lends divine authorization to human constructs and patterns.

In the late twentieth century, women attempted to revise this founding myth in order to replace the divine authority with a human one and to displace the gods' sanctions by human responsibility. What is troubling for women in Klytemnestra's story is precisely the fundamental determining of male/female roles and the setting of male/female "responsibilities" in such a way that killing the mother is vindicated while killing the husband cannot be.

As Zeitlin demonstrates in her analysis of the *Oresteia*, women—and particularly the rebellious Klytemnestra—must be redefined in order to accomplish their subjugation. Klytemnestra's depiction in the course of the trilogy underscores this move. As Zeitlin summarizes it:

Clytemnestra, the female principle, in the first play is a shrewd intelligent rebel against the masculine regime, but by the last play, through her representatives, the Erinyes, female is now allied with the archaic, primitive, and regressive, while male in the person of the young, Apollo, champions conjugality, society, and progress, and his interests are ratified by the androgynous goddess, Athena, who sides with the male and confirms his primacy. Through gradual and subtle transformations, social evolution is posed as a movement from female dominance to male dominance, or, as it is often figuratively phrased, from "matri-archy" to "patriarchy." (151)

Zeitlin recalls Bachofen's view that true historical development occurs when ancient *Mutterrecht* (Mother Right), "represented by the telluric, the mate-rial and the feminine," gives way to the "higher Uranian, spiritual, and mas-culine values" (Zeitlin, 175 n. 4). While Zeitlin stresses that actual matriar-chy (defined as the genuine political and economic supremacy of women) is not a demonstrable historical reality and may itself represent another myth,[29] the need to inscribe the movement from female- to male-dominat-ed order is central to the founding of Western culture.

What partly fuels the myth of matriarchy is men's fear that women are unruly and violent, that they must be kept in check in order to form a viable society. Marriage is the institution designed to accomplish the task. By mur-dering her husband and her king, and valuing her female child over the male legal spouse, Klytemnestra clearly mounts a dangerous challenge to conju-gal as well as political order. Rule by women threatens to overthrow rule by men—and the whole social order based on it. To accentuate this threat, Kly-temnestra is compared in *The Libation Bearers* to a series of murderous wom-en, who represent the main female roles—mothers (Althaea), daughters (Scylla), wives (Klytemnestra herself), and finally women who destroy the male en masse, the Lemnian women. Plainly, if we let one murderous wom-an off, her crimes will escalate to wipe out all males. Klytemnestra represents a danger from within the system itself, a dissident who threatens to overthrow the male order as a whole—both domestic and political. This provides strong justification for Orestes' defense by Apollo in the *Eumenides*.

The attempt to curb female violence also calls for an institutional means to enforce social arrangements, thus the founding of the law court of Athens to preserve traditional male dominance and to end the threat of anarchy. The Furies, daughters of ancient Night, must be brought to accept the judgment of Athena's new legal institution. Athena, the male-loyal virgin, who "cannot set more store by the woman's [Klytemnestra's] death" (l. 754), must find a way to persuade the female principle represented by the Furies to become both benevolent (Eumenides) and repressed (occupying a space beneath the earth).[30] Athena's power of persuasion (*Peithō*) is a mixture of clever argu-mentation, flattery, and threat. She placates the Furies by pointing out that they were not defeated, since the votes of the jurors were equal and only Athe-na's vote can break the tie. She lures them with promises of fame and honors from the Athenians. But just in case, Athena also reminds the Furies that she is the only god who knows the key to Zeus's armory of thunderbolts. *Peithō*, or persuasion, thus takes on many guises in Athena's hands.

When Athena finally succeeds in convincing the Furies to become the Eumenides and to protect Athens rather than to wreak vengeance on it, the subjugation of the female principle is complete. The female is not removed entirely; she is installed comfortably underground, where she can be flattered or threatened into supporting the now firmly established male social order. Ironically keeping watch over fertility and wedlock, the virgin Furies give way to the virgin Eumenides as female sexuality is safely constrained within marriage. Now that the Furies have been tamed, the Athenians

> poised by the side of Zeus
> loved by the loving virgin girl
> [can] achieve humanity at last
> nestling under Pallas' wings
> and blessed with Father's love.
> (ll. 1007–11)

Returned by the Furies to the Father and to the Father's loyal, virgin daughter, Athens can now become the fount of Western civilization. The blood-red robes that snared Agamemnon and the torchlight that presages his death are now redefined to serve the Eumenides and to ensure the safety and prosperity of Athens. The female principles are firmly planted "deep, deep" below and will serve to support patriarchy. Klytemnestra's rituals in celebration of her slaying of Agamemnon from the first play are reenacted as rituals to confirm the dominance of the male rule of law and the safe suppression of the female Furies.

Sophocles

In Sophocles' *Electra* (between 418 and 410 B.C.),[31] produced almost forty-five years after Aeschylus's *Oresteia*,[32] we see Klytemnestra predominantly through the eyes of her abused and relentlessly mourning daughter Electra. Sophocles' Electra believes her mother a monster who slays Agamemnon unjustly in order to reign with Aegisthus. The chorus agrees. They refer to Klytemnestra as "the wretchedest of mothers" (Grene, l. 121), "treacherous," and "evil" (ll. 125–26). Electra identifies completely with her murdered father and awaits Orestes' return so that he may slay Aegisthus and Klytemnestra and restore the House of Atreus. Electra also laments her mother's shoddy treatment of her, making her live childless, unmarried, and poor while Klytemnestra sleeps with Aegisthus in Agamemnon's bed. Electra claims that vengeance and justice compel her to act as she does.

The chorus, too, condemns Klytemnestra's actions when they attribute her murder of Agamemnon to lust rather than vengeance for Iphigenia. Sophocles' treatment of Klytemnestra is not entirely biased by Electra's point of view; he does allow Klytemnestra to speak for herself. She refuses to deny her mariticide; she argues that her killing of Agamemnon was an act of justice in retribution for his brutal murder of his own daughter. Defending Mother Right, Klytemnestra feels that Electra should side with her dead sister, Iphigenia, and the mother who avenged her.

Electra responds that it was not maternal justice but the seduction of Aegisthus that prompted Klytemnestra to kill. She rejects Klytemnestra's maternal defense and argues that Agamemnon was constrained to sacrifice Iphigenia by the gods (a defense that would resurface in the cyberspace trial of Klytemnestra in the 1990s) and the country's military aspirations. Like her brother, Orestes, in the *Eumenides,* Electra denies Klytemnestra as her mother, defining her rather as Aegisthus's mistress only. Having failed to sway Electra, Klytemnestra appeals to Apollo to protect her and allow her to live out her life with Aegisthus and the children who love her. The classical audience, who might well have known Aeschylus's *Oresteia,* must have found it the height of irony that Klytemnestra would appeal to the god who would later win an acquittal for the son who murdered her. If ever there was a misplaced trust in the god of light, it is here. Klytemnestra and the daughters of night, who haunt her son in the *Oresteia,* cannot be protected by the god of light and the defender of the father-engendered theory of parenthood.

Sophocles has Orestes announce his own death. Klytemnestra's reaction to the supposed death recalls her maternal claims. She regrets that her own good fortune as queen in being freed of the threat of destruction can only come at her expense and pain as a mother who loses her son. But she quickly acknowledges that Orestes' death frees her of fear, leaving only Electra's poisonous hate to taint her life. In this short interchange, we are reminded of the ambiguous motivations for Klytemnestra's actions. Does she kill justly in a mother's act of vengeance, or does she murder to usurp a throne with a paramour? Although Sophocles presents both possibilities, his Electra clearly believes only the latter.

Orestes is wary of Klytemnestra's warlike spirit and knows she can be as dangerous as a man. Electra prays to Apollo to oversee the murder of Klytemnestra and to demonstrate what punishment awaits the wicked. We know from Aeschylus that Apollo answers Electra's prayers rather than her mother's. The last we hear (literally) of Klytemnestra is her lament that the House of Atreus has left her friendless and confronted by her murderers. She calls for Aegisthus and then entreats her son to pity her as his mother. He does not. Sophocles completes the play with Aegisthus's return.

Sophocles does not follow Orestes' story any further. He allows Klytemnestra's death to go unchallenged and unavenged by the Furies. Sophocles acknowledges both possible motivations for Klytemnestra's mariticide, but Electra keeps the more negative explanation uppermost in our minds. Electra, however, relentless in her vengeance (as is her mother before her), is not an entirely noble character. She demands the two most barbaric acts in the play: the murder of the mother and the casting of Aegisthus's body to the dogs—two actions that parallel those of Creon from *Antigone*. Sophocles leaves us with mixed emotions; his Klytemnestra does not seem entirely evil nor his Electra altogether positive. The gods have sided with Electra and Orestes, but the denial of pity to the mother must have troubled audiences. We leave wondering why Orestes does not go mad or at least seem more traumatized as he marches Aegisthus off to his death. This may indeed be the last murder in the House of Atreus, as Sophocles' closing lines remind us. But this is "justice by death" as Orestes puts it, not a firm foundation on which to found a polis and legal system to replace the self-devouring House of Atreus.

Euripides

After the tragic grandeur of Aeschylus and the troubling negative view of Sophocles, Euripides humanizes Klytemnestra. In his *Electra* (417 B.C.),[33] Klytemnestra claims to have avenged her daughter's sacrifice by her father, but she also admits that it was Agamemnon's additional adultery with Kassandra that finally pushes her to murder him. Euripides' play, situated close to Electra's point of view, is highly critical of Klytemnestra. As Agamemnon and Klytemnestra's daughter, Electra sees her mother as a usurper and as the adulterous lover of Aegisthus. She brooks no excuses for Klytemnestra and denies her the defense of avenging mother. Electra explains to the disguised Orestes that her mother condones the abusive treatment she (Electra) receives at the hands of Aegisthus. She comments bitterly that women are their husbands' friends, not their children's—a particularly ironic accusation to make about Klytemnestra. Electra thus attacks Klytemnestra's one acceptable defense, that of a mother distraught enough to avenge her sacrificed daughter, Iphigenia. Indeed, the audience must wonder why Klytemnestra can be so loyal to one daughter while allowing the other to be exiled and abused. This emphasis on the mother-daughter conflict (stronger finally than the enmity between Orestes and Klytemnestra) calls into question any claim Klytemnestra may have to fierce maternal loyalty. This intense female hatred between mother and daughter, in a more general sense, isolates Klytemnestra from other women. This problematic relationship to women will haunt the twentieth-century Klytemnestras and make the job of reclaiming her as a strong female figure all the more complex.

Euripides, too, shows us a jealous Electra (who will find a sister in Dacia Maraini's Elettra in the 1980s). She is almost as deeply offended by having been ordered out of her royal home as she is by her father's death. She does not appreciate that her mother probably saved her life by accepting Electra's removal to the countryside and to poverty. She argues that Klytemnestra should have been submissive to her husband Agamemnon in all things— although Electra herself only follows this tenet with her own (remarkably benevolent) peasant husband in order to demonstrate her abused and miserable state. The mixed motives of Euripides' Electra make her retributive slaying of her mother less tragically grand than she wants to believe—a fact that becomes clear to her once the deed is done.

Ironically, Electra uses Klytemnestra's clearest virtue to trap her. Her plan to kill her mother depends on Klytemnestra's maternal feelings for a daughter who has supposedly just given birth. Electra can count on Klytemnestra coming to her aid as a child in need, thus turning Klytemnestra's maternal instincts into her fatal flaw—but strengthening Klytemnestra's claim that motherly feeling forms part of her motive in slaying Agamemnon. Klytemnestra was not brutal and ruthless enough to kill Electra when she slew Agamemnon, and she responds to Electra's needs in this play as well; the price of Klytemnestra's irrepressible maternal devotion is death. Maternal loyalty is thus not only endangered but also dangerous—a point patriarchy is only too happy to establish. The whole complex of motherhood is a central issue in Klytemnestra's story in which maternal, blood rights are under attack. Klytemnestra's motherhood, finally, facilitates her destruction; she dies at the hands of her own children.

In the classical tradition, mothers can be fiercely loyal and willing to enact violence on behalf of their own rights and those of their (loved) offspring. Therein lies Klytemnestra's danger: she values blood relationships over the male right of dominion. Her struggle with a husband is also woman's struggle with man who claims authority to dispose of women's bodies and rights. Her attack on Agamemnon undermines both the father and the king. Her maternal violence rocks patriarchy and must, therefore, be stamped out by patriarchy in the persons of Orestes and Electra, who regain their own positions of power in the male-identified structure by killing their mother.

Euripides uses the technique of having the daughter rather than the son urge the vengeance. To discredit a woman, it is preferable to have another woman lodge the accusations. Electra must indict her own mother to demonstrate that her crime is so heinous that even other women will condemn her. Athena is the perfect arbitrator in Orestes' case for this reason. The advantage to this technique is clear: it tears apart from the inside any sense of community among women and any loyalty between mother and daughter. This internal wrenching within the female community remains a problem in the twentieth-century texts.

Euripides' *Iphigenia in Aulis* (first performed in 405 B.C., a few months after Euripides' death) gives us perhaps the clearest look at Klytemnestra's motivations of any of the classical texts. In this play, Klytemnestra is a dedicated mother attempting by reason and emotional appeal to dissuade Agamemnon from "sacrificing" his daughter at the priest's demand. Klytemnestra possesses more nobility than her husband, whose ambitions, desire for power, and fear of his own army call his "heroic stature" into question. Klytemnestra, on the other hand, has overcome her own early hatred of Agamemnon for killing her first husband and "dashing [her] living baby upon the earth, / Brutally tearing him from [her] breasts" (ll. 1151–2, 276). Even though she is forced to marry Agamemnon, Klytemnestra becomes an exemplary wife. She points out the senselessness of sacrificing the innocent Iphigenia for the beautiful but evil Helen; she asks Agamemnon to imagine her plight as a mother, always seeing her daughter's absence; and finally, she gives him fair warning that his horrific deed of murdering his own child might produce just the homecoming that he deserves. Klytemnestra becomes the fierce warrior fighting for her child, while Agamemnon betrays himself as an ambitious yet cowardly schemer. The chorus, the young but valiant Achilles, and the audience side with the mother. Agamemnon knowingly destroys Klytemnestra's love and loyalty to him; by his actions, he places the *labrys* in her hands.

Iphigenia finally stops Klytemnestra's attempts to save her. Iphigenia realizes that she alone can make Greek victory possible and goes to her death willingly, asking her mother not to hate her father. The audience must question whether the Greece that is represented as a bloodthirsty mob demanding the girl's death to satisfy its frenzy for war is worthy of her sacrifice. Early on it is evident that sparing Iphigenia would end the violence. Only the destruction of the innocent virgin makes the war possible. In a recurrent gesture, Greek (and Western) civilization is empowered by violence against women: the abduction of Helen, the "sacrifice" of Iphigenia, and the murder of Klytemnestra. The final step in the founding of the polis is to have the surrogate male, Athena, silence women's subconscious or "prerational" powers in the form of the Erinyes. The fall of Troy and the rise of Athenian democracy are steeped in the blood of women and the privileging of male needs over female rights.

One last irony is the role that marriage plays in Euripides' plot. Klytemnestra brings Iphigenia to Aulis on the understanding that she is to marry Achilles. The mother's joyous celebration is desecrated by the ruse of Agamemnon, and marriage becomes a death trap for Iphigenia just as it will eventually be for Klytemnestra. Society's constant demands that women be good wives (and its complaints that they are not) seem highly ironic when marriage becomes a deadly ploy in patriarchal hands. Why, we wonder, should women honor marriage when men do not?

As both wife and mother, then, Klytemnestra has been betrayed. Her later actions are more comprehensible after viewing this play, where she is most valiant as the defending mother and offended mate. She gives Agamemnon clear warning of the repercussions of his actions. Her only miscalculation seems to be her assumption that Iphigenia's siblings will be as strong in their condemnation of Agamemnon as she is. The audience already knows that Electra and Orestes will side not with their sister and mother but with their father who sacrifices his own children for public position and glory. Like Iphigenia, they will become part of the founding of the patriarchal Western tradition in which the female and mother's blood rights must be suppressed.

In some ways, the issue of female sacrifice needed to found the Western tradition reaches its conclusion not with the acquittal of Orestes but with his rediscovery of his sister Iphigenia in Tauris. Euripides' *Iphigenia in Tauris* (produced c. 412 B.C.) could be read as society's reincorporation of the female virgin (both Iphigenia and the virgin goddess Artemis), who remains necessary to marriage as an institution and to the male's assurance of leaving his legacy to legitimate heirs. Once the violent and powerful matriarch Klytemnestra has been substituted as the female sacrifice necessary to maintain the new patriarchal order, Iphigenia can be reintroduced by the same mechanism as her aunt, Helen.[34] The gods have swept her off to safety. But they have done so in a way that makes the Old Testament test of Abraham and Isaac look benevolent by comparison. Abraham at least knows his son is spared; Klytemnestra believes her daughter sacrificed by her father. She never learns otherwise. This play helps to exonerate Agamemnon's act of cruelty while making Klytemnestra's seem more misguided. If Iphigenia was not sacrificed, Klytemnestra's act of vengeance is futile.

Klytemnestra is almost entirely missing as any kind of human presence in Tauris. She is acknowledged by Iphigenia as the mother who, with Agamemnon (who is mentioned first), bore her. Orestes mentions killing Klytemnestra almost in passing, "My mother shed my father's blood, I hers" (l. 78). But it is not his mother Orestes is concerned with but rather the Furies unleashed by his killing. He seeks to escape their torment; this is his mission in going to Tauris to steal Artemis's statue.

Iphigenia and her brother could be seen as trauma survivors in this play.[35] Like all trauma survivors, each must relive the traumatic scene in dream, flashback, or reenactment, but neither can come to any sense of completion. Iphigenia imagines that her sacrifice at Aulis could be expiated by another sacrifice—that of her aunt, Helen. I would argue (although Euripides does not do so in his play) that the expiating sacrifice has already taken place, but it was Klytemnestra, not Helen, who served as sacrifice. The beautiful and less directly threatening Helen is reaccepted into her husband's house. Klytemnestra, not Helen, must be eliminated to keep patriarchy intact.

Orestes in Euripides' *Iphigenia in Tauris* seems more favorably disposed toward women at this stage in his life (with the exception of Helen, whom he hates).[36] He is overjoyed to find his sister alive. It is Iphigenia who finds a way to turn the murder of the mother into the salvation of the son. She uses Orestes' sin against the mother to demand the need for a purification rite, which is a ruse to allow their joint escape from Tauris. Matricide remains such a shocking crime that even the land of "savage men ruled by an uncouth King" (l. 31) find it repulsive and in need of special purification. Unlike her mother, Iphigenia seeks the help of other women, her chorus of Greek attendants, who aid her with their silence and distractions.

Orestes has apparently learned to value women through his matricide and his acquittal in Athens, which in Euripides' version does not free him of all the Furies. When his sister offers herself again as a sacrifice to gain his safety, Orestes refuses. No longer willing to sacrifice the female for the male, Euripidean Orestes decides that he and Iphigenia will have one fate—life in Greece or death in Tauris. We begin to understand why this adventure will finally earn Orestes rest from the female Furies. Having slain the dominant female, he now risks his life to return the virgin (human) female and the virgin (divine) statue to Greek culture. The real expiation of his guilt comes not in the law court of Athens but in a realignment of his attitude toward the female.

Having turned some of the Furies into the Eumenides, Greek culture must now placate the remaining Furies, who cannot accept the verdict that makes women less important than men, by reimporting women—in a safe, virginal form—back into the tradition. Although it is Apollo who sets this action in motion, it is Athena who intervenes to see the task through. The father-aligned Athena saves the human brother and sister from King Thaos by threats and persuasion (the same tactic she uses in the *Eumenides*). The virgin Iphigenia with her brother's help can now found a new site of worship for the virgin Artemis as Artemis's brother, Apollo, has demanded. Tellingly, these virgins become patronesses of women who die giving birth. Thus two crucial aspects necessary to marriage and to legal heredity are united—the necessity that the bride be a virgin and that she become a mother. Women are reinscribed in the social system in a configuration most supportive to patriarchy.

But Orestes and Iphigenia also reevaluate the male role in their experiences. Both now see Agamemnon as culpable. Both acknowledge the treachery and deception involved in Agamemnon's action. Although Orestes still sympathizes with his father's "haunted face," he sides with Iphigenia in withholding his pity for "this pitiless man" who began it all. The siblings see this new attitude and their reunion as the beginning of a miracle that will end the self-devouring nature of the House of Atreus.

Only the reevaluation of the roles of men and women and their reconciliation can end the gender struggle as well as the struggle for political power. However, Orestes will go back to rule; Iphigenia must remain subdued, virginal, and dutiful. Euripides' play in Tauris rethinks the roles of men and women in Greek society—perhaps enabling him to be more sympathetic to Klytemnestra in his treatment of Aulis. Although they do not rise to the level of equality, *Greek* men and women are at least on the same side here. It is as though (as Wolf argued in the 1980s) Greece was not convinced by Athena's famous use of persuasion at the close of the *Oresteia*. The female Furies, defenders of blood relationships and Mother Right, were not entirely subdued; they demanded that Orestes learn to value the female more fully by being saved (again) by women and goddesses.

Characteristics of the Classical Klytemnestra and Her Offspring

The most striking feature of Klytemnestra's story in the classical texts is her function as a focal point of violence—violence both against and by women. The sacrifice of her daughter Iphigenia to the military aspirations of Agamemnon as well as his murdering of Klytemnestra's first husband and child begin the tapestry of violence. The threads of violence wind more complexly as Klytemnestra herself kills Kassandra and slays Agamemnon upon his return from the Trojan War, thus moving from violence against women to violence by women. Klytemnestra weaves a web of violence to trap and destroy husband and king.

Violence is further problematized in Klytemnestra's story because her ferocity is sparked by maternal rage. Klytemnestra's maternal anger is so powerful that it must be suppressed in order for paternal civilization to endure. The Erinyes must become the Eumenides, "kindly ones," for the polis and the rule of law to be established. As Luce Irigaray suggests, Orestes' murder of his mother, which precedes and supersedes Oedipus's murder of the father so crucial to Freud in the Oedipus myth, becomes a necessary founding gesture for Athens and for the rule of law and patriarchal civilization itself (*Le corps-à-corps*, 15–23).

Klytemnestra's connection to violence undoubtedly forms part of her fascination for late-twentieth-century women writers who seek to come to terms with violence against women in the modern world. But modern women must also question Klytemnestra's violence against her own children—or at least her estrangement from them. Electra is a particularly troubling figure in this regard. Electra's loyalty to her father and to patriarchy cannot in itself account for Klytemnestra's estrangement from her daughter, since Euripides suggests in *Iphigenia in Aulis* that Iphigenia, too, submits to patriarchal wisdom in accepting her own death and in urging Klytemnestra not to hate Agamemnon. But the Klytemnestra who murders Agamemnon, who rules with Aegisthus, and who agrees to have Electra sent from the palace is no longer defined primarily by her position as the protecting mother but rather by her position of power in the public arena. Her role shifts from nurturance and protection in the private realm to defending power in the public realm. She moves from family to polis and from mother to queen. At this point, Klytemnestra becomes a distinct liability to all men who would rule.

Electra sees her own position in society as linked to her father and thus to the male power structure. She can act, however, only through her brother. Electra thus chooses her father and brother over her mother and dead sister. Women in their closest relationship, that of mother and daughter,[37] are wrenched apart by the laws and needs of patriarchy; one cannot be loyal to both father and mother, to both polis and blood bonds. The logic of the classical plays demands a choice. This splitting of the mother-daughter relationship allows Orestes finally to kill his mother. The loyalties of women to one another are outweighed by the allegiance to the father but also to the hierarchical position that Electra hopes to gain by being restored to the royal household. Economics and jealousy thus figure in Electra's anger—as both Sophocles and Euripides imply.

Electra's reward for her loyalty to the world of men is not public status, however. In Sophocles' *Electra,* she seems to have lost all sense of humanity as her fury demands that Aegisthus's body be thrown to the dogs—a gesture not merely cruel but also an offense against religion and human decency, as Grene points out in his introduction to the play (124). In Euripides' *Electra,* she regrets her rage and her mother's murder. Ironically, the murder does not restore Electra's position in her father's house, but rather further exiles her in marriage to Pylades, which will remove her from Argos and return her to the private realm and role of wife and mother—thus reversing Klytemnestra's own career.

Finally and most crucially, the classical versions of the Klytemnestra story (and particularly the *Oresteia*) spotlight the fact that a critical founding moment for Western culture hinges on the subjugation of women in the service of a new patriarchal order and on the suppression of the female "irrational," kin-related principles beneath the newly arising male social and legal arrangement of the polis. Women artists at the end of the twentieth century focus on the repercussions for women of that founding act of violence and subjugation. What ongoing social actions against women does this original violence sanction? What value do women have as time goes on in this kind of Western democracy? Does the original suppression of women authorize continued repression in the name of marriage, social order, and economic necessity? Does the female ever climb up from the cave of the Eumenides to participate fully in Western culture? Or do modern women endlessly reenact Klytemnestra's rebellion only to be cut down again by symbolic or real sons and husbands?

These are troubling questions—especially when most of us feel that Western democratic principles clearly do represent a step forward from the feud and blood lust of more ancient times. But we must still question whether that progress must necessarily depend on choosing the male over the female, on opting for one side of a binary opposition that Western philosophical tradition constructed in the first place. Do we really need to make women scapegoats for irrational and blood-centered drives so that the suppression of women signifies the successful repression of those drives? Might it not be possible to envision a configuration that did not force the choice, that imagined a different—and perhaps even more democratic and laudable—social configuration? The women writers we are about to examine take on these vexed questions and often arrive at equally vexing conclusions.

Notes

1. Scholars have long debated whether Aeschylus's Klytemnestra wielded an axe or a sword to slay Agamemnon. Fraenkel's commentary convinced many scholars that a sword was the murder weapon. Davies argues strongly for the axe and discusses vases to support his assertions, including the Boston Krater (depicted at the opening of this chapter). Sommerstein argues that Aeschylus's *Oresteia* may have been the first version of Agamemnon's murder that combined the bath, robe/net, and sword: "By means of this innovation Aeschylus was enabled *both* to present his Klytaimestra in the traditional feminine role of the beguiler and entrapper . . . *and* to have her, a woman, slay a man and a warrior with a masculine, warrior's weapon—the extreme manifestation of the reversal of standard gender roles which she embodies" (301). While this comment is enticing, I think Klytemnestra embodies both a gender role reversal and the capacity of women to exert violence themselves. I link Klytemnestra with the axe in my discussion because the double-headed axe, or *labrys,* has particularly feminist overtones that late-twentieth-century women writers highlight in Klytemnestra's story.

2. I have chosen to spell Klytemnestra with a *K*—as is the habit of many classicists—rather than a *C.* In this volume, however, a number of variations on the name occur de-

pending on how a particular author spells this character's name. Differences in usage in the various languages (French, Italian, German, and English) also cause disparate spellings. When speaking about a character from a particular text, I use the spelling chosen by the author of that text.

3. Keuls presents a typical example of such a vase painting on page 337. She points out that it is more likely that the scene represents Klytemnestra's "attempt to save the life of her lover, Aegisthus, from attack by Orestes, rather than her assault on Agamemnon" (338). Keuls argues that either interpretation makes Klytemnestra the symbol of "violent female revolt against male authority." Gantz discusses Klytemnestra's role in the murder of Agamemnon. He cites a number of ancient artworks as well as literary texts. Although he does not give her her own entry heading (she is discussed under the heading for Agamemnon [vol. 2] as well as for Leda [vol. 1]), Gantz provides much detail on the various versions of Klytemnestra's story.

4. Tripp describes Klytemnestra's early history as follows: "A daughter of Tyndareüs, king of Sparta, and Leda. Tyndareüs married Clytemnestra to Tantalus, son of Thyestes (or Broteas). Agamemnon, king of Mycenae, killed her husband and her baby, whereupon Tyndareüs gave her to him in marriage" (167). Bethe's entry "Klytaimestra," in *Paulys Realencyclopädie der classischen Altertumswissenschaft,* cites Euripides in acknowledging Klytaimestra's first husband and child, both slain by Agamemnon (11, 1:890–93).

5. Robertson and Rose in *The Oxford Classical Dictionary* and Seyffert in *Dictionary of Classical Antiquities* identify Klytemnestra primarily as the daughter of Tyndareos and the wife of Agamemnon—whom she slew. Strangely, in *Der neue Pauly: Enzyklopädie der Antike,* Harder mentions only the first husband killed by Agamemnon and omits the earlier child (6:611–12).

6. Gantz also discusses this first marriage in the context of Thyestes' children: "Klytaimestra herself in Euripides' *Iphigeneia at Aulis* (1149–52) . . . says that she was originally married to one Tantalos, and that Agamemnon killed both him and their child. She adds that Agamemnon then married her by force, and the implication is thus that his motive for the murders was to obtain her, although the text does not actually say that. Apollodoros repeats the story, calling the Tantalos in question a son of Thyestes. . . , and Pausanias agrees with this genealogy and the marriage" (2:549).

7. See Zeitlin for the most compelling discussion of this point. She outlines the necessity of bringing women under patriarchal control in order to found the polis and Western culture. This point will be discussed in detail below.

8. "Mother Right" derives from Bachofen's *Mutterrecht.* Bachofen proposed that matriarchy and kinship-related rights predated patriarchy. While historians probably cannot validate the theory of the literal supremacy of women in politics and the economy in a prepatriarchal time, Western culture marks the crucial moment of the rise of the patriarchal order and the subjugation of the female in artworks such as Aeschylus's *Oresteia.*

9. Aeschylus (525?–456 B.C.). The *Oresteia* trilogy (along with the lost satyric *Proteus*) was produced in 458 B.C.

10. Warner points out that Michael Crichton makes a similar point with the dinosaur matriarchy of his novel *Jurassic Park* in 1990 (3–6).

11. See Robertson and Rose's entry on Clytemnestra in *The Oxford Classical Dictionary,* 256–57. They point out that "Her name occasionally occurs as a common noun meaning

'adulteress' (as Quintilian, *Inst.* 8. 6. 53), or 'murderess' (see Horace, *Sat.* 1. 1. 100, where 'fortissima Tyndaridarum' stands for Clytaemnestra)."

12. For a recent discussion of the long history of this debate, see Marquardt. Marquardt analyzes earlier entries into the debate by Eduard Fraenkel, Charles Beye, M. Platnauer, B. Mader, Pierre Chantraine, Gregory Nagy, W. B. Stanford, F. Dornseiff, and B. Hansen, as well as Stephanie West, among others.

13. Little is known about Klytemnestra's first husband, Tantalus. We cannot know, therefore, if he—unlike his two successors—won her by wooing.

14. For an extended discussion of the complexities of Helen's story and the competitions for her hand, see Austin, 40–50. Helen is also sometimes identified as Iphigenia's mother. Gantz summarizes the events as follows, "From Pausanias we learn that in Stesichoros Helen gives birth to a child by Theseus, Iphigeneia, the same girl usually thought to be the daughter of Klytaimestra (191 PMG)," 1:289.

15. Marquardt's argument builds on the idea that Klytemnestra was so named to serve as a foil to the much wooed Penelope and her faithfulness. For additional comparisons of Klytemnestra and Penelope, see D'Arms and Hulley, 212–13; Carpenter, 166–67; Lord, 160; and Beye, 97. All highlight the contrast between Klytemnestra's adultery and Penelope's faithfulness. Although both may be cunning, Penelope is virtuously so. Penelope's cunning parallels that of Odysseus, whose epithet is "the cunning Odysseus."

16. See Marquardt, 242 n. 2, "'Wooed for her fame' would also make good sense. Though apparently an active agent suffix, -*mnestra* was undoubtedly also understood in a passive sense in the name Hypermnestra ('much wooed' or 'wooed by many')."

17. The classical scholar Arnold Band proposed this reading in a conversation. Auffret suggests a similar reading that I discuss in chapter 3.

18. Scholars debate Homer's dates with estimates ranging from 900 B.C. to 700 B.C.

19. See, for example, Euripides' *Hippolytus,* particularly Aphrodite's opening speech, Phaedra's complaint of being overthrown "by some god's spite," or the choral ode that follows it.

20. As early as 1949, Simone de Beauvoir declared that the *Eumenides* represents "the triumph of the patriarchate over the matriarchate. The tribunal of the gods declared Orestes to be the son of Agamemnon before he is the son of Clytemnestra—the ancient maternal authority and rights were dead, killed by the audacious revolt of the male!" (89 n. 9).

Millett agreed with this assessment two decades later in her *Sexual Politics* (111–15). Although both Beauvoir's and Millett's analyses agree with Zeitlin's, I find her nuanced readings of details more compelling than these early generalized statements. Later feminist critics such as Hartsock and Case in *Feminism and Theater* also build on Zeitlin's work.

Case does not specifically cite Zeitlin, but she does acknowledge Hartsock, who refers to Zeitlin. While I find Case's general reading of the *Oresteia* persuasive, and I agree that "the pathos the feminist reader feels may be for Iphigenia and Clytemnestra rather than for Agamemnon," I cannot agree that "In fact, the feminist reader might become persuaded that the Athenian roles of Medea, Clytemnestra, Cassandra and Phaedra are properly played as drag roles. The feminist reader might conclude that these roles contain no information about the experience of real women in the classical world" (15).

While the roles mentioned may not precisely reflect "the experience of real women in the classical world," they are crucial in determining the "proper" roles of women in ancient Greece and for centuries thereafter. The fact that so many contemporary women find it necessary to reenvision these roles marks their crucial impact not just on the theatrical practice of the West but on the very definition of gender roles in the West.

21. Ziolkowski discusses the *Eumenides* as it traces this movement from blood vengeance toward institutionalized law (20–41). He notes that "the literary representation of legal crises, the dislocations of law and morality, often take the form of a struggle between men and women—a struggle that usually displayed pronounced sexual or gender overtones, as in the battle between matriarchy and patriarchy in the *Oresteia*" (18).

22. For an extended discussion of Agamemnon's transgression in treading the tapestries, see Fagles and Stanford, 24–25.

23. As Goldhill points out, this attempt to master words is a common trait of "Shakespearean 'villains', whose violence is as much verbal as physical. . . . It is in societies' interest (it even constitutes society, some might say) to attempt to maintain rigid distinctions in naming, the use of language. It is not surprising to see the 'villain' who stands apart from society, as having a special relationship to language, particularly as the powerful distorter, manipulator. This, perhaps, adds to the paradoxical attraction of these characters (including Klytemnestra?)" (35 n. 70).

24. For more detailed discussion of Klytemnestra's ironic use of language, see D. Porter and Lebeck.

25. Well over a century after Aeschylus's suggestion, Aristotle claims scientific status for Apollo's assertion of male supremacy. As Keuls notes:

> [Aristotle] sought to prove scientifically not only that the male is superior to the female, but also that the female, despite her nurturing of the fetus during pregnancy, has no genetic input into procreation, thus making the father the only real parent.
>
> . . . Aristotle's reasoning, set forth in the most detail in his *Generations of Animals,* goes as follows (726f). Since the male secretes sperm and the female menstrual blood, conception takes place during menstruation. Since blood is merely nutritious and not procreative, the female has no genetic power, but provides temporary nourishment. It follows logically that the female is merely a male without genitals (728a 18); she is a maimed male, Aristotle says (737a 28–3), anticipating Freud's "penis envy" theory. (145)

26. For detailed discussions of the tenuous theoretical relationship between mother and fetus throughout the ages, see Huet and Laqueur.

27. See Ziolkowski's analysis of the movement from vengeance to structured legal process in the *Oresteia* for more discussion.

28. Patterson argues that Zeitlin's view of Klytemnestra as representing female interests defeated by the arguments of patriarchal authority "does not do full justice to the complexity of the dramatic representation of adultery or to the trilogy's conclusion, in which Athena's female persuasion brings the still-powerful Furies into the circle of Athenian public religion as the guardians of marriage and the *oikos*" (267 n. 22). While I appreciate Patterson's emphasis on complexity, I cannot but remember that Athena's "female persuasion" is reinforced by her access to Zeus's thunderbolt and her not so veiled implication that she would use it if "female" persuasion failed. Patterson contends that Klytemnestra makes the *oikos* corrupted and "sick" "not because of any adulteration of

the patriline but because of the violation of responsibility" and the "perversion of male/ female roles" (145). On the clash between polis and *oikos,* see also Blundell, 176–80.

29. In this view, she cites Bamberger, 263–80.

30. While we could argue that the Erinyes were always closely associated with the Mother Earth and that this return to earth is a return to chthonic powers, I would like to stress the need for Aeschylus to return the female powers to their safe subterranean position in order to ensure the health of the new Athenian patriarchal democracy.

31. Sophocles (c. 496–406 B.C.). I am citing Grene's translation in *Sophocles 2.*

32. Between Aeschylus's and Sophocles' plays, the lyric poet Pindar (518–438 B.C.) in his odes (Pythian XI) depicts Klytemnestra as a grievous traitress who mercilessly slays Agamemnon and Kassandra and threatens to destroy Orestes. Pindar posits two explanations for Klytemnestra's violence: the loss of Iphigenia at Agamemnon's hands and his unfaithfulness in returning with Kassandra as paramour. In either case, Orestes returns to slay his mother and Aegisthus. Scholars date Pythian XI as written either in 474 or 454 B.C.

33. Euripides (c. 485–c. 406 B.C.). *Electra* was probably produced around 417 B.C.; some scholars give a date of 413 B.C. because of internal references.

34. In his introduction to Witter Bynner's translation (*Euripides 2,* 118), Lattimore points out the almost identical plots of Euripides' *Iphigenia in Tauris* and his *Helen.*

35. In fact, much recent trauma theory proves quite useful in providing psychological models of behavior to examine the actions of Klytemnestra and her children. Caruth's and Herman's volumes on trauma are particularly helpful. The progression of actions described here for Iphigenia and Orestes match those observed in trauma survivors. I will return to this similarity in my conclusions.

36. This is a distinctly different attitude than Orestes displays in Euripides' later play *Orestes,* in which the rather unappealing matricide is only too eager to murder his aunt Helen and her daughter (his future wife) Hermione. In this play, Argos clearly condemns Orestes for Klytemnestra's murder and demands his death. Klytmnestra figures here primarily as the murdered mother who should have been spared by her son. Although everyone disapproves of her adultery, the majority clearly feel that Orestes should be condemned to death for her murder. Only Apollo's intercession prevents the death of Orestes, Pylades, Electra, and Hermione as well as the burning and final destruction of the House of Atreus.

37. For an extensive discussion of mother-daughter relationships, see Hirsch.

2. Klytemnestra Takes Center Stage: Klytemnestra in the Pre- and Early 1980s

Klytemnestra and her female offspring have continued to fascinate both male and female authors through the centuries. In the first century A.D., Seneca produced a Latin *Agamemnon*, which informed many medieval texts. Benoît de Sainte-Maure's twelfth-century *Roman de Troie* became very popular. Klytemnestra was certainly known in the Middle Ages. In Chaucer's *Canterbury Tales* (c. 1387–1400), for example, the Wife of Bath recalls in her prologue that her husband, who had a book of "wikked wyves," read aloud to her "Of Clitermystra, for hire lecherye, / That falsly made hire housbonde for to dye" (3 [D] 737–38).[1] And in 1474 or 1475, William Caxton's translation of Raoul Lefèvre's French romance, *Recuyell of the Historyes of Troye*, became the first book ever printed in English. Pierre Matthieu produced the late-sixteenth-century cautionary piece entitled *Clytemnestre: De la vengeance des injures perdurable à la postérité des offencez, et des malheureuses fins de la volupté.* In 1679 Jean Racine composed the tragedy *Iphigénie en Aulide;* in 1774 Christoph Gluck presented his opera of the same name; Johann Wolfgang von Goethe put Iphigenia into both a prose (1779) and a verse (1787) play in *Iphigenia in Tauris.* John Galt's *The Tragedies of Maddalen, Agamemnon, Lady Macbeth, Antonia, and Clytemnestra* appeared in 1812, Michael Beer's tragedy *Klytemnestra* in 1823, and Edward Bulwer-Lytton's *Clytemnestra, The Earl's Return, and Other Poems* in 1855. William Makepeace Thackeray even included a charade "The Triumph of Clytemnestra" in his 1848 novel, *Vanity Fair.*[2]

The twentieth century teems with women from the House of Atreus. In 1903 Hugo von Hofmannsthal wrote his *Elektra,* which he and Richard Strauss turned into an opera in 1909. Henry B. Lister composed a play from pieces of Euripides', Aeschylus's, and Sophocles' tragedies entitled *Clytemnestra* in

1923, while Eugene O'Neill produced his trilogy of plays, *Mourning Becomes Electra,* in 1931. Marguerite Yourcenar presented a lyrical prose Klytemnestra monologue in her 1936 collection *Feux.*[3] Jean Giraudoux composed his drama *Électre* and Laura Riding published her novel *A Trojan Ending* in 1937. Gerhart Hauptmann drafted a massive treatment of the House of Atreus in his tetralogy *Atriden-Tetralogie,* which includes *Iphigenie in Delphi* (1941), *Iphigenie in Aulis* (1943), *Agamemnons Tod* (1947), and *Elektra* (1948). Jean-Paul Sartre's drama *Les mouches* was produced in 1943. Ilse Langner published her tragedy *Klytämnestra* in 1947 and her dramatic poem *Iphigenie kehrt Heim* in 1948. Michael Cacoyannis's 1977 film *Iphigenia,* with Irene Papas as Klytemnestra, was nominated for both the Cannes Film Festival's Golden Palm and an Academy Award for Best Foreign Film. And the American poet W. S. Merwin translated Euripides' *Iphigenia in Aulis* in 1978.

Tellingly, from the Enlightenment on, male authors tend to pay more attention to Klytemnestra's patriarchally aligned daughters, Elektra and Iphigenia, than to Klytemnestra herself, while female authors (Yourcenar and Langner, for example) concentrate on Klytemnestra. Violence against the woman seems a more attractive topic than Klytemnestra's violence against husband and king.[4] However, this ongoing literary interest by both men and women in Klytemnestra and her family helped to keep her alive as a cultural figure of crucial importance and available for feminist revisions at the end of the last millennium.

In the final decades of the twentieth century, women writers rediscovered Klytemnestra in a particularly intense way. Klytemnestra took the 1980s by storm; she appeared, often in eponymous pieces, on stage, in dance, and in literary texts by women authors writing in English, German, French, and Italian. The 1980s might even be labeled "the decade of Klytemnestra."[5] Precisely why this is the case must be a matter of speculation. Perhaps the strength of the women's movement as the 1970s came to a close made the powerful and dynamic ruler Klytemnestra an appealing figure. Or perhaps the superwoman syndrome of trying to juggle career, husband, and children made the idea of taking an axe to one's absent or inadequate spouse an enticing thought.

Economic conditions may well have played a role. A number of countries suffered high unemployment and economic hardships during the 1980s. In the early 1980s, the international economic recession caused West Germany's unemployment rate to rise to greater than 10 percent. Then Chancellor Helmut Schmidt attempted to reduce unemployment by moving funds from social welfare, thus triggering other social pressures. In 1982 when he took office, Chancellor Helmut Kohl was faced with taming unemployment and reforming the finance system. In the United States, inflation rose to double digits in 1979 and began a mild recession. By July 1982 unemployment reached 9.8 percent. President Ronald Reagan promoted "union busting," deregulation, and tax cuts but was eventually forced to raise taxes. By 1984 the U.S. economy began to recover (partly on Reagan's platform of deficit spending for military defense), but the disparity between the very rich and the very poor grew even worse. In France, socialist leader François Mitterand, who began his presidency in 1981 with sweeping economic reforms (including the nationalization of major industries and banks, increased government spending, and a minimum-wage raise), was forced by rising unemployment and a devaluation of the franc to adopt conservative policies known as "economic realism" in order to fight unemployment and inflation. And in Italy, the 1980s were marked by growing recession and rising inflation. Major banking scandals (and bank liquidations), as well as earthquakes and landslides in 1980 and 1982 and a severe drought in 1989, put the country in economic jeopardy.

Given the stress of these economic hardships, women's home lives may have become more violent. Many countries evidenced such domestic violence and an unbelievably unsupportive response to the women damaged by it. In 1985 Italian courts sentenced a husband to three years imprisonment for beating his wife to death.[6] The battered wife also became a focus of attention in the 1980s through media coverage of actual cases as well as films (such as the made-for-television film *The Burning Bed* [1984]) based on actual cases. Other abused women also made headlines. The acquittal of convicted gang-rape suspects in Italy,[7] the refusal of spectators in an American bar to come to the aid of a gang-rape victim, and the particularly harsh sentencing of violent lesbian lovers in Germany (referred to in Reinig's *Entmannung*) might all contribute to the desire to see a strong female character willing to retaliate with violence. With the issue of battered women given so much exposure in newscasts, literature, and film, the idea of a woman exerting violence against her husband becomes alluring.

Rethinking Klytemnestra's condemnation for retaliating against a husband who enacts violence on women might have been particularly relevant in the 1980s, when a number of women were sentenced to prison terms because they could not use their years of being battered as a legal defense. Courts eventually recognized the battered woman syndrome as important evidence. In 1991 the California legislature made such evidence admissible in defending women who had killed their batterers.[8] In 1998 Brenda Aris, who was imprisoned in 1987, was released on the basis of clemency granted by the governor of California, Gray Davis, after she served eleven years of a sentence of fifteen years to life for killing her abuser.[9] As a figure of justified female retribution, Klytemnestra became crucial for women in the 1980s as they struggled to cope with the many permutations of violence enacted upon them.

Another kind of violence—and ownership—became contested territory for women in the 1980s as well. A woman's right to control her own reproductive activity and to assert ownership of her own body became a heated debate during these years. After the 1973 proabortion decision of *Roe v. Wade,* feminists in the United States were immediately faced with an antiabortion backlash. Women such as Phyllis Shafley (who on her Web site <http://www.eagleforum.org> espouses conservative principles for women and the country at large) declared themselves "pro-family." Shafley, who has been nationally active since 1972, became prominent during the Reagan years (<http://www.Reagan.com> often features her articles and speeches). In addition to her media opposition to abortion, Shafley led the battle against the Equal Rights Amendment (which, after its defeat in 1982, was reintroduced into Congress in 1985 and every year since—and is held in committee). In addition in the 1980s, Reagan's conservative Supreme Court began to threaten the rights of women to control their own bodies, and public funding for many types of abortion was banned. (In 1981 congress eliminated rape and incest as grounds for obtaining federal funds for abortions.) In 1989 the Food and Drug Administration issued an import ban on the abortion drug RU486 (although it would eventually be approved for use in the United States in September 2000). Violent (and sometimes deadly) physical attacks on abortion-clinic doctors, staff, and patients became acute in the mid-1980s. The conservative agenda of the 1980s thus threatened basic rights of American women to decide their own physical and moral fates as well as their attempts to gain equal status under the legal and constitutional systems.

But America was not unique in this respect.[10] In 1975 France legalized abortion (with counseling and a waiting period) until the tenth week of pregnancy. But the controversy sparked again in 1988 by the abortion drug RU486 reveals the strong antiabortion undercurrent present in the country. Antiabortion groups succeeded in temporarily halting the sale of the drug, but the French government later ordered its sale to be reopened. Over the fierce opposition of the Vatican, Italy passed a law in 1978 allowing women over eighteen to seek abortions in the first ninety days of pregnancy (with counseling, a doctor's certificate, and a minimum seven-day wait). Italian doctors, however, may register as "conscientious objectors" to abortion on religious, moral, or social grounds; about 70 percent of Italian doctors have done so.[11] Although Italians overwhelmingly rejected a referendum supported by the Catholic Church in 1981 to overturn the abortion law, abortions remain difficult to obtain due to the scarcity of doctors and waits of up to thirty days at public facilities. East Germany's remarkably liberal 1972 law permitted abortion on request during the first twelve weeks of pregnancy. In contrast, West Germany passed a law in 1976 that allowed abortion (with the approval of two doctors, mandatory counseling, and a three-day wait) up to the twelfth week. However, abortions were so difficult to obtain in many parts of West Germany that women often went to the Netherlands for the operation. (The disparities between East and West Germany's laws caused major and lingering debates when the two countries reunified.) And the strong antiabortion sentiments in Catholic Bavaria led to the conviction and two-and-a-half-year prison term for the gynecologist Horst Theissen in 1989. Theissen performed abortions without the costly and lengthy abortion certification process required in Bavaria. One hundred thirty-seven of Theissen's patients were also fined or jailed.[12] Despite apparent legal protection, then, conservative agendas in many countries threaten women with the loss of control of their own bodies, reproductive rights, and lives. Klytemnestra's position as a woman who battles for these issues at the very inception of the Western sense of law and democracy makes her a crucial figure.

In addition, in the academic world, feminist scholarship gained strength and recognition in the 1970s. This vitalization of women in the academy might have helped stimulate female creative artists of the 1980s to take a feminist look at the sacred texts and figures of Western culture. As Deborah Epstein Nord points out in her 1996 essay commemorating the twentieth anniversary of the publication of Ellen Moers's *Literary Women,* the 1970s "launched feminist scholarship in a manner that ultimately remapped academic disciplines, rerouted individual careers, and reshaped our culture."[13] Nord cites a number of important academic pieces that fueled this movement in several areas of study, including the art historian Linda Nochlin's "Why Have There Been No Great Women Artists?" (1971); the anthropologist Gayle Rubin's "The Traffic in Women: Notes on the 'Political Economy' of Sex" (1975); the sociologist Nancy Chodorow's *The Reproduction of Mothering: Psychoanalysis and the Sociology of Gender* (1978); the American historian Linda Gordon's *Woman's Body, Woman's Right: A Social History of Birth Control in America* (1976); and the Europeanist Natalie Davis's "Women on Top" (1975). In addition, *Feminist Studies* came onto the academic scene in 1972 and *Signs* made its appearance in 1975.

From Kate Millett's *Sexual Politics* in 1970 to Sandra Gilbert and Susan Gubar's *Madwoman in the Attic* in 1979, the 1970s provided both academic and creative women writers with new inspirations. In 1975 Patricia Spacks explored the *Female Imagination,* and in 1977 Elaine Showalter examined women having *A Literature of Their Own.* In French criticism, *l'écriture fémi-*

nine was fueling femininist criticism on the Continent. Hélène Cixous published "Le rire de la méduse" (The Laugh of the Medusa) in 1975, and Luce Irigary's *Ce sexe qui n'en est pas un* (The Sex Which Is Not One) appeared in 1977. In Germany in 1979 Sylvia Bovenschen explored *Die imaginierte Weiblichkeit* (The Imagined Feminine), and in the early 1980s Argument-Verlag published several important volumes of feminist criticism, including *Die verborgene Frau* (The Concealed Woman) in 1983, and *Feministische Literaturwissenschaft* (Feminist Literary Criticism) in 1984, both edited by Inge Stephan and Sigrid Weigel. In Italy, volumes such as Abba, Ferri, Lazzarello, Medi, and Motta's *La coscienza di sfruttata* (Women's Experience of Exploitation) from 1972, Frabotta's *Femminismo e lotta di classe in Italia, 1970–1973* (Feminism and Class in Italy, 1970–1973) from 1973, and Balbo's *Stato di famiglia* (The State of the Family) from 1976 helped to raise women's consciousness of their own positions.

Finally, the scholarly focus on Klytemnestra intensified in the late 1970s and 1980s—particularly among critics concerned with gender issues. In addition to Froma Zeitlin's seminal essay on misogyny and the *Oresteia* (1978), Nicole Loraux (1981), Helene Foley (1981), Nancy Rabinowitz (1981), and Mary Lefkowitz (1986) produced studies concerned with gender aspects of Klytemnestra's tale. Sally MacEwen's *Views of Clytemnestra, Ancient and Modern* collected essays from a Classical Association meeting in 1987; her introduction analyzes the various critical positions that arose in the 1970s and 1980s. Many male scholars clearly helped to shape the debate as well; Simon Goldhill focused on rhetoric and language (1984), and R. P. Winnington-Ingram underlined the treatment of women by Athenian men (1983).

All of these many forces—economic, political, legal, sociological, and academic, among others—are at work to varying degrees in helping to make the 1980s Klytemnestra's territory. These forces play themselves out in the texts by women writers who rethink Klytemnestra, her actions, and her reputation in the 1980s. Before turning to these texts, I would like to examine two works that predate 1980 but actually form a part of this group—Martha Graham's 1958 ballet *Clytemnestra* (revived in the 1980s) and Christa Reinig's 1976 novel *Entmannung*.

Klytemnestra in Motion: Martha Graham's Ballet *Clytemnestra*

The American choreographer and dancer Martha Graham (1893–1991) was fascinated by classical figures and strong women. She created dance works ranging from *Letter to the World* (1940), based on the life of Emily Dickinson, to *Clytemnestra* (1958). Although her famous ballet, first performed on

April 1, 1958 (with Graham herself, nearing the age of sixty-five, as Clytemnestra[14]), falls outside my parameters for this study, I include it for a number of reasons. First, it enjoyed a major revival in 1987 in the United States (by the Martha Graham School of Contemporary Dance in New York).[15] Graham herself gained special prominence in the 1980s when she was decorated with the Legion of Honor (1984) by Jack Lang, the French Minister of Culture, and was awarded Denmark's highest distinction for contributions to the arts, the Ingenio et Arti medal (1987), by Queen Margrethe II of Denmark.[16] Given the clustering of Klytemnestra revisions in the 1980s, I believe that Graham's prominence during that time and the revival of her *Clytemnestra* belongs to the same impulse as the literary texts I examine. Second, this piece, considered the very height of Graham's choreographic work and the first program-length work in modern dance, raises many of the issues investigated in later attempts to rehabilitate Klytemnestra.

In her autobiography, *Blood Memory,* Graham writes that she was surprised to be claimed by the women's movement as a "women's liberationist" (25). Always surrounded by men, Graham nonetheless asserts that she never felt competition. She declares, "I never had the feeling that I was inferior. . . . I always got whatever I wanted from men without asking" (25). But Graham produced a series of unforgettable women, many of them from classical antiquity, including Medea, Jocasta, and, most memorably, Clytemnestra. Graham saw these figures as participating in what makes up "every woman." And in most of her ballets, Graham's women have "absolutely and completely triumphed" (25). She may not see herself as a feminist (an attitude that she shares, surprisingly, with Brückner and the early Wolf), but many of her admirers—particularly in the 1980s—envision her as one.

Graham reveals early in her autobiography an affinity for the character of Clytemnestra: she feels that "Clytemnestra is every woman when she kills." She goes on to explain women's capacity to exert violence and destruction as well as a powerful will:

I know that in a woman, like a lioness, is the urge to kill if she cannot have what she wants. Much more than in a man. Woman kills, intends to kill. She is more ruthless than any man.

. . . You do what is attractive and wonderful to you at the time. That's why I did women like Clytemnestra. It comes out of that deep desire for creation. One girl came to me and said, "But I am not Clytemnestra. I would never kill anyone."

"On the contrary," I said, "I have seen you look at a man in such a way that you have killed him right there on the spot. If that is not murder, just as the other, then I do not understand it."

Clytemnestra struggles with Orestes. In Martha Graham's *Clytemnestra*, with Graham dancing Clytemnestra. (Photo by Martha Swope. Martha Swope/Timepix)

After a few moments of silence she looked at me and said, "I think you're right." (*Blood Memory*, 26)

Graham's figure is Clytemnestra as everywoman—with a conscious capacity for violence. This is not an aberrant woman who is terrifying in her destructiveness; this Clytemnestra figures the capacity for ferocity in each woman. Whether they wield a psychological or a physical axe, women are willing and able to strike in Graham's world. The non-women's-liberationist Graham has no difficulty in seeing women as both powerful and violent.

She also has no difficulty in reimagining classical tales. When she was a child, her father recited stories from Greek myths. Graham remembers hearing the story of Achilles and his being dipped in water from the river Styx—except for his famous heel. She remembers thinking about "the error of the foot, how it was his heel, some small part of the body, that became his undoing" (27). Graham's response is immediate, "I wanted to redip him into the water to protect him." Not delayed by any view of the classical myth as sacrosanct, Graham's first impulse was to revise. She exercised this same impulse when dealing with Clytemnestra, whom she dips back into her own reflective consciousness in order to save her.

Graham's Clytemnestra is a figure redeemed and triumphant. In the underworld, she faces her deeds and accepts them. She revisits her actions in dream so that the ballet stage becomes a "highly theatrical presentation— unreality & beauty of remembered things. . . . The scenes are enacted for[/]in the theater of the mind" (Graham, *Notebooks*, 248). In dream, Clytemnestra is given the distance and time to reflect on her own actions; she becomes her own spectator. This allows Clytemnestra to reevaluate her retribution and violence. It is striking that in a world composed of movement and action, Graham creates a space for reflection and thought. When the scene opens in the underworld, Clytemnestra is haunted by the question, "Why am I dishonored among the dead?" (*Notebooks*, 262, 266, 268). This is a Clytemnestra who contemplates and reevaluates all of her past experiences. Her dreams include Helen and Paris as well as Agamemnon and her children, Orestes, Electra, and Iphigenia; Clytemnestra thus revisits the whole scope of the Trojan War and its links to the roles and reputations of women.

Like Aeschylus's figure, Graham's Clytemnestra has the strength to accept her fierce justice in slaying her husband to avenge her child. When Agamemnon kills Iphigenia, he also kills Clytemnestra's own creative instinct. Her underworld is really "The private hell of a woman who has killed her love because her love killed her creative instinct—her child—" (*Notebooks*, 255). Clytemnestra is thus both victim and avenger, abused and destructive. She must sort out her part in the tragedy in the "Underworld of her imagination" (*Notebooks*, 255). But in doing so, she also gains the wisdom to forgive and be reconciled with her son and murderer, Orestes. In the ballet, after Orestes is found not guilty, he and Clytemnestra dance a duet in which she is carried on her son's shoulders in a scene of rebirth. As Orestes assumes his new kingship, Clytemnestra dances off in triumph and reconciliation. It is she—and not Athena or Apollo—who "changes the Furies into beneficent powers" (*Notebooks*, 258) by forgiving herself and Orestes. In this gesture, Mother Right retains its power; it is not driven underground but rather reborn. Clytemnestra's role of mother has been reestablished; her role as irrepressible heroine is amplified. She is a woman of psychological as well as physical courage.

Graham's vision of Clytemnestra in the *Agamemnon* is quite vivid. In Graham's words:

She is the glittering, regal, hate-breathing woman—
The woman whose creative instinct—her child Iphigenia—has been
   killed by her husband—
   by her need for home,
   (her woman's nature has betrayed her)
   In a sense she is a "career woman" or a woman with
   creative gifts—in that part masculine in her strength
   of will & need to propagate her power—
passionate
autumnal woman—
she kills her womanhood in killing Agamemnon, her
    husband.

                                   (*Notebooks,* 258)

But if Graham's Clytemnestra kills her womanhood in killing her husband, she regains it in reconciling with her son. The woman of strength, passion, and creative gifts is reborn when she adds reflection and forgiveness to her talents.

    Graham clearly envisions her title figure killing Agamemnon as a reenactment of a religious ritual. Graham sees Clytemnestra as a queen, a temptress, a woman, but also as "a high priestess about to perform the sacrifice" (*Notebooks,* 250)—a trait she shares with Aeschylus's figure. Clytemnestra restages Agamemnon's sacrifice of Iphigenia by taking his place and making him her sacrifice. In a classic response to trauma, she must replay the traumatic incident and give it a different ending that reempowers her and restores her system of meaning and experience. She sets her world right by reestablishing her sense of justice. Graham stresses this role reversal in her *Notebooks* by underlining Clytemnestra's vision of her act as a mystical ritual: "And as [Clytemnestra] speaks we realize that she is using the language of mystical initiation. With blasphemous audacity, she imagines herself as the officiating priest, Cassandra as the candidate for initiation, & the impending murder as a holy mystery" (251). Shortly after this episode, we see the bodies of Cassandra and Agamemnon. Significantly, the female, Cassandra, here is not seen as another sacrifice to Clytemnestra's rage but rather as an initiate in a religous ritual, whose rite of passage is necessary to complete the sacrifice of Agamemnon.

    In finally playing out her traumatic memory, Graham's Clytemnestra really redefines her self. She remakes the loving and subservient female into a dominant, powerful, and hate-wracked avenger. As Graham explains, "In the course of 10 yrs. her love for her firstborn has been corrupted into hatred of the man who wronged her, & the whole of her passionate nature dedicated to revenge. Yet this hate was the outcome of love. . . . For her the murder was a necessary act of purification, a perfect sacrifice by which the family has been purged of its hereditary madness" (*Notebooks*, 252). Clytemnestra's reenactment and reversal of the loss of her daughter finally completes the traumatic experience and frees her. She has finally made sense of her loss and her powerlessness is overcome. In the trial that takes place within her imagination, Graham's Clytemnestra reaffirms and accepts her actions. Her ability to do so allows her also to be reconciled with her son, Orestes.

In Graham's world of images in her *Notebooks,* a net or web entraps each of the characters in turn—Iphigenia, Agamemnon, Clytemnestra, Orestes— until it is finally broken or transformed by the final reconciliation of mother and son. The web of dreams impinges on the net of fate to allow Clytemnestra to escape both and be reborn as a heroine who does not regret her actions but who can be reconciled with her death. Clytemnestra breaks the nets by rethinking her life, affirming her pursuit of maternal justice, and reacknowledging her son. The Italian writer Dacia Maraini also would employ dreams in her 1981 revision of Klytemnestra, *I sogni di Clitennestra,* but Maraini's dreams do not have the reconciling power of Graham's. Maraini's are nightmares of destruction dreamed by a debilitated Klytemnestra; Graham's are a theater of the mind in which the nightmares of reality can finally be laid to rest.

One of the most striking uses of physical props by Graham is Clytemnestra's blood-red scarf that wraps her as she enters and that becomes the carpet on which Agamemnon treads toward his death. In the *Oresteia,* the red carpet spread for Agamemnon is also the path of justice that Klytemnestra lays as a road to her vengeance. Graham continues this concept by making her Clytemnestra's long red scarf also serve as screen or tent behind which Agamemnon and Cassandra are murdered that is opened to reveal their dead bodies. Graham's Clytemnestra manipulates this symbol to figure mourning, death, justice, and retribution. Like Aeschylus's Klytemnestra, this Clytemnestra, even in her most destructive actions, is a reflective intelligence—just as her creator is.

From Graham's revision of Klytemnestra we gain the following insights. First, it is not mandatory to change Klytemnestra's destructive actions in order to see her positively; it is, however, necessary to allow her a mind and a space to reflect and give meaning to her apparently bloodthirsty behavior. Second, Clytemnestra's redemption lies in coming to understand and accept herself and in rejecting tradition's condemnation. Third, Clytemnestra redeems herself and her children by reclaiming her female role of mother and regaining her female "creative instinct," her child; when she reconciles with Orestes, she can be saved. If, as Graham argues, Clytemnestra kills her

Clytemnestra's reconciliation with Orestes. In Martha Graham's *Clytemnestra*, with Graham dancing Clytemnestra. (Photo by Carl Van Vechten. Courtesy of the Carl Van Vechten Trust and the Robert D. Farber University Archives and Special Collections Department, Brandeis University Libraries)

womanhood in killing her husband, she reclaims it in forgiving her son. The female blood bond remains the strongest one for Clytemnestra. The capacity for forgiveness and reconciliation based on the strength of her own mind makes Graham's Clytemnestra an attractive figure for later feminists.

From Graham's own comments, we might have expected her to align herself with Athena rather than Klytemnestra. When, after a performance, a woman asked Graham about her role in the women's liberation movement, Graham rather surprisingly responded, "My father raised me to be a woman" (*Blood Memory*, 26). This apparently patriarchal allegiance recalls Athena, but if Graham is sprung full blown from a mind, it is from her own powerfully female mind, from her own creative instincts. It is also a powerful female mind that she provides for the character of Clytemnestra. Restoring Clytemnestra's thoughts, her psychology, allows her to be redeemed as a fierce but positive archetype for contemporary daughters and sons.

The Late-1970s Klytemnestra—Brutality on All Fronts: Christa Reinig's *Entmannung*

The startling title of German author Christa Reinig's 1976 novel, *Entmannung: Die Geschichte Ottos und seiner vier Frauen erzählt von Christa Reinig*, might well call up a Klytemnestra taking direct aim at phallocentrism. The title could be rendered as "Castration: The Story of Otto and His Four Women Narrated by Christa Reinig," but perhaps "Emasculation," "Demasculinization," or even "Unmanning" would be more accurate than "Castration." This process refers principally to the central male character Otto Kyra, whose last name is related to the Greek *kyros*, meaning power or authority and *Kurios*, which designates a master or lord (a title that is eventually extended to Christ). The fact that Otto's name ends in the feminine, *Kyra*, already signals his proclivity for arguing on behalf of women (which he does frequently in the text). Kyra undergoes a transformation, a demasculinization, in the course of the novel, in which he moves from a successful and authority-wielding surgeon to an eccentric surrounded by women and finally to being dressed as and representing a woman.

It should be noted, however, that Kyra's predilection for siding with women does not keep him from destroying them in particularly patriarchal ways. In fact, when I read Otto Kyra's name aloud to a group of classicists, they heard the Greek *autocheiria,* which means "murder perpetrated by one's own hand." Although Kyra does not technically murder anyone in the novel, he certainly deserves responsibility for several deaths. For example, he becomes angry when Xenia, his friend and housekeeper, does not want to have sex with him, so he orders her out of the car in a dark woods at night. This act leads to her brutal gang rape and Xenia's overdetermined suicide. The fact that the repentant Kyra takes only a few paragraphs to recover his appetite and his equilibrium after Xenia's death makes his theoretical transition away from the crassly masculine problematic.

Although Kyra provides the recurrent thread, "his" four women form the real center of the narrative. The women represent various female role options: Doris, a doctor, is the intellectual; Thea is an artist and prostitute; Klytemnestra is a housewife and mother; Xenia is a housekeeper. The female characters' ultimate fates convey Reinig's feminist protest over the lot of women. Doris ends in an insane asylum; Thea dies of cancer; Klytemnestra is sentenced to prison; and Xenia commits one of literature's most resolute suicides (she takes pills, slits her wrists, sticks her head in an oven, and is blown up by the leaking gas). The classical Klytemnestra must indeed have presented an appealing example for Reinig of female frustration successfully vented.

Born in 1926 in Berlin, Reinig studied Greek along with her courses in art history and Christian archaeology at the Humboldt-Universität in Berlin from 1953–57. Following her studies, Reinig worked as a technical assistant at the Märkisches Museum in East Berlin until 1963. She began writing in the late 1940s and had poems and stories published in the early 1950s in East Germany. Censorship eventually compelled her to publish in West Germany instead of East Germany. In 1964 Reinig was awarded the Literaturpreis der Freien Hansestadt Bremen. She took the opportunity of accepting the prize to leave East Germany and emigrate to West Germany. She has lived in Munich since 1964.[17]

Reinig remained an outspoken and prominent feminist voice into the 1980s and beyond.[18] The feminist publishing company Frauenoffensive issued *Erkennen, was die Rettung ist* in 1986; in this interview with Marie-Luise Gansberg and Mechthild Beerlage, Reinig describes finding her feminist and lesbian voice after writing *Entmannung*. She recalls that she knew in the 1950s that she was a lesbian sexually but that she did not have a lesbian identity until she became a feminist in the 1970s. Reinig also discusses the need for women to learn to use both violence and cunning to survive various attacks by men (123–26). Clearly, she was exploring precisely these characteristics in Klytemnestra's story in the late 1970s. This exploration grew in her works in the 1980s and contributed to the impulse of other women writers to explore similar issues.

Making good use of her language studies in *Entmannung*, Reinig underlines the connection of her characters to Greek classical literature by using names that derive from Greek.[19] In addition to Kyra and Klytemnestra, the other Greek names have etymologies that prove relevant. Thea signifies "goddess," Doris "spear" or "gift." The housekeeper has a name appropriately derived from the Greek *Xenia,* which means "the state or privileges of a guest, hospitable reception." Her name also calls up the concept of stranger, but in the sense of one who should be treated in a friendly way. Although Xenia is the one who provides such hospitable reception, she does not receive the same from Kyra, who abandons her to a gang rape because of his injured pride. Xenia's name is thus both appropriate and ironic.

Entmannung emplots Klytemnestra's story not simply by retelling it in a modern setting but by embedding it in varied depictions of German women in the late 1970s. The novel designates a specific Klytemnestra (van der Leyden), a housewife submissive to her husband, Albert, and mother of two children, Edgar and Herzel. Her rather regal Greek name is turned into the diminutive "Menni" just as she herself is reduced to a lower scale of action. This "Menni" does not vie for political power but rather is confined to a diminished version of Klytemnestra's "House" in which her role is clearly and confiningly defined. But Reinig also uses motifs from Klytemnestra's tale in the narratives of other women in the story. Klytemnestra's characteristics and actions are thus spread out among several female characters. Killing with an axe is particularly prominent.

A real-life case of two lesbian lovers who hired an assassin to kill the husband who stood in the way of their being together appears at the center of Reinig's text;[20] an axe was the murder weapon, and the two women each received life in prison for the deed—a particularly severe sentence in Germany, even for murder, and one that outraged many German women, including Reinig, who cites this episode as the triggering point of her conversion to feminism. The enthusiastically strenuous condemnation of female love and the need to reassert patriarchal law and to sacrifice the women who violate it, in the case of these two murderesses, recall the classical Klytemnestra's fate. The axe motif is also implicit in the real-life figure of Valerie Solanas, who appears in Reinig's text. Solanas produced the *SCUM Manifesto* in 1967; SCUM stands for Society for Cutting up Men, a strategy Solanas was willing to turn into praxis in her very nearly successful attempt on the life of Andy Warhol. Although Solanas presents a particularly extreme position, she clearly envisions a battle between those who support strong women of authority and those who side with "Big Daddy."[21]

The axe surfaces also in the hands of Reinig's fictional character Doris, who, dressed as Marilyn Monroe, attacks the novel's central "male" character, Otto Kyra. Ironically, Reinig's Klytemnestra never gets to swing the famous *labrys;* she is convicted of attempted manslaughter when she defends herself from her husband with a vegetable slicer. An overly fastidious jury decides that the tiny scar that the husband suffers is sufficiently close to a vein to call the attack attempted murder and sentences Klytemnestra to a year and a half in prison.

Although Reinig's Klytemnestra lacks the power and authority of her classical counterpart, her story emphatically points up discrepant power distributions between men and women. Reinig's Klytemnestra laments the lack not only of authority in the political arena but even of control over her own body. Because she cannot tolerate birth-control pills, she relies on luck to avoid conception. This method fails on more than one occasion, and Menni conceives a child during an affair with Kyra. In need of an abortion to save her marriage, she must seek illegal means and then risk prison. As she points out: "It's about my belly. Everyone gets to possess [my body/womb]: husband, son, judge, doctor. I alone, I have no property claim on it" (*Entmannung,* 49). Klytemnestra sees herself as a piece of raw flesh to be used and controlled by men.

The 1970s Klytemnestra, then, struggles for survival as a person rather than for dominion over a kingdom. Like her Italian counterpart in Dacia Maraini's *I sogni di Clitennestra,* she can only wound her husband, not kill him. Her children are lost in abortions, not as ritual sacrifices. Her son tries to crush his sister in a doorway but doesn't have the tragic grandeur to attack his mother. Menni is sent off to prison, leaving her husband in possession of the house as well as the children, who are almost instantly consoled at the loss of their mother by a trip to the toy store. Modern women, Reinig suggests, do not have the power successfully to attack their husbands. They have lost political ground by having been tamed into the Eumenides. The modern tragedy consists in the fact that not enough women reached for their axes in earlier times so as to keep women's power and authority alive. As Reinig puts it, "one can't avoid the reproach to women that they have spared the axe. The only woman who is innocent of the downfall of the world is Klytemnestra" (*Entmannung,* 79). The modern Menni has lost the capacity to exert sufficient violence to assert her own rights.

Reinig is concerned with male domination in all fields. She reveals the repercussions of the triumph of Father Right and patriarchal law in the lives of late-twentieth-century women by staging a conversation between Freud and Hitchcock and later introducing a monsignor to debate various gender issues. In all cases, women are objects to be studied or obsessed with but never subjects with their own rights. Thea laments at one point that the "rule of three" for women's existence is: "Irrenhaus, Krankenhaus, Zuchthaus" (153) (insane asylum, hospital, and penitentiary). In addition to the mad women in the attics, there are the physically broken women and those imprisoned for rebelling against the male rule of law and abusive husbands. Doris, Thea, Xenia, and Klytemnestra herself reify these limited female social options.

Competing voices and perspectives mark the text as dialogic. They produce a cacophony of voices that both assert the traditional patriarchal positions and challenge them by showing the repercussions of those positions on women's lives. The dialogic is extended into intertextual conversations between Aeschylus and Goethe (with murmurings from Solanas) as the novel concludes, but Reinig pushes this multivocality even further as she merges competing voices, archetypes, and even gender roles within single characters in the final scene.

Perhaps Reinig's most complicated moment in the novel is the ending, in which she produces a play within her novel and restages the close of Aeschylus's *Oresteia*. Reinig focuses on the crucial moment at which matriarchal blood rights give way to patriarchal rule by law in Aeschylus's play. In her restaging, Reinig fuses Goethe's *Faust 2* scene that calls Helen up from the underworld with the close of the *Oresteia*. Most crucial in the scene is the necessity for Goethe/Faust to attain to the realm of the Mothers in order to achieve his desire. By using *Faust* and the realm of the Mothers, Reinig reinvokes the female, and specifically the mother, in order to reinterpret the judgment of Athena in the *Eumenides*. If mothers are reinscribed in the myth as necessary and powerful, Klytemnestra cannot but fare better than she did in Aeschylus's version.

And indeed, in Reinig's restaging, Athena (played by Doris, whose name, appropriately for this role, means "spear"[22]) withdraws her patriarchal protection from Orest (played by Klytemnestra's son, Edgar) who is returned to Klytemnestra. Much as in Graham's ballet, Klytemnestra refrains from punishing her son, thus ending the eternal recurrence of violence. Orest (who is referred to as Klytemnestra's "Opfer," "victim or sacrifice") then reveals himself as Apollo and frees the imprisoned female Furies. This gesture of Apollo freeing the female principle reverses his famous speech in Aeschylus's *Eumenides* in which he argues that mothers are merely the containers for the fathers' fertile sperm and therefore have no rights in regard to their children. Reinig thus essentially reverses the outcome of the *Oresteia;* in her version, women and Mother Right triumph over patriarchy as represented by Athena and Apollo. Blood rights vanquish again the patriarchal rule of law.

The text ends, however, on a more problematic note. The stage is held by a trio composed of Sappho, Solanas (played by the now demasculinized Kyra), and Porkyas (played by Mephisto as in Goethe's *Faust 2*, who in turn is played by Gustaf Gründgens, the German actor and theater director who collaborated with the Nazis). Three female principals command the scene, but two are played by men. This gender confusion is also built into Goethe's *Faust 2,* in which Mephisto takes on the form of one of the Phorkyaden and refers to himself in this guise as a hermaphrodite.

Gender confusion is also inherent in the classical theater itself, in which men played all the female roles. Christa Wolf takes up this point in her essays preceding *Kassandra:*

> [Aristotle in Chapter 15 of the *Poetics*] goes on: "Woman, too, and even a slave can be good, although in general woman is perhaps an inferior, and the slave a worthless being." For this reason it was logical that women never attended Greek tragedy, not even as actresses. Iphigenia, Antigone, Clytemnestra, Electra, Medea, Hecate, the Trojan women, were all men in women's dress, . . . possibly homoerotic—but men. . . . This throng of women, mothers, and goddesses . . . was brought under control, ... The prohibitions of that day still tell us what things made people feel threatened. Aristotle: "For example, character is good when a man has courage; but in general it is not appropriate for a woman to be brave and manly or even alarming." (*Cassandra,* 282)

Aristotle's words make only too clear his view of the subordinate status of women and the fact that men are alarmed by a bold, let alone violent, woman. The depiction of such women as Medea and Klytemnestra could only provide negative incitements to females.[23] But such figures played by men must have reassured the fearful male audience; men, after all, dominate the action and the roles. Wolf and Reinig both demonstrate that one way to bring women under control is to displace them by having men adopt their clothing and eventually their positions as priestesses, rulers, and goddesses. Kyra's appropriation of female garb and roles thus takes on a more sinister tone.

Does Reinig's closing scene with its confusion of male and female finally complete the demasculinization of the males and create a kind of equality? Or does it simply represent a usurping of female roles by men? Clearly, Gründgens, a male, controls the action and the characters. He is the lord of the theater whose will reigns. In addition, the entire re-presentation of the *Oresteia* takes place in a chapter entitled "Letzte Vorstellung," meaning either "last performance" or "last ideas/images," which could be read as a dream by the male character, Kyra. Indeed, Margret Brügmann in *Amazonen der Literatur: Studien zur deutschsprachigen Frauenliteratur der 70er Jahre* (Amazons of Literature: Studies of German-Speaking Women's Literature of the 1970s) (204–8) reads the ending as a male wish fulfillment in which all the female roles are usurped again by men, and women are eliminated from the stage of history.

I find it difficult to understand, however, why any man would find his wishes fulfilled by a rewriting of Aeschylus's depiction of the triumph of father rights over mother rights. Men are already the winners in the *Oresteia;* they successfully repress female fury and found the Western tradition of law. Reinig reverses this patriarchal happy ending. While I agree that Reinig is not presenting a simple utopian reversal that reinscribes matriarchy as dominant (the text is much too satirical for that), I do feel that she is successfully confusing gender roles in at least one fevered male imagination: Kyra's. The wish to have a male at the center is still prominent, but that male is not Kyra (whose lordship has indeed been demasculinized by the end of the text) but the more problematic Gründgens, who represents a false idol of German culture. The last gesture we see from Kyra in the surface of the text is his attendance on Thea ("goddess"), who is dying of cancer. Referred to as "Mama Kyra," he functions here not as a doctor (a profession usurped from women according to Kyra himself) but as a nurturer.

This Mama Kyra persona finally supplants that of Kyra as playboy surgeon as well as a number of his other roles. Early on, Kyra serves as a modern Paris in the text, who seems to award the apple of discord to each of the women who vie for his attention. Kyra is responsible in some way for the destruction of each of the main female characters. Xenia dies as a result of the rape Kyra sets up; the intellectual Doris goes insane from unrequited love; Thea (who later plays Aphrodite), the prostitute whom Kyra marries, dies of sexually related cancer; Klytemnestra (who later plays Hera), has an affair with Kyra leading to an abortion, loses her husband and children, and ends up in prison. None of the traditional female roles has proven viable. Mother or whore or intellectual, women in the modern world cannot succeed in any social arena. In the course of the text, Kyra establishes a modern parallel to the House of Atreus, populated entirely by women—and by Kyra. The self-devouring character of the house is visited exclusively upon women, however, as all the women are removed from the scene, leaving only Kyra to escape disguised in his dead wife's clothing.

The gender role confusions at the end of the text, where Kyra becomes Solanas (a woman dedicated to eliminating men) and Gründgens becomes the female Porkyas, certainly do not present a "happy ending" to the problems of gender suppression and inequality. But they may, at least, provide a troubling productive confusion, particularly in light of a comment by Reinig herself, who suggests that Kyra's attempts to demasculinize himself represents to some extent Reinig's own attempt to rid herself of her own patriarchally engendered thought patterns.[24] What we have then is a woman using a man to become less masculinely determined (a gesture not unlike the gender confusion inherent in designating Gründgens to play the male Mephistopheles playing the female Porkyas.) The point finally is not for matriarchy or patriarchy to triumph but to call the clichéd ideas about both thoroughly into question.

As Brügmann points out, Reinig is as critical of unexamined romantic notions of naive feminism (the ur-matriarchy, the inherent creativity of women, the nurturing role of women, and the idealized notion of motherhood, for example) as she is of the male images of women projected in psychology, the arts, and religion. Klytemnestra may be an appealing character for Reinig precisely because she is not easily assimilated into the definitions of the female proposed by either feminists or masculinists. Klytemnestra allows Reinig to explore women's loss of power in their traditional roles and to conceive of a different narrative for men and women. By relocating Klytemnestra's story in many characters—both historical and fictional—Reinig can investigate new configurations of gender roles and the relationship between masculine and feminine. Reinig uses the many multiple-gendered voices in her novel to create a kind of gender dialogic—a concept I explore more fully in my concluding chapter.

The Early 1980s—A Human Face for the Female Monster: Nancy Bogen's *Klytaimnestra Who Stayed at Home*

In her 1980 novel, *Klytaimnestra Who Stayed at Home,* the native New Yorker Nancy Bogen (b. 1932) chooses to revise the Klytemnestra story by humanizing all its characters. Bogen, who earned her undergraduate degree at New York University and her master's and doctoral degree at Columbia University, is a professor emerita of English literature at City University of New York's College of Staten Island.[25] She conceived of writing about Klytemnestra after teaching an interdisciplinary course "The Greeks" with the historian Phyllis Roberts at Richmond College.

Keeping the ancient setting, Bogen begins by focusing on the love story between her Klytaimnestra and Aigisthos. Both of them are disappointed with their lives for reasons apparently controlled by Agamemnon. Klytaimnestra finds Agamemnon a brutal, unfeeling, and sexually inadequate husband, but, more importantly, she cannot forgive him for sacrificing their eldest daughter, Iphigenia, at the supposed behest of the gods (but, we find out later, really only at the demand of his fellow Greek commanders). She is also driven by a secondary, but very human, motivation of jealousy over Agamemnon's new captive princess, Kassandra. Aigisthos knows that Agamemnon murdered his father (Thyestes) and that Agamemnon's ancestors usurped the throne that should have belonged to Aigisthos himself. Thus both Klytaimnestra and Aigisthos have motives of revenge for blood murders carried out by Agamemnon. Klytaimnestra and Aigisthos also share a tender love relationship based on communication and caring intimacy. These details humanize and soften Bogen's Klytaimnestra.

Agamemnon, too, is shown as a confused and broken man whose exploits at Troy have profited him nothing. His treasures have been lost at sea; his men don't respect him; his wife hates him. The war, which in this version is entirely engineered by Odysseus (who talks Agamemnon into the plan), has caused nothing but death and destruction for Greece as well as Troy. Agamemnon feels regret, sadness, and confusion. He hates slaughter and killing and wants to return to a "normal" home life. In fact, everyone who fought in the war comes back degraded and disillusioned. None of these characters has the godlike tragic stature of the classical version of the story. Indeed, Bogen passes up a chance to justify Klytaimnestra's vengeance more strongly at Agamemnon's expense when she chooses not to use the part of Klytemnestra's legend that suggests that Agamemnon killed her first husband (Tantalus, son of Thyestes) and her baby, and thus gained her as his own wife. By suppressing this part of the story, Bogen maintains a more humanly sympathetic and less monstrous Agamemnon. This makes Klytaimnestra's task more confusing and troubling for her as well as for the reader.

The murder scene is also underplayed and humanized. Klytaimnestra does not appear wielding her famous double-headed axe but steals up behind a drunken and nostalgic Agamemnon in his bath and virtually unnoticed, with a small knife, opens a vein in his neck as he had done years earlier to Iphigenia. Bogen consciously presents this death as a distinctly female form of execution by merging the fluids of the bath with Agamemnon's own blood. The victim is not terrorized as he might be by a frontal (and more phallic) assault with the knife[26] but drifts into a comfortable sleep of death.

This Klytaimnestra must struggle with her own mixed feelings and pity for Agamemnon. Not the screaming banshee of vengeance, Bogen's Klytaimnestra is a middle-aged mother who knows her son will not feel much regret at killing her. She and Aigisthos imagine in great detail their own deaths at Orestes' hand. They foresee a blind singer relating the tale after they are gone; Klytaimnestra understands that "Orestes and Elektra and doubtless the others too will want to hear it" (238). An aside by the narrator suggests that "while it was possible that he, her son, would experience some uneasy moments over it now and then," Klytaimnestra the realist comments, "that is how the whole thing will be received forever and ever" (238). This Klytaimnestra understands that she and her beloved will play the parts of the villains throughout time. In a decision similar to that of Virginia Woolf's Mrs. Dalloway, Bogen's Klytaimnestra invests her remaining energies in the small moments that she can savor with Aigisthos before they are both killed.

Bogen, then, presents a very human Klytaimnestra who cares about love and sex. She is a tormented wife and mother who would prefer to run away with her lover if that were possible. It is not power and dominion she desires (she knows in any case that she will not have them for long), but rather peace; she is the Klytaimnestra "who stayed at home." She evokes our compassion as an all-too-human figure. Closing on an image of nurturance, Bogen's text hopes for small moments of fulfillment for Klytaimnestra and Aigisthos. Theirs is a fate writ small but not to be escaped. The reader is asked to understand them as human beings rather than as mythic symbols. While this move sparks our sympathies, it also creates a diminutive female figure of the once fierce Klytemnestra. Far from an embodiment of female destruction, this Klytaimnestra is a confused human being who reacts from personal feeling. She is a less dominant woman than her classical counterpart and a more humbly human one.

Bogen is also concerned with a female perspective on a very physical level. Kassandra, for example, on experiencing sharp pains, wonders if it is her "bleeding-time" or if she may be pregnant with Agamemnon's child, and worries about the embarrassment of bleeding in public (199–201). Many of the women in the text discuss the need to masturbate as well as the quality (or lack of it) of intercourse with various men. Klytaimnestra, for example, thinks of Agamemnon's harsh and hurried sexual treatment as opposed to Aigisthos's tender consideration; and Helen (not of Troy, but rather a minor character) actually does a shopper's comparison of male sexual technique. Bogen incorporates these unavoidable physical concerns that women face— but that few texts by men are willing to address—as well as a female perspective on the pleasures and pains of sex. The female stream of consciousness includes these details as a self-evident part of experience in a way not usually employed by male writers (Joyce's Molly Bloom might be an exception).

Bogen also includes a number of scenes that reveal women's inferior position in the society. Both wives and captured women of Troy are deemed to be at the sexual disposal of the men with whom they live. Even the sanctuary of religion does not save them, as Kassandra's rape in the temple demonstrates. Many women are raped—Kassandra, various slaves and captives, and a ten-year-old girl. Even Klytaimnestra (like Reinig's character) has no sovereignty over her body; it belongs to her husband when he wants it. Any woman walking along the road seems fair game. (It should be noted that boys in the text often experience the same fate. Adult male dominance here extends to all those of lesser strength or standing.)

Frederic Leighton's *Clytemnestra from the Battlements of Argos Watches for the Beacon Fires Which Are to Announce the Return of Agamemnon,* 1874. (Leighton House Art Gallery Museum, Royal Borough of Kensington and Chelsea)

In another instance of distinctly female perspective, a small girl watches boys compete in having intercourse with a goat. She is both disgusted and envious. Finally, she is disillusioned to realize that the position she will occupy when she grows up and marries is that of the goat. Freud might rejoice at this instance of penis envy, except that it is not the penis (the maleness) but the dominance that is envied. The warrior heroes that the young girl had idolized are totally debased as her long-expected and now degraded warrior-father returns home to rape his captive woman while the daughter listens in disgust and pain.

Bogen more than counters any penis envy in the text by hatred of the penis and the scepter for which it stands. In a delirium of vengeance, Klytaimnestra dreams of castrating Agamemnon. She will "take his phallus and put the knife to it, and then as I watch the pain spread across his face when he realizes what is going to be, say—'This is what you made the child with, this is what you hurt me with again and again, and it is because of this that the people all follow and serve you right or wrong.' And with this draw the blade over it and—'Now look at it!'—fling it in his face" (145). It is not that the women in this revision want to be men; they clearly do not envy the penis. (One is reminded of the 1990s real-life version of this scene enacted by Lorena Bobbitt on her husband.[27]) Bogen's women just want the men to be human beings who think with their hearts and heads rather than their sexual organs.

Bogen's text, like many of the others I examine, is determinedly dialogic. All important male and female characters (and several minor ones) are given a voice. First-person passages and stream of consciousness predominate. These many voices call into question the gender roles and cultural assumptions inherent in Klytaimnestra's story. The definition and value of traditionally lauded concepts such as "heroism" become more problematic as we hear various versions of characters such as Agamemnon. As a result, although our sympathies lie with the lovers Klytaimnestra and Aigisthos, our views are tempered by Agamemnon's pitiable weaknesses and fears. Like Klytaimnestra herself, the reader is not sure she should kill him. Finally, the social rules and the rituals of power and dominion make his death unavoidable. Klytaimnestra has her vengeance, but she has also come to pity Agamemnon in a way her classical predecessor does not. Many of the cultural values of the ancient texts are met by competing values in Bogen's twentieth-century version.

All in all, Bogen's revision is a low-key version of the story. She sees the confusing human weaknesses of everyone. She does, however, justify Klytaimnestra's actions to a large degree by her need to avenge her daughter as well as by the political and social pressure imposed on her. There are few possible ways out for the lovers—ultimately, there are none. Nevertheless, the text closes on a nurturing image of the landscape as a giant golden mother bird looking after her young. Klytaimnestra's own powerful maternal instincts are thus projected onto the world at large as she and Aigisthos look forward to their remaining savored moments.

Bogen's text is not the shrill feminist protest that we have from Reinig and will see again in Maraini or Brückner. Rather it is a touchingly human and mundane revision; it attempts to understand what real people might have felt before the exaggeration of song and legend rewrote their experience. Physical and even earthy (recalling another feature of Kristeva's carnivalesque), this tale is about normal human beings struggling to live with one another under always inadequate emotional and physical circumstances.

The Hand That Rocks the Cradle Wields the Axe!: Dacia Maraini's *I sogni di Clitennestra*

Very unlike Nancy Bogen and her gentle touch, the Italian author Dacia Maraini (b. 1936) presents a voice of loud and clear feminist protest about the figure of Klytemnestra. In her play *I sogni di Clitennestra* (*Dreams of Clytemnestra*),[28] Maraini reexamines Aeschylus's conversion of the female Furies into the Eumenides at the close of the *Oresteia* and outspokenly laments the decision to replace Mother Right and blood relationships with Father Right and law. Lifting whole passages directly from Aeschylus, Maraini reassesses the ascendancy of patriarchy that the *Oresteia* records.

Born in Florence, Maraini, the daughter of the famous ethnologist Fosco Maraini, lived in Japan from 1938 to 1946. After finishing her studies in Sicily, she worked in Rome as a journalist and writer. She lived for a time with author Alberto Moravia and published her interviews with him as *Il bambino Alberto* (1986). Maraini is well known for her novels and poems, in addition to her plays, and has won a number of prestigious Italian literary awards.[29]

Unlike either Bogen or Wolf, Maraini modernizes the classical materials. She sets her *Clitennestra* in contemporary Italy, with Agamennone as a Sicilian who has emigrated to Prato and Clitennestra as an ex-prostitute turned textile worker. This connection between women and weaving (or embroidery), common in the classical materials, persists into the twentieth century. Marie Cardinal also makes her main character in *Le passé empiété*[30] an embroiderer, but Cardinal raises hers to the status of an artist. Weaving and sewing represent some of the earliest acknowledged connections of women with artistic creation. The tapestry is frequently portrayed as a weaving of meaning and a visual speech (as Helen's tapestry is in the *Iliad;* indeed, the modern word text derives from *texere*, "to weave.") Classical female figures often resort to this visual speech when deprived of spoken language (Philomela, for example, embroiders the story of her rape after Tereus cuts out her tongue to silence her) or when spoken language was ineffectual (Penelope must buttress her attempts to dissuade her suitors verbally by weaving her father-in-law's shroud). Weaving is also frequently linked to the negative weaving of plots or nets (such as the one Klytemnestra uses to trap Agamemnon in his bath). Art, signification, and clever plotting (the famous cunning of Klytemestra) are all tied to weaving and sewing.

In Maraini's text, however, weaving emphasizes women's degraded state. Maraini's Clitennestra is almost chained to her loom—which is her husband's property, just as (Agamennone argues) Clitennestra herself is. The loom represents both her economic repression and inferiority and her being tied to a traditional female role (as Ifigenia will appear tied to a bed). The symbol of weaving remains, but here it is subverted by Maraini to become an image of protest.

Maraini also recasts her other characters to reflect their modern social, political, and cultural context. Oreste becomes a restless young emigrant to Germany who returns to Italy as a communist and homosexual; Egisto is an unemployed opportunist; Elettra is an apprentice weaver; Cassandra is an American peasant; Ifigenia is a pregnant fourteen-year-old who is married off for a dowry. But the most striking figure of all is Athena, who has become a female psychoanalyst preaching the Freudian way to submission and health for the unfortunately penisless female race.[31] Clearly the daughter of her fathers, Zeus and Freud, this Athena, too, "honors the male" in all things—including marriage.

Suffering under the poor Italian economy, Agamennone decides to move to America. To finance his emigration, he agrees to give his pregnant daughter, Ifigenia, as a bride to the father of her child; the dowry will finance his trip. The doctors say, however, that the frail child-mother Ifigenia will not survive the birth—which she in fact does not. It is this "sacrifice" of her daughter, who dies as a result of Agamennone's economic exploitation of her sexuality, that Clitennestra cannot forgive.

Ifigenia's plight as doomed child-mother is underscored by her brief appearance, during which she is tied to the bed (of childbirth) that will be her tomb. Like Reinig's and Bogen's Klytemnestras, Maraini's Ifigenia as well as her Clitennestra have no claim to their own bodies or to their labor—either in childbirth or at the loom. Maraini borrows lines directly from Aeschylus to counterpoint her present-day setting and to mark the sacrifice of the daughter Ifigenia to the modern needs of the family, or rather those of patriarchy, for money. Maraini gives the lines of the chorus from Aeschylus's *Agamemnon* quite pointedly to the female fate, Moira (also identified as a female avenging fury, an Erinys), who describes in gory detail Agamennone's sacrifice of the defenseless Ifigenia:

> MOIRA: The gods worshipped,
> the father makes a sign to the servants
> [the following four lines are quoted by the chorus as Agamemnon's
>   in the *Oresteia*]
> because like a goat covered
> by his bindings and desperately
> tethered to the earth,
> she was taken, gagged, suspended.
> DONNA: [Woman and Prostitute]:
> He kills his daughter with his own hands
> and thus the armada can leave.
> MOIRA: . . .
> And she seemed an image, a mute image.
>
> (9–10)

As in the case of the original Iphigenia, Ifigenia's betrothal becomes her death sentence. No longer given to the bravest warrior, Achilles, the modern Ifigenia is given to a nameless male who takes her as his "paternal duty" dictates. Sacrificed not for the glory of Greece but for the financial survival of her father, Ifigenia has become a more mute and meaningless sacrifice than her classical namesake. Maraini challenges the classical definitions of "duty" and "heroism" to produce a dialogic text that relativizes many cultural icons. The difference in rhetorical levels between Maraini's modern, lower-class Italian and the classical text emphasizes the deflation of the "heroic tradition" and lays bare the blatant use of women for the needs of men.

Clitennestra's other daughter, Elettra, is infinitely closer to her father than to her mother.[32] She has incestuous fantasies about him that will be matched by Oreste's incestuous desires later in the play. Elettra hovers over Clitennestra like an avenging spirit even before Agamennone dies. Clitennestra attempts to enlist Elettra's sympathy as a sister female, tied to the same tasks, anchored to the same looms whose clashing bobbins recall the Furies. But Elettra's love belongs to her father and to the house. Much akin to Euripides' Electra, Elettra accuses Clitennestra of never having loved the house but only thinking of her body and its pleasures and needs, now filled by the unemployed Egisto. A modern audience might well take Elettra's accusation as evidence rather of Clitennestra's sane realignment of priorities, since the "house" here must be the incestuous, cannibalistic House of Atreus engaged in an endless male power struggle in which women are pawns, seduced and betraying as well as betrayed. This is a house that even a mother finds hard to love—and rightly so. The only problem is that Clitennestra has nowhere to turn but to the unemployed opportunist Egisto. He may fulfill her physical needs, but he has nothing more to offer. Not able to exist as a woman alone in her society, Clitennestra has only the weakest examples of the male species to choose from.

Agamennone returns after ten years with his own Cassandra, an American who, like her namesake, has visions of dead children and a murdered Agamennone. This Cassandra, however, accompanies Agamennone out of love—an emotion that Agamennone neither seeks nor respects. What he wants is fidelity built on fear. Fear is the single driving emotion in Agamennone's own life, and he wants to impose it on others to relieve his own sense of inferiority. Agamennone attains a feeling of power from his ability to order Cassandra around and from the security that Clitennestra is "his property" (taken in as a thirteen-year-old prostitute to make love to Agamennone and his lover and therefore molded to Agamennone's needs). Women, whose own social and economic position is inferior to his own, make Agamennone feel like a "man." Clitennestra, who as a child was grateful to have food and a place to stay, once loved Agamennone. She comes to realize that he did not save her but rather consumed her. She suffers beatings, abortions, and a number of illegitimate births before Agamennone condescends to marry her. Only Ifigenia's death finally kills Clitennestra's love. In the end, Clitennestra is trapped in another "love" triangle with Cassandra.

Although Maraini's depiction of men is certainly harsh, she complicates the picture by revealing that men in the society fare no better than women. Young men are reduced to pimping, stealing, living off their mothers—or all three. Oreste and his homosexual partner, Pilade, are adrift, looking for a means to enter into a society that is economically and socially closed to them. Only Agamennone's death opens the way for Oreste to become husband, father, and man in this degraded world.

Agamennone, like Clitennestra, dreams that she stabs him to death with a knife ornamented with a head of Diana (Artemis, who demanded the sacrifice of Iphigenia) in a symbolic act of revenge for Ifigenia. He actually dies of a heart attack, but Maraini implies that Clitennestra's hatred of him, even though repressed, helps to kill him. Moira returns to mourn the "lord" Agamennone who has been caught in the spider's web of Clitennestra's hate, just as his ancient counterpart is caught in Klytemnestra's net. But here the spider's web (*tessuto di ragno*) is also related to *tessile*, or "cloth," and *telaio*, the "loom." The loom, in turn, represents both the female weaving of Clitennestra and the economic pressures that give Agamennone his heart attack.

In the modern world, female fury is given a hand by economic necessity. The loom that would have made Agamennone a happy capitalist instead becomes his death web as Clitennestra vividly imagines driving the blade into his heart. Elettra is left to mourn her father's body that she so fervently desired.

Oreste, jealous of his mother and Egisto as well as imagining his sister/mother as a vengeful lover, listens to Elettra's pleas that he save the "house" and the looms and avenge his father. But Oreste is reluctant. Elettra then sets about inspiring Clitennestra with guilt for her failure to be a model woman who cared only for the family and the house: "I'd have liked you to have been different. Like grandmother was, the mother of our father: a quiet woman, who smelled of basil; a body dedicated to the family, ready for any sacrifice. . . . Instead you do as you like. You decide things as though you were the boss, you take, you give, but only as you like. And you treat us like strangers, without a thought" (33). Much like Euripides' Electra, this monomaniacal daughter would like her Clitennestra to be the perfect, self-sacrificing, submissive mother, dedicated to house and family and never asserting a self.

The irony, of course, is that the modern Clitennestra does not really have the option of being boss, of deciding her own fate or that of Agamennone. She is in a very inferior position, both economically and socially, to her classical counterpart. Clitennestra is a cog in an economic wheel whose profits she does not share, unlike the wealthy ancient Queen Klytemnestra. Also unlike her ancient counterpart, Clitennestra belongs to the lower rather than the upper class. She does not wield political power or influence when her husband is away. She cannot even successfully exert her will through violence by actually killing her husband. According to Maraini's critical depiction, women's lot has obviously not improved over the thousands of years since the first Klytemnestra ruled in Agamemnon's absence.

Elettra insists on keeping alive an image of the family and the mother that is even more repressed than the classical original. Clitennestra, however, wants to live a new life. She and Egisto announce they are having a child. Both Elettra and Oreste urge Clitennestra to abort it. Elettra, speaking as "neither woman nor man" but as "the family," urges Oreste to kill his mother—which, in another dream sequence, he does. Elettra, in a complete about-face at her mother's dream bier, now professes her love for her mother and her admiration for her defiance of patriarchy. She tells of her mother's resentment at Elettra's growing up—which reminded her of her own increasing age. Menstruation marks Elettra as a rival so that the father-son Freudian struggles are rehearsed also by the mother and daughter who compete for the father's love—and also the son's love, since the now insane Clitennestra later asks Elettra jealously if she has made love with Oreste.

Maraini innovates in several ways. First, she portrays Clitennestra as pregnant, emphasizing her maternal, fertile, female aspects usually suppressed in favor of her masculine aggressiveness. In turn, her children's desire to abort the new baby marks their dedication to the old patriarchal order. Second, Clitennestra is not killed by Oreste (just as she does not kill Agamennone), but rather she goes insane. Taking over Oreste's role in the original story, Clitennestra is the one to lose her senses rather than her life. While Orestes is pursued by the Furies, who avenge blood killings, Clitennestra is driven to the insane asylum by her own children and their desire to defend patriarchy. Not able to act out her repressed revenge, the modern Clitennestra goes mad instead. In going mad, Maraini's Clitennestra joins a long line of female characters (including Reinig's Doris) who become the madwomen in the attics or asylums.[33] She is conveniently locked away so that her opposing views are not available to disrupt her family or patriarchy. And while Orestes' pursuit by the Furies is ended by Athena, Clitennestra's insanity is verified by the Athena figure in the person of the female psychoanalyst. Females in Maraini's text do not avenge one another but rather are complicit in having women who rebel against patriarchal rule committed.

Maraini commented in an interview in 1984: "My . . . *Clytemnestra* is the story of female madness, as rejection, incongruence, nonrelationship with the male world. . . . Madness is not adjusting to the world. Women find themselves . . . in a nonadjusted condition, because this is not a world made to a woman's measurements. . . . So many women don't fit in it, and the damage that this does to some women is so severe that. . . . the most sensitive . . . go crazy, the ones who feel the most strongly this violence that is being done to their psyches, to women's psychological integrity, by the male world, which is very powerful" (Anderlini, 150). Maraini's "male world" also contains women who support the patriarchal order. Maraini's Clitennestra is defeated by both men and patriarchally loyal women; she loses her mother rights and her human rights without being able to loose the Furies on those who destroyed her.

Oreste, on the other hand, retains his senses and the family fortune to develop into a non-Fury-pursued capitalist. Oreste (who Clitennestra reveals is the son of his grandfather rather than Agamennone) already lives in a world in which male right has been long established. There is no need for him to feel guilt; he simply steps into the family fortune and lives happily on while Clitennestra is safely locked away. The women, Clitennestra and Elettra, are finally sisters indeed in their sexual and social needs and in their economic dependence. Clitennestra's only revenge or "glory" is to be as scandalous as possible in the midst of her bourgeois, patriarchal community.

In a rather startling moment of hallucination in the insane asylum, Clitennestra merges Agamennone and Christ—in the most sexual terms possible. Describing an act of fellatio on Agamennone, Clitennestra complains that during the act a nun came in and hurled Agamennone against the wall, nailing him to the cross where he can still be seen. Agamemnon, sacrificed by Klytemnestra for his sins against a woman, becomes Christ, sacrificed by mankind to redeem the original sin of woman. In both cases, the male sacrifice will eventually help to inscribe the patriarchal order and male dominance; the sacrificed males are thereby redeemed. In its modern version, a female (nun) returns the male sacrificial victim to his cross in the midst of sexual activity. Both the female and the religion she represents help to restore patriarchal order. From a modern religious perspective (here, that of Catholicism), sex itself has become the sin for which man (symbolically in the crucifix) and woman (physically in all the abortions) must pay. The death of the father (Agamemnon) and the son (Christ) both help to keep patriarchy in power and the woman in her place—dead (Klytemnestra or Ifigenia), insane (Clitennestra), or virginal (or in Elettra's case, frigid).

Another passage from the opening scene of Aeschylus's *Eumenides* introduces the modern equivalent of Orestes' being pursued by the Erinyes—which in this case is Oreste's being tempted by the female fate, Moira (as Adam is tempted to knowledge and sexuality by Eve). Moira becomes specifically the spirit of the young Clitennestra who appears to her son, Oreste (as Clitennestra had appeared to the father, Agamennone), as a thirteen-year-old prostitute. Oreste, despite his homosexuality, has intercourse with the girl and then attempts to strangle her (unsuccessfully, although he hallucinates having succeeded). The desire to kill the mother here merges with the desire to have her sexually. The incest motif is complicated by a misogynist streak in Oreste, the representative of paternal right and domination. The Erinyes, in the persons of three streetwalkers, put Oreste on trial for the hallucinated murder. Oreste defends himself less than nobly by pointing out that the girl wasn't a virgin anyway. He also attempts to align himself with the prostitutes by claiming to be an exploited worker like them.

The echoes of the Marxist attempt to enlist women as fellow exploitees rings clearly through this scene. But despite his offers of "brotherhood," Oreste is one of the economic rulers, not the ruled. With the looms taken from his mother, he will start a small factory and buy himself a pistachio-colored Ford Escort (just like his late father had in America) by the end of the play. Finally, Oreste confesses that he had to kill Moira (his fate or his "doom"—the Greek word implies both) because he was afraid of being lost in her enormous feminine darkness, of being devoured by her—a confession that would make

Freud proud and that wakens Oreste from his nightmare to find Moira alive next to him. In a parody of psychoanalytic thinking, Maraini implies that Oreste, having symbolically slept with and killed his mother, is "cured" of homosexuality; Oreste is reported married in the next scene and can then get on with a "normal" heterosexual life. He has literally returned to the womb, as Clitennestra recalls he had asked to do when he was younger.

Oreste being acquitted, however, Clitennestra must now face her own condemnation. She has obviously been too aggressive. Clitennestra challenges her accuser, the female psychoanalyst, by pointing out that she too is a penisless woman ("that the bird in her shorts has lost its point"). The psychoanalyst is identified as Athena; both Athena and the psychoanalyst are born of their fathers (Zeus and Freud), not of mothers, and both side with patriarchy against women. The psychoanalyst/Athena believes in and is living proof of Apollo's argument in the *Eumenides* (ll. 666–71) that the father, "the one who mounts," is the real creative force. Demonstrating a clear case of womb envy, men usurp the female contribution to birth in order to gain dominion.

In Maraini's text, Agamennone makes precisely Apollo's argument to Elettra before he departs for America:

> AGAMENNONE: They say that the daughter is hers. . . . And me? Who am I? . . . Who put the sacrosanct seed in her belly? Who thought of that white flesh, who wanted it, did it, guessed it? She's not hers, but mine.
>
> ELETTRA: Daughter to the father, daughter to the grandfather, sole progenitor. [Vode translates this more directly as: "From father to grandfather, it's men that make us."]
>
> AGAMENNONE: Elettra, learn something: from here, from this head comes your well-being. That I have with my imagination given you birth. Your mother has contributed the flesh/guts. I the truth. Understood? (9)

And to be quite certain that women accept the argument, men then claim that the envy is on the woman's part. The psychoanalyst argues with Clitennestra that her aggression, her filthy talk, her sexual obsession, and her infantile exhibitionism are all indications of envy—good solid envy of (male) virility—penis envy! (54). The woman (Clitennestra) cannot accept the feminine part of herself, her sweetness, gentleness, and passivity (54). She wants to compete with men, with power, and become hard; this causes her hysteria. In an unrivaled bid to have women accept their inferior state (their penisless selves) the psychoanalyst/Athena tells Clitennestra that to be healthy, she must be submissive to the male. Having usurped the female powers of prophecy and even of procreation, the male must finish the job by demanding physical and psychological submission. That Maraini makes the psychoanalyst female demonstrates the extent to which she feels that women have bought into the roles assigned them by their fathers in order to participate in the power structure, to play at being Freud's and Zeus's favored offspring.

During this entire exchange, Clitennestra taunts the psychoanalyst sexually. Finally, "the blameless physician" threatens to have Clitennestra tied up. She answers quite appropriately that she is already tied up or caught in a web herself. Maraini points here not just to the physical ropes that hold Clitennestra but to the entire patriarchal tradition that binds her to the female role of subservience and forbids her to rule or to avenge. Wielding the axe or knife that can only signify castration in the Freudian world, Clitennestra is a threat even if she only dreams of using it.

The psychoanalyst explains to Clitennestra that her problem is that she has not developed properly into the correct "receptive" role of the woman. She has failed, as modern women have been instructed, to reach "mature," internal (vaginal) orgasm and is stuck, instead, at the level of immature, external clitoral stimulation:

> PSYCHOANALYST: As a child you concerned yourself a lot with your body and justly so. . . . As a child you masturbated, you were languid and aggressive; justly so, for you still had to discover your femininity. . . . But then, you see, you grow up, you become a woman and transfer your pleasure from the outside to the inside, you learn to be receptive, docile, maternal. . . . This is the path of the woman who matures sanely. . . . you, no, you remained a child, aggressive, undocile, clitoritic. And it is this which makes you crazy. . . . The conflict . . . is always alive in you and corrupts your soul. (55)

Aeschylus's great tragic struggle between Mother Right and Father Right, between female prerogatives and the patriarchal power structure, is translated here into its more crass and straightforward Freudian terms, which Maraini critiques and satirizes—the woman has simply not learned to be submissive to the male—"receptive, docile, maternal." She has been driven mad by her refusal to repress sexual desire and pleasure and the aggressive and exploratory parts of her own personality. Clitennestra has not learned to internalize sufficiently enough to become the well-adjusted, "mature," sexually repressed mother that society can praise and use as it needs.

The psychoanalyst is quite right in suggesting to Clitennestra that she "corrompe l'anima" (corrupts her soul). *Anima* here can be rendered as soul, but it also calls up the Jungian term "anima"—or the male projection of female-ness.[34] As Demaris S. Wehr puts it: "The anima is a component of male psychology and the feminine a component of female psychology. Although both terms seem to refer in some way to women, 'anima' is not synonymous with 'the feminine.' The anima is the soul-image of men's imaginations which they often project onto real women. Men must disentangle themselves from the anima in order to be able to relate to real women and to allow real women the space to be themselves" (38). Clitennestra is indeed corrupting her "anima," that is, the male projection of what she should be, by struggling to gain a real feminine self. The growth of a Clitennestra who has her *own*, female identity retards and destroys the Clitennestra that patriarchy would like to develop.

Clitennestra responds to the accusation by stubbornly concentrating on seducing the psychoanalyst. This attempt finally infuriates the "good doctor," who disposes of Clitennestra by labeling her definitively insane, a "manic regressive, expulsive schizophrenic." Even twenty years (or twenty centuries?) of shock treatment may not make her normal. Clitennestra at this declaration unleashes on the psychoanalyst/Athena a speech that a good many modern female analysands might applaud. (Unfortunately, this speech is cut entirely from the published English translation, thus depriving Clitennestra of one of her most powerful feminist protests.) It goes as follows: "CLITENNESTRA: Your father has thrown his semen among the innards of his hot, wet brain. He made up all of you. He made his member explode with pleasure playing with thoughts of a solitary Narcissus. Then the furious seed spilled towards the stars, he spread out the folds of his paternal brain to collect that foggy, falling rain. The seed took root, made leaves, flowers. And after nine months of brooding thought in masculine hate you were born. While your mother died of love in a kitchen full of smoke. . . . Women like you make me vomit" (55–56).

The "father" here is Athena's father, Zeus, from whose head she sprang in full battle armor like an angry thought. Conceived by the male rational tradition alone (according to patriarchy, which finds it convenient to forget Athena's swallowed mother Metis—from whom, ironically, Athena obviously inherits her own intelligence, or *metis*), Athena would be entirely her father's daughter, who would decide in favor of male right against the female at the end of the *Eumenides*. But Maraini makes clear that the "father" is also Freud, whose own version of the rational tradition gave the man—and the penis—dominance in Western tradition, thus displacing the mother and the female. For Maraini's Clitennestra, Freud represents the final bourgeois, patriarchal plot to keep the failing male power structure and dominance intact. The women who participate in the Freudian game of phallogocentrism would indeed make the great upholder of Mother/female Right, namely Clitennestra, vomit.

The play moves toward its conclusion as Clitennestra confronts (as she does in Aeschylus's *Eumenides*) the Erinyes, now three prostitutes, who were supposed to have upheld her right and tormented the male order into recogni tion of her murder. She accuses these modern Erinyes of having betrayed her. They defend themselves by arguing that science (modern Freudian knowledge?) has changed them, that they were converted by democratic reason (thus evoking Athena's speech as she tames the Erinyes into the Eumenides at the end of the *Oresteia*). Having been lulled to sleep by the sexual attention of men and the tranquilizers of science, the modern Eumenides announce to Clitennestra that she, too, has lost, that killing an adulterous mother is not an unpardonable crime, that man is born of the paternal seed, and that woman is only the receptacle. Justice has been instituted as the law of patriarchy.

Defeated anew in history, Clitennestra gives up the dream of being herself and of being another—of having a self that can accommodate multiplicity and otherness. Clitennestra realizes that such dreams of an independent female identity are in vain, and she decides to die, as Elettra wants, in the name of "truth and the family order" (58). Not knowing if it has all been "a dream of life or a life of dream" (58), Clitennestra continues somewhere, among the dead dreams, to live in order to continue to dream. With this speech, she dies. Clearly a call to contemporary women to keep her dream of a female self alive, this last speech resituates Clitennestra in a literary tradition that has been changed by *I sogni di Clitennestra*.

As the play's title indicates, Clitennestra's dreams are particularly important. While the Greek Klytemnestra could kill her lord and master—for whatever reason—the Italian Clitennestra can only dream of doing so, implying that women's realms of action have become even more restricted in the late twentieth century than they were in classical times. Clitennestra's dreams during the play are of two types. First, she dreams of men doing violence to her—her husband wanting to slit her throat (10) and her son being a serpent who sucks her blood (32) and later cruelly tugs at her breasts. In these dreams, the immediate representatives of patriarchy, the husband and the son, exert a sadistic sexual and physical control over the mother's body. They are dreams of fear born of an inferior social position in which Clitennestra's sexuality and her self are controlled first by the husband and then by the son who replaces him. In the dream world, Oreste plays out the fantasy of replacing his father sexually. He shares Clitennestra's dream of violent sex when he dreams of strangling his mother's ghostly representative, Moira, after intercourse (47). He both desires to be taken back into the womb and fears that it will happen. He must finally destroy the woman whose womb he cannot reenter. Penis envy seems a pale comparison to the violence spawned by womb envy.

Second, Clitennestra dreams of doing violence to the man who subordinates her, her husband (24). The dream of stabbing migrates from Clitennestra to Cassandra, who dreams that someone has stabbed Agamennone, to Agamennone himself, who dreams that Clitennestra has taken her revenge by stabbing him to death (while he, in fact, dies of a heart attack). In this dream, Clitennestra (recalling Aeschylus's version) throws herself upon Agamennone, who is a beast to be slaughtered (just as he had thrown himself upon Ifigenia in order to sacrifice her); she watches his blood flow as he squirms and dies. A wish-fulfillment dream, this vision allows the actually impotent Clitennestra to take action and vengeance in order, she explains to Egisto, to get back her daughter (or at least avenge her) and her looms. She repossesses her maternal right and the economic (and signifying) capacity to maintain it. Only in her dreams does Clitennestra have the power of maternal vengeance to avenge her own years of physical and sexual abuse and her daughter's death.

Clitennestra's final dream is of being herself and the other simultaneously. She dreams of having an identity that is communal and powerful. With her parting words, she dreams of an independent female self supported by other women: "I dreamed of being me. I dream of being another. Between the two dreams there is no link. The dream gives me strength. The dream takes away my strength. Women of my dreams, don't betray me, help me! Can a dead woman dream of reviving, dreaming, her most mutilated dreams? . . . If I die dreaming maybe I'll die happy. But is it a dream of life or a life of dream? Somewhere, among the dead dreams, I continue to live, in order to continue to dream. (*Clitennestra dies*)" (58–59). The lost dream is one of female and blood rights. The dead Klytemnestra has passed her dream on to the contemporary Clitennestra, who must now hope to pass it on to women who would follow her. Perhaps somewhere in the long dream of restoring women's rights and independent selfhood the poison and mutilation will be replaced by a happier ending. But not yet, Maraini implies. This Clitennestra, too, is killed by the family and the house; her dream remains unfulfilled— but alive in the minds of the women—and men—who view the play.

The closing speech of the play goes to Moira, the female fate. Citing Aeschylus (ll. 792–805 of Fagles's translation of *The Eumenides*), she delivers the bitter speech of the defeated Erinyes in the *Eumenides* that threatens poison and plague upon men and terror for the city of Athens since it has instituted patriarchy and law over female, blood rights. Aeschylus positions this speech before Athena's final persuasion of the Furies to become benevolent, tamed spirits, the Eumenides. Maraini, on the other hand, places this speech of rage and sadness by the wounded daughters of Mother Night at the very end of the play. The psychoanalyst/Athena has already had her say—and the Erinyes are still furious. Maraini suggests that the death of Clitennestra and the instituting of patriarchy at her expense is not a settled point of history. Clitennestra's and Klytemnestra's dreams live on among women who share the image of a whole and multivalent self. The repression of this modern Clitennestra seems only to resurrect the festering hate of the female Furies.

When Clitennestra's death calls forth once more the female Furies tamed by Aeschylus, Athena, and Freud, the female will to fight for a self is resurrected. Clitennestra's deathbed becomes the childbed of a new feminist anger and aggression. While she cannot reinstate female right over the current patriarchal power structure, she can, at least, unleash the female Erinyes and fate, Moira, upon world literature again. Maraini's primary revision of Aeschylus's work, then, is to invoke again the repressed female Furies, who have literally gone underground at the end of the *Oresteia*. They do not have a particularly pleasant message for patriarchy, promising poison, plague, leprosy, and terror upon the city of man. Maraini may be shrill, but she is also clear.

Although less experimental in form than Reinig's *Entmannung* or Wolf's *Kassandra* and its accompanying essays, Maraini's play is strongly dialogic in structure. Her use of passages taken directly from Aeschylus in the midst of her own modern class and family struggle (with its Freudian underpinnings) creates a revision of the *Oresteia* that demonstrates both the survival of basic human gender conflicts and the deflation of their heroic nature. We begin to see conflicting definitions of the "heroic" and of traditional gender prescriptions. Aeschylus, Freud, and Maraini generate competing voices that are all present in this text. Maraini's dialogue (which recalls Kristeva's carnivalesque), full of crass obscenities and worries about money, sex, and the burdens of the family, starkly contrasts with the elevated rhetoric of Aeschylus's language. But Ifigenia is sacrificed for her father's success just as Iphigenia is. The actual ritual slaughters of the *Oresteia* may be turned into nightmare and hallucination in the modern text, but the hatreds and loves that fuel them lose none of their intensity.

Clitennestra remains the avenging mother and the deserted wife. Patriarchy still sanctions her "murder" by Orestes and Electra, or in this play their having her committed for insanity. In fact, disposing of Clitennestra remains necessary to keep patriarchy intact. Clitennestra's disappointment with the Erinyes for not upholding female rights of motherhood and blood over the male right of inheritance and rule by law becomes a crucial challenge of the original decision in favor of Orestes and patriarchy at the end of the *Eumenides*. We hear competing voices that relativize our views of the founding tenets of Western culture. The justifications put forward by Athena on behalf of Orestes and Zeus are translated into the mouth of a modern female psychoanalyst preaching the Freudian form of patriarchy.

Maraini's play clearly protests the situation of women, who are driven mad or sacrificed or co-opted by patriarchy. No woman in the play survives whole and female. The original decision reached in the *Oresteia* in favor of the father, of patriarchy, still holds and binds women to childbed, the loom, and the family—that is, to the traditional "female" roles that have kept women repressed since the Erinyes became the Eumenides. Maraini's loosing of the Erinyes once more to agitate for female right represents a parting gesture of hope.

The Unredeemed Klytämnestra: Christine Brückner's "Bist du nun glücklich, toter Agamemnon?"

Originally published in 1981, Christine Brückner's twelve-page monologue, "Bist du nun glücklich, toter Agamemnon?" (Are You Happy Now, Dead Agamemnon?), was included in a 1983 collection entitled *Wenn du geredet hättest, Desdemona: Ungehaltene Reden ungehaltener Frauen* (If You Had Spoken, Desdemona: Angry [or Indignant] Speeches of Angry [or Indignant] Women), which contains monologues by those women who never got to have their say in the recorded tradition. Martin Luther's wife, and Goethe's, the Blessed Virgin, Sappho, Petrarch's Laura, Desdemona, the terrorist Gudrun Ensslin, Brückner herself, among others, and Klytämnestra all finally get to speak their minds. The volume contains much suppressed rage and revealed psychological torment—women ignored, degraded, silenced. It is understandable that Klytämnestra should get the final speech, should at last have the chance to justify herself for her "crimes." Hers is a powerful voice of suppressed rage overflowing into destructive action.

Brückner (b. 1921) was raised and lives in West Germany and became a successful writer of popular novels, children's books, and radio plays. Although it drew a large audience, her work was snubbed by critics as *Trivialliteratur* (trivial literature). Many of her works, however, deal with the survival of women in difficult situations and are clearly of interest to a broad audience and particularly to feminist readers.[35]

Brückner opens her Klytämnestra monologue in a much angrier voice than Bogen ever approaches. The title query reflects Agamemnon's tenet (borrowed from a saying of Solon[36]) of never calling anyone happy who isn't already dead. In Fagles's translation of the *Oresteia*, Agamemnon's line reads, "Call no man blest until he ends his life in peace, fulfilled" (*Agamemnon*, ll. 923–24). In the Greek trilogy, Agamemnon utters this line in a dialogue with Klytemnestra, who is tempting him to blaspheme and commit an act of hubris by treading on the tapestries of the house—an honor fit only for a god.

Brückner's Klytämnestra has already slain her husband when the story opens. She ironically asks her murdered husband if he can now be counted among the happy. Her voice still spews hatred for Agamemnon and the House of Atreus, whose members must either kill or be killed. She feels that any pain inflicted on her dead husband was more than merited. In this, Brückner's Klytämnestra is the equal of her classical counterpart in the *Oresteia*.

In Brückner's text, Klytämnestra matches her female strength (symbolized by water in Brückner's iconography, such as the water of the bath in which she drowns Agamemnon) against his male power (symbolized by fire, the fires of Troy, and destruction). She claims that the female water kills Agamemnon, not the phallic knife (which was probably wielded by Ägisth). While both Agamemnon's phallic fire and Klytämnestra's fluid water can be deadly, she insists that the power to dispatch the tyrant husband and king is female. She does not want simply to replace Agamemnon as the male principle of dominion or destruction; she wants the female to vanquish the male. Although a bit symbolically reductive, this gesture is a clearly feminist critique on both Klytämnestra's and Brückner's parts. Going beyond most feminist positions, however, Klytämnestra embodies an intensely projected hate that must claim the credit for Agamemnon's murder even if Ägisth did the actual deed. But her claim also privileges female retribution over the male battle for political dominance. Long ignored by her husband, Klytämnestra is now in a position to make him listen to the female world he has suppressed.

By opening the monologue after Agamemnon's death, Brückner avoids depicting the murder itself; this makes Klytämnestra a less bloody and more sympathetic figure (since we have only her point of view). In addition, we realize that *only* a dead Agamemnon can be made to listen—a frustrating fact that also increases our sympathy for Klytämnestra as a suppressed and silenced wife.

Very much at odds with the heroic tradition of the ancient times in which her story takes place, Brückner's Klytämnestra cares nothing for heroic reputation; indeed, she counsels her son to run from battle.[37] She berates men for wanting to play gods in their aping of the gods' heroic exploits, in their desire for war and "honor." Finally, she decides that the war is the desire of the king, Agamemnon, and not any decree of the gods who are invoked as an excuse.

The only spoils Klytämnestra requests from Troy are flower seeds, something that might grow from the slaughter. The garden becomes one of her emblems (just as the now shattered stone lions that flank the citadel gates figure Agamemnon). But she realizes that no gardens will grow, that none of her children will play in them. She bore her children and gave them to a nurse to raise, as was proper for the ruling class, thus allowing enmity to grow between mother and daughter just as animosity reigned between fathers and sons, "as it does by the gods" (157). What might have been a garden in Mykene becomes wasteland.

Klytämnestra indicts Agamemnon for never having listened to his subjects any more than he listened to her; in a familiar patriarchal gesture, he suppressed all speech but his own. But despite everything (including Agamemnon's murder of her first husband and child), Klytämnestra claims to have loved Agamemnon. Perhaps her hate is intensified by the murdered love. In any case, Agamemnon's sacrifice of Iphigenia marks the end of love and the beginning of Klytämnestra's hate, even though she acknowledges that Artemis has saved the child to serve in her temple. Klytämnestra's only momentary regret is Kassandra's murder. Perhaps she might have let Kassandra live; but Kassandra represents the last of Agamemnon's captured lovers and is the seer who foretells Orest's vengeance; for both she must die.

Kassandra, the embodiment of Agamemnon's infidelity, becomes part of the list of justifications for Klytämnestra's actions. Klytämnestra (like Bogen's character) dreams of debilitating both Agamemnon's spear and his penis, his supposed heroism and his sexual betrayal. Even his grave, she asserts, resembles a phallus, but she foresees that the glorious grave will deteriorate and be used by vagrants; the generative symbol thus becomes a figure of death and decay. How can she feel regret or remorse when remembering her dead first husband and child, and Iphigenia taken from her? She argues that Agamemnon's cruelty has made her a murderer—a role with which she feels many wives would identify if they were honest.

Klytämnestra mourns not for Agamemnon but for her self, the loving self that existed before the Trojan War and wanted to nurture gardens and children. Earlier in the monologue, she declares: "I, Klytämnestra, sister of the beautiful Helen of Sparta! I, Klytämnestra, mother of three daughters and a son. I, Klytämnestra, beloved of Ägisth. I was not only the wife of Agamemnon!" (158). But these "definitions" only describe Klytämnestra's relationships to the outside world—sister, mother, lover, and wife—the roles traditionally assigned to women. Interestingly, queen is not among them; Brückner's Klytämnestra does not see power or dominion as her major role. She does not lust after prestige or immortality; indeed, she wants her name forgotten by history. Agamemnon has robbed Klytämnestra of the self she knew when he went off to Troy. She was forced to forge a new identity out of her abandonment and hate.

But this Klytämnestra's new identity is not one to be hallowed or admired; it is comprised of antipathy and vengeance. She will have no grave masks carved; she would rather be a vague legend or a shadow over Mykene. Hers is not a female role she wants perpetuated. Her hate has poisoned everything she has touched and will continue to do so after her death. Klytämnestra's last desire is to return to Gäa, Mother Earth, who will take pity on her. Only release into a larger and more nurturing female principle can release her from her hate.

Brückner's Klytämnestra then is the opposite of Bogen's gently human lover. Brückner depicts the potency and depth of hate. Her Klytämnestra has plenty of justification, including the murder of a first husband and child, which Bogen suppresses. But even Klytämnestra realizes she is defined by hate. Her self has been constricted into a venom that kills the poisoner as well as the victim. The reader can feel the fury of Klytämnestra's hate but also pity for her self-destructive obsession. This is not, finally, a liberating figure. She is more akin to those modern-day women who suffer from physical and psychological battering and finally destroy the batterer. The intensity of her hate is proportionate to the violence and destruction she feels has been visited upon her, her family, and her people.

Perhaps this single-minded ferocity leads Brückner to simplify other aspects of style. She uses very traditional male and female symbology—fire versus water, or sword versus seed, for example—whereas Reinig, in contrast, confuses gendered symbology whenever possible. Brückner indicts the male rather than questioning all gender definitions. She also presents women warped and destroyed by their social and gender role limitations. She would prefer a social and gender equality to domination by either group. Some of the essentializing tendencies of Brückner's narrative may be due in part to its straightforward presentation. Spewed forth as a single last address by an enraged woman—who has been trapped in a reductive patriarchal view of women's role and place—to the vanquished man who imposed that role on her, Brückner's text treats Klytemnestra as a woman with intense and immediate feelings and resentments.

However, neither the classical Klytemnestra nor her modern German counterpart precisely fits the stereotyped mold that some critics label "naive" feminism.[38] These figures call into question ideas of sisterhood, of female nurturance and benevolence, and fixed gender designations. Brückner's Klytämnestra is isolated and alienated by her hate. She is thus not able to establish an open female self, a self *en procès* that would allow her to change and adapt. She has been forced into an ossified role she cannot escape. Despite her strength and her "triumph" over male suppression, Brückner's Klytämnestra remains a difficult figure to reclaim for contemporary feminist tradition.

There is a great deal of debate as to whether Brückner can, in fact, be labeled a feminist at all. Brückner herself did not accept the designation. She declares, "I won't let myself be locked into any feminist camp" (*Mein schwarzes Sofa*, 56). Sigrid Bauschinger argues, "It would be the greatest misunderstanding to bring Christine Brückner into connection with the feminism of her time" (258). Brückner's early novels, children's books, radio, and dramatic work did, indeed, draw a considerable conservative audience. While I agree with Bauschinger that Brückner's ideal society shows some Christian-patriarchal characteristics, I believe that her depiction in the *Desdemona* collection of the limitations that society places on women is a loud and clear protest over the prescribed and repressive roles doled out to women throughout history. I would, therefore, agree with Robert von Dassanowsky-Harris when he argues that Brückner eventually emerges as "an important feminist voice" (331).

Comparisons and Contrasts

The Klytemnestra revisions from the pre- and early 1980s display a number of striking similarities. Graham, Reinig, Bogen, Maraini, and Brückner all demonstrate that marriage limits women's choices and actions. Its psychologically, socially, and economically repressive nature means that women do not control their bodies, their labor, or their children. This abusive state causes women to react in two ways: they can either exercise real violence to destroy their oppressive husbands (Graham, Bogen, Brückner), or, if they cannot successfully enact violent revenge, they end up in insane asylums (Maraini's Clitennestra) or prison (Reinig's Menni). These choices forced on women by social institutions (both marriage and the legal system) reveal that the public and private spheres are intertwined as they were for the original Klytemnestra when she slays her king and husband. Even the twentieth-century women who take physical revenge and slay their abusers (Bogen's Klytaimnestra or Brückner's Klytämnestra) do not revel in their triumph. They do not see themselves as role models to be emulated (although Reinig sees them as such); they know that they will face violent ends themselves.

Graham's *Clytemnestra* moves in the opposite direction by restoring Clytemnestra's regal grandeur and her conviction that she has acted justly. Graham's figure is close to Klytemnestra's best moments in the *Oresteia* with the revision that her powerful articulation comes in movement rather than in words. Graham creates a Clytemnestra who is not forever trapped in a cycle of violence but who breaks the cycle by reconciling with her son, Orestes. Genders and generations are brought together in a peaceful and hopeful final gesture in Graham's ballet. We must note, however, that this reconciliation comes in the underworld. Even Graham's Clytemnestra has paid with her life, but she, at least, has halted the violence and the endless male-female battle by changing the direction of the House of Atreus. She has struck back against husband, king, and abuser to create a more gender-integrated world. Graham's is the one vision of hope among the darker canvases painted by the other four women writers.

Two more striking similarities arise in these early texts. First, the issue of abortion (which was anticipated in examining the social battles of the 1980s) surfaces directly in Reinig's and Maraini's texts. Here, the women lament the lack of control over their own bodies and over their children. They feel themselves reduced to simple flesh, to the very receptacles Apollo describes women as being in the *Eumenides*. Women's bodies become the site in which control of the children and family is played out in the 1980s. In the other texts (particularly Bogen and Brückner), women also lose their children, but they lose them to the patriarchal social code that demands allegiance to the father. Marriage again proves destructive of any mother-child bond and of children in general. The children in these modern texts are not sacrificed directly by their fathers (with the exception of Maraini's Ifigenia), but they are thoroughly co-opted by patriarchy and turned against the mother. Again, the exception is Graham, whose Clytemnestra reunites with her son in a triumphant gesture of reconciliation.

Second, castration becomes a prevalent wish or symbolic background for many of these texts. Reinig's title presents it most obtrusively, but even the otherwise subdued text of Bogen presents a Klytaimnestra who fantasizes slicing off Agamemnon's penis and flinging it in his face. Brückner's Klytämnestra also dreams of debilitating Agamemnon's penis and his spear, thus linking the male's generative power to his political and military power. The penis as sign of male dominance becomes the symbolic—but, in these texts, never real—target of women's hate and revenge. Maraini moves the issue of castration to the psychological arena as her female analyst argues that Clitennestra suffers from penis envy—a particularly ironic accusation given that the patriarchal establishment is attempting to force Clitennestra into an abortion. If there is envy or fear involved, it is patriarchy's envy of Clitennestra's womb. Generative power as well as political and social dominance remain contested in these texts, but women generally are not in control of any of these.

The issue of violence—exercised against and by women—also forms a focal point for these women revisionists. Each writer works to undermine traditions that present male violence as heroic but female violence as an unpardonable sin that must be purged by eliminating the women who are willing to exert violence to protect their own interests—particularly Klytemnestra (but, as we will see in the next chapter, in Wolf's case, Penthesilea also). Each author also ends complexly, not willing to advocate violence as a useful strategy for women but not able to escape it in Western culture. These women writers work to provide the underlying psychological motivation for women driven to violence, but they do not provide an alternate female narrative that survives (although Graham implies that one might yet be possible). They cannot release the Eumenides from their subterranean habitat to reinstill the modern world with a newly invigorated female principle (although Maraini calls for just this move). They do, however, mount a clear critique of the cultural assumptions and practices that perpetuate violence and its use in the gender hierarchies that still exist in Western culture.

Graham confronts violence directly—both Agamemnon's violence and Clytemnestra's. Graham reveals the moral and psychological motivation for Clytemnestra's actions and allows Clytemnestra to think through the consequences of her deeds. Clytemnestra comes to understand and accept her own violent conduct as retribution necessary to realign patriarchal assumptions. But she also comprehends that there must be forgiveness and reconciliation to break the cycle of violence in male-female struggles. The murder of husband and king gives way for Graham to a reconciliation with the son; blood bonds are thus reestablished over legal bonds of marriage. Graham's Clytemnestra can be reborn as a positive maternal figure in her dance of reintegration with Orestes. Both his violence and hers can be turned to serve a more positive future in which gender equality might be possible. Always the most positive of the artists we have so far examined, Graham can turn even the vexed issue of violence to a positive use.

Reinig demonstrates throughout her novel various kinds of psychic and physical abuse heaped on women—ranging from repression of wives and mothers to brutal gang rape. Many of her women feel that they are simply objects at the mercy of the men who control them. One response to this condition comes in Reinig's use of Valerie Solanas and her 1967 *SCUM Manifesto* (Society for Cutting up Men). Reinig appropriates this historical text to demonstrate her intense concern for abused women as well as her understanding of and, to some degree, sympathy for violent remedies to that abuse. Reinig also responds sympathetically to the contemporary real-life case of the two lesbian lovers who each received life in prison for the murder of a husband. Reinig's immediate historical and cultural context thus fuels her retelling of Klytemnestra and her experiences in a modern guise. Reinig is clearly appalled at the need to stamp out exclusively female love that undermines patriarchy—precisely Klytemnestra's crime in avenging her daughter. Reinig's satiric presentation of a woman being sentenced to prison for nicking her husband with a vegetable slicer marks her attempt to deflate men's extreme fear of female violence (even in self-defense). Neither male nor female violence retains any heroic stature in Reinig's Germany of the late 1970s. Reinig's novel presents a complicated narrative riddled with interpolated stories and texts, which gives her a broad canvas on which to explore male-female relationships in which violence is a recurrent theme for both sexes. Whereas Brückner concentrates the archetypal characteristics of Klytemnestra into a single speech, Reinig teases the many strands of Klytemnestra's story apart and embeds them in several intertwined narratives. Reinig, therefore, can more effectively resist the essentialist models she is intent on questioning. Indeed, she confuses gender categories whenever possible by having characters in her surface narrative take on opposite-sex roles from earlier texts. Reinig's complex gender intertextuality forces a reconsideration of the male-female conflict and violence inherent in the original Klytemnestra story.

Finally, Reinig leaves us with her complex and gender-confusing restaging of the ending of the *Oresteia*. Her ultimate point is not for matriarchy or patriarchy to triumph but to lead her readers to reexamine and interrogate both systems and our cultural attitudes toward them and the violence against women that helps to perpetuate cultural roles.

Bogen underplays Klytaimnestra's moment of violence in slaying her husband, but she depicts violence as permeating every level of the daily existence of those who inhabit Agamemnon's kingdom. Violence for Bogen is insidiously present everywhere power is abused by men. Klytaimnestra's mariticide is intended to change that long history of both personal and public abuse by the dominant males. Bogen has her character come to realize, however, that this strategy will not work. Klytaimnestra knows that she and her lover will be remembered as villains and that their own end will still remain part of a violent cycle. Bogen thus seems most intent on criticizing the inescapable nature of violence for both the men and the women of her text.

Maraini depicts both physical and psychological violence in her play. She sees violence as related to economic exploitation as well as male dominance. Battered physically and psychologically and exploited sexually, her Clitennestra can only dream of enacting the real vengeance that Graham's and Bogen's characters execute. This Clitennestra is most victim and least villain among the texts examined here. She is related to Reinig's women in their inability to gain control on either the personal or public level. Like Aeschylus's Klytemnestra, Clitennestra is defeated by a patriarchally co-opted woman. Her desire to act "like a man" transgresses the boundaries of appropriate female behavior; she must, therefore, be relegated to the social cave of the insane asylum so that the patriarchal order can continue. Clitennestra can only invoke the resurrection of the Erinyes in hopes that women can regain some social equality—even if it means exerting violence on their own behalf.

Maraini laments women's loss of the capacity for action—even violent action—in the 1980s.

Brückner presents a Klytämnestra who has seen through the war's facade of heroic rhetoric and divine decrees to understand it rather as the desire for glory and power of an ambitious and insensitive man, Agamemnon. Male violence is unmasked, and Brückner implies that only a reciprocal female violence on Klytämnestra's part can end it. This Klytämnestra is a woman abused and robbed of her own identity; she is forced into a violence she does not want to see perpetuated. In the volume *Wenn du geredet hättest, Desdemona,* Brückner surrounds Klytämnestra with other women who are psychologically abused, ignored, or condemned. Most interesting in terms of violence, however, is Gudrun Ensslin, a member of the terrorist Baader-Meinhoff Gang, which in the 1970s robbed banks, raided military installations, and, in 1977, kidnapped and murdered prominent industrialist Hans-Martin Schleyer.

Within her monologue, Ensslin examines and rejects her roles as wife, mother, and daughter in the capitalist and patriarchal tradition. A well-educated intellectual, she quotes Rilke, Kafka, and Beckett—much to her own dismay since she knows that her mind has been so saturated with what she is supposed to know that she finds it difficult to think for herself. In response, she spews obscenities to try to eradicate the platitudes ingrained in her by her father. Like Reinig, Brückner here appropriates a recent, historical incident to underline the problematic construction of gender roles—for men and women. Ensslin sees no way out but destruction. Hurling bombs at all of capitalist culture seems the only act of liberation. She sees herself not as a criminal but as a political martyr. The difficulty is that this politics can only destroy; it does not fight *for* any specific goals. And while Ensslin argues that her actions represent a kind of female liberation ("We rebel like the men and throw bombs like the men" [117]), this gender equality hardly inspires the reader with new found hope for women.[39] Ensslin seems accurate in describing the nonsignificance of gender in terrorism, "'From what do we get the high proportion of women among terrorists?' As if that played any role now. Men—Women. We are all genderless, hunted creatures" (117). But despite the claim to gender equality, women have more at stake than men. They participate in higher numbers because, as Ensslin's monologue reveals, they feel themselves more abused than men and with nothing to lose by exercising violence. But Ensslin's defiant monologue ends in the realization that, for all her violence, she will die unremembered by history. Her monologue is entitled "Kein Denkmal für Gudrun Ensslin" (No Monument for Gudrun Ensslin). As she crosses the fine line between reason and insanity and retreats to a childhood memory, we realize that Ensslin was right; history has not given her a prominent place. Terrorist violence does not finally liberate women. Brückner's Klytämnestra also realizes that the violence she exerts rebounds against what was best in herself. Although there is an understanding of and sympathy for women who exercise violence, Brückner does not advocate it as a solution. It cannot be molded into an acceptable feminist strategy. The issue of violence will remain prominent as we move into the later 1980s.

In addition to these many similarities, the pieces we have examined so far also have significant contrasts, most notably those of genre, strategy, and setting. To begin with the latter, Graham, Bogen, and Brückner choose to retain the ancient setting for their Klytemnestra revisions. This allows each revision to reconsider the issues at stake in the original Greek tragedies and to add psychological depth to the classical Klytemnestra's motivations. Both the cultural impact and the personal responsibility of Klytemnestra's actions can thus be reexamined with the benefit of hindsight. As twentieth-century artists, these women can suggest the negative impact of Klytemnestra's story on later generations of women, who remain trapped in the same cycles of violence as their classical counterpart. The revisionists can also help the reader/viewer to understand what social and psychological pressures drive women to maternal vengeance or self-defensive violence.

The strategy in Graham, Bogen, and Brückner is to give Klytemnestra her own "voice" with which to discuss her deeds and her reasons for committing them. Although the genres are widely divergent (including dance, multivoiced narrative, and monologue), the strategy of presentation is similar. Tellingly, this statement of having her own "voice" also applies to Graham's nonverbal dance piece. Her Clytemnestra may express herself visually and directly through the body, but she has a powerful "voice" to reassert the justice of her deed and to find reconciliation with her son. We could call all of these "first-person" presentations (whether in dance, direct quotations, or stream of consciousness). Each of these Klytemnestras can still exercise violence successfully by wreaking vengeance upon Agamemnon. The modern texts do not dispute her slaying of her husband and king, but they do reveal the mitigating circumstances. Klytemnestra presents herself directly and explains herself, thus giving the audience personal insight into the cultural icon. These twentieth-century Klytemnestras gain sympathy and understanding from the audience/readers by doing this, but they also gain a critical self-awareness. This allows Klytemnestra to rejoice in her just deed (Graham) or lament that the patriarchal world left her no choice but violence (Bogen and Brückner).

Reinig and Maraini, on the other hand, present Klytemnestra in a modern context. Their updated settings allow them to suggest that Klytemnestra's story is continually—in fact, ineluctably—replayed throughout the cultural history of the West. The classical characters may be spread across several modern ones (as in Reinig), or the modern characters may closely correspond to their classical namesakes (as in Maraini). Either way, the forces at work remain the same. A male-dominated society persists; women are controlled economically, physically, and psychologically by the men in their lives—husbands, lovers, or sons. The strategy here is to present this recurrent story from the outside. The Klytemnestras may get their individual speeches, but they do not themselves comprehend all the forces at work to repress them. Reinig and Maraini are more intent on critiquing their societies and cultures than on justifying or explaining Klytemnestra's actions. We might call these "third-person" presentations, or perhaps social context presentations. Reinig and Maraini both include economics, politics, morality, psychoanalysis, and gender expectations in their analysis of Klytemnestra's story. Reinig embeds this exploration in a multistrand narrative with many interpolated conversations and stories; Maraini chooses drama for her presentation. Both women use pieces of the classical texts to foreground the constant interaction of late-twentieth-century Western culture with its own beginnings and to highlight the extent to which those ancient beginnings still control gender definitions. Reinig undermines and challenges those gender roles; Maraini laments that women have surrendered an even more ancient female power to patriarchy and calls for its resurrection.

Notes

1. We might also remember the Wife of Bath's comment that "By God, if wommen hadde writen stories . . . They wolde han writen of men more wikkednesse / Than all the mark of Adam may redresse" (III [D] 693–96), which stresses how crucial it is to have a voice in literature.

2. DiBattista's "The Triumph of Clytemnestra" is a fascinating essay on this charade and its meaning. Jadwin, too, investigates this use of Clytemnestra and incorporates Bakhtin's notion of "double discourse" in her discussion. Male revisions of Klytemnestra thus occupy women literary critics as well as women writers in the 1980s and 1990s.

3. Yourcenar's is a particularly intriguing text that was revived along with the general interest in Klytemnestra in the 1980s. Yourcenar's Clytemnestre really kills out of love and neglect. She cannot stand to have Agamemnon, who has returned with a "Turkish" beauty, act as though she is not worthy of a thought. He doesn't even care that she has been unfaithful with Aegisthus. Clytemnestre kills Agamemnon to make him acknowledge her value as a human being and as a woman. She is haunted by his ghost and envisions loving him again in hell, where he will again abandon her in favor of conquests in war. Women may dream of getting their husbands' undivided attention through violence, but they certainly would not wish for Clytemnestre's literally undying love for the man who deserts her in Yourcenar's text.

4. Klytemnestra's sister, Helen, who is successfully reincorporated into the patriarchal order, is also frequently featured—particularly in dramas. Male dramatists tend to place her in a comedy of errors, while women tend to focus on Helen's confused identities (Helen of Troy v. Helen in Egypt). For an analysis of Helen revisions from the classical texts to the Renaissance, see Suzuki.

5. Klytemnestra is also present in the 1980s in countries outside my area of cultural and linguistic expertise. Tadashi Suzuki, a theater director and playwright, wrote *Clytemnestra,* which he produced in August 1983 in Toga, Japan; the Japanese production also played in Los Angeles on April 7, 1987, helping to fuel American interest in Klytemnestra in the 1980s. McDonald provides photos from both productions in her analysis of Suzuki's work. She also comments more generally on his use of Greek materials. In Chile, Alabau published a series of poems entitled *Electra, Clitemnestra* (1986); and in Spain, Maria-Josep Ragué i Arias produced a Catalan *Clitemnestra* (1987).

6. For details of the case of Bruna Odinotte, who was fifteen when she married Mario D'Onofrio, ten years her senior, see Bassi. The same courts allowed a husband to return to the family home after repeated requests for protection by his wife; he subsequently killed her (Bassi, 199–200).

7. The reason given for the acquittal was that so many men attacked and immobilized the female victim that "the violence done to the passive party was minimal, given her limited capacity to defend herself" (Bassi, 212).

8. In 1996 the California Supreme Court ruled that experts should be allowed to testify to a battered woman's state of mind and her fear for her life when she committed murder.

9. For a woman's view on this issue, see Mills's editorial.

10. For information on abortion laws in European countries, see International Planned Parenthood Federation (European Region); Tietze; and Childbirth by Choice Trust.

11. See Childbirth by Choice Trust, 46 n. 64, which cites "Defending the Law in Italy," *Women's Global Network for Reproductive Rights Newsletter* 31 (October–December 1989): 28.

12. See Childbirth by Choice Trust, 46 n. 48, which cites "The Globalization of the Abortion Debate" *Time,* August 21, 1989, 52–53.

13. For further discussion of Moers and feminist scholarship in the 1970s, see Nord, "The 'Epic Age'"; O'Brien; and DiBattista, "Memorializing Motherhood."

14. Terry suggests that this role "was a triumph for [Graham], her last true triumph as a dancer, and it took every ounce of strength and willpower and, perhaps, desperation that she had within her" (127). Clearly, this ancient figure held a very special significance for the aging Graham.

15. Freiert provides a number of photos of the October 1987 American revival of *Clytemnestra.*

16. The Martha Graham Dance Company was also featured on the *Great Performances* series on public television (WNET, channel 13), recorded in February 1976. *Clytemnestra* is not one of the pieces presented, but the television documentary kept Graham's work vital during the 1970s and 1980s.

17. Among Reinig's other main works are *Die Ballade vom blutigen Bomme* (1972; The Ballad of Bloody Bomme), *Die himmlische und die irdische Geometrie* (1975; Heavenly and

Earthly Geometry), *Der Wolf und die Witwen* (1980; The Wolf and the Widows), *Mädchen ohne Uniform* (1981; Girl without Uniform), *Die Frau im Brunnen* (1984; Woman in the Well), and *Sämtliche Gedichte* (1984; Collected Poems).

18. She was featured in Jurgensen's *Deutsche Frauenautoren der Gegenwart* (German Women Authors of the Present Day) along with Ingeborg Bachmann, Christa Wolf, and other major writers. For an early review of *Entmannung,* see Ester. For an analysis of Reinig's radical views, see Bammer.

19. Elstun discusses the Greek connections of the names in Reinig's novel. Rather than focusing on etymologies, Elstun seeks mythological figures of the same name. Doris, for example, is a sea goddess, daughter of Oceanus and Tethys and sister of the rivers and fountains. Xeni is a naiad, a minor female deity of fountains, lakes, brooks, and springs. While I find this enlightening, I believe the etymologies provide more relevant interpretative possibilities.

20. See Brügmann (173–74) for more discussion of the case of Ihns and Anderson in 1974.

21. As Solanas puts it: "The conflict, therefore, is not between females and males, but between SCUM—dominant, secure, self-confident, nasty, violent, selfish, independent, proud, thrill-seeking, free-wheeling, arrogant females, who consider themselves fit to rule the universe, who have freewheeled to the limits of this 'society,' and are ready to wheel on to something far beyond what it has to offer—and nice, passive, dependent, scared, mindless, insecure, approval-seeking Daddy's Girls, who can't cope with the unknown; who want to continue to wallow in the sewer that is, at least, familiar, who want to hang back with the apes; who feel secure only with Big Daddy standing by, with a big, strong man to lean on" (39).

22. There are two possible Greek roots for Doris. The first is *dōron,* which means "gift." The second is *doru,* which means "stem of a tree" or "spear."

23. There is disagreement as to whether women attended classical theater. Auffret discusses this in *Nous, Clytemnestre* (see my discussion in chapter 3). She points out that nineteenth-century scholars favored the restrictive theory that women were excluded, and later twentieth-century scholars argue that women could attend.

24. "In a certain sense Otto's ideological 'Entmannung' [castration or unmanning] is my own path, and Kyra (originally Otto had a different name), Kyra is Christa. I test on myself how much 'masculine illusion' I can do away with in myself." Reinig, *Mein Herz ist eine gelbe Blume,* 20.

25. Bogen's earlier research focused on William Blake; she produced a facsimile edition and new interpretation of his *Book of Thel* in 1971. She also authored *Bobe Mayse: A Tale of Washington Square* (1993) and *How to Write Poetry,* which went into its third edition in 1998.

26. While readers might object that Bogen's use of the fluid for the female and the phallic (knives, spears, fire) for the male may be a bit simplistic, Bogen does build a consistent iconography from them.

27. For more on Bobbitt's trial for cutting off her husband's penis, see <http://www.eon.law.harvard.edu/vaw/bobbitt.html>. The site discusses articles from the *Chicago Tribune* (Jan. 19, 1994) and the *Washington Post* (Jan. 11, 1994) in considering the case.

28. Maraini, *I sogni di Clitennestra e altre commedie* (Milan: Tascabili Bompiani, 1981). All page numbers refer to this edition. Translations in the text are by my able research

assistant, Dr. Amy Morris. An English translation of the play, *Dreams of Clytemnestra*, was published in 1994. It is one of four plays by Maraini in *Only Prostitutes Marry in May.* The play was first performed in English translation by the City Troupe in New York in 1989 using Vode's translation and directed by Greg Johnson. I have retained Morris's translations because Vode's has some important deletions and because Morris's were the translations I used in my article "The Hand That Rocks the Cradle Wields the Axe." I note where these diverge greatly from Vode's published translation. I would like to thank my colleague Lucia Re for making me aware of Maraini's work and that of other Italian women writers.

29. Among Maraini's other works are *L'eta del malessere* (1963; *Age of Discontent,* 1963); *Memoria di una ladra* (1972; *Memories of a Lady Thief,* 1973); *Donna in guerra* (1975; *Women at War,* 1984); *Lettere a Marina* (1981; *Letters to Marina,* 1987); *La lunga vita di Marianna Ucria* (1990; *The Long Life of Marianna Ucria*).

30. The title, in fact, is a kind of stitching, as explained on page 249 of the text. It can also signify, however, "the past appropriated."

31. The New York production in 1989, which used Vode's published translation, strangely changes the psychoanalyst into a male, thus losing the association of her as the daughter of Zeus as well as Freud. It is crucial that this figure, who replaces Athena in the original story, be female in Maraini's complex indictment of modern social forces that oppress women. Maraini's choice of a woman makes it clear (as does Elettra's attitude) that the patriarchy is not entirely populated by men.

32. For a discussion of other mother-daughter relationships in Maraini's work, see Dagnino.

33. For a discussion of madness and female characters, see Gilbert and Gubar as well as Chesler; Showalter, *The Female Malady;* and Yalom. Showalter's and Yalom's volumes are both from the 1980s, and Gilbert and Gubar's was published in 1979. The 1980s interest in Klytemnestra thus seems coupled with an interest in the psychological abuse women suffer in being driven to madness or simply declared mad.

Maraini also discusses her own experiences of being locked away in a Japanese concentration camp during World War II; see her interview with Ceccatty and Nakamura.

34. This passage represents a slight confusion of Jungian terms, since a man should have anima (as his feminine component of consciousness) and a woman animus (as her male component of consciousness). But anima and the feminine are often confused in common usage—and sometimes even by Jung himself, as Wehr points out (38–40).

35. Some of her major works include *Ehe die Spuren verwehen* (1954; Before All Trace Fades Away), *Der Kokon* (1966; The Cocoon), *Jauche und Levkojen* (1975; *Gillyflower Kid,* 1982), which was made into a successful series for television in West Germany in 1978, and the radio play *Die Burgerinnen von Calais* (1997; The Female Burgers of Calais).

36. The saying gained fame in the Croesus-Cyrus anecdote in which Croesus was said to have called out Solon's name as he remembered his counsel, thus saving Croesus's own life. In Brückner's monologue, in contrast, the question comes, ironically, only after Agamemnon *is* already dead. Some scholars point out that Croesus's and Solon's dates do not coincide and that, therefore, the classical tale is impossible. In any case, the saying was a popular proverb and appears in a number of places, including the final lines of Sophocles' *Oedipus Tyrannos.*

37. Several of the monologues are directed against war. In addition to Klytämnestra's, Brückner's Hetäre Megara suggests that female sexuality could be used to keep men's minds off war. For further discussion of the *Desdemona* collection, see Dassanowsky-Harris; Biener; and Jens.

38. Early notions that women would necessarily be more nurturing or that if a woman were president we would have no wars or that all women are linked by an overriding feeling of sisterhood and would therefore support one another over other politicial needs would all fall into what later, more politically experienced feminists (or antifeminists) would call "naive" feminism. See, for example, Moi's critiques of early American and French feminism. As issues of race and class began to work through the women's movement, naive or essentialist concepts were questioned and rethought. See Minh-ha, *Woman, Native, Other;* Smith, "The Truth"; and Kaplan.

39. Passerini points to a similarly distressing gender equality among terrorists in Italy in the 1970s: "Other less positive aspects [of the feminist movement in Italy] should not be ignored, as they are no less a part of this process of women's full involvement in the public sphere, such as the numerous terrorists in the 1970s who were women (Guidetti Serra 1988); here, tragically, equality was achieved" (180).

3. Klytemnestra in the Mid- to Late 1980s

Klytemnestra as the Strong Woman Wronged but Unrecuperated: Christa Wolf's *Kassandra*

Unlike the majority of the 1980s texts, Christa Wolf's 1983 novel and essays do not focus directly on Klytemnestra. They do, however, offer a fascinating portrait of her through the eyes of the woman she eventually slays, Kassandra. This unusual look at Klytemnestra from the point of view of her victim gives us a unique insight into some of the more problematic aspects of her character for late-twentieth-century women revisionists.

One of Germany's most widely published authors, Wolf was born in Landsberg (now Poland) in 1929 and grew up during World War II.[1] Wolf strongly supported East German socialism, although she was critical of the abuses of the Communist regime. Many of her books examine women's roles and their struggle to establish a viable female self.[2] She is outspokenly antiwar and antinuclear.[3] After the fall of the Berlin Wall, Wolf was accused of cooperating too closely with the East German secret police, but she was herself an object of their surveillance for many years.[4] In 1996 Wolf published *Medea*, another revision of an ancient female figure who shares much with Klytemnestra.

In her essays focusing on the Trojan War, *Voraussetzungen einer Erzählung: Kassandra* (Conditions of a Narrative)[5] and her novel *Kassandra*,[6] Wolf examines the issue of heroism from a uniquely critical point of view—that of the female victim of "heroic" action, the priestess of the losing side, Kassandra.[7] Given Wolf's intense resistance to the violence of war, the perverse rhetoric and hypocrisy needed to fuel it, and the cultural destruction it wreaks, how does Wolf reconceive Klytemnestra's bloody reputation? If we see through Kassandra's eyes, how do we envision the woman who will murder her and (in Wolf's version) her children? How does Klytemnestra's victim respond to being slain by another woman?

When Wolf stepped to the podium to participate in a prestigious series of lectures on poetics at Frankfurt University in 1982, she did not speak directly about poetics, but rather she took her audience on a journey, the journey that led Wolf to the narrative *Kassandra*. Taking a highly personal approach to the masses of classical material, an approach that is not "tidy" ("nicht ganz ordentlich") or easily reduced to a neat linear plot, Wolf nonetheless formulates a problem for poetics, which is: "There is and there can be no poetics which prevents the living experience of countless perceiving subjects from being killed and buried in art objects. So, does this mean that art objects ('works') are products of the alienation of [the German actually says 'within'] our culture, whose other finished products are produced for self-annihilation?" (*Cassandra*, 142). Although Wolf investigates the dehumanization of modern and classical humanity in toto, she focuses on those subjects who have been most excluded from history and buried in art objects—women.[8] In addition to the general alienation of Western culture, women experience a secondary alienation *within* the culture. They find themselves silenced or missing from the historical record. This deletion or suppression necessitates a female revision of literary history. As Wolf explains: "To what extent is there really such a thing as 'women's writing'? To the extent that women, for historical and biological reasons, experience a different reality than men and express it. To the extent that women belong not to the rulers but to the ruled, and have done so for centuries. . . . To the extent that they stop wearing themselves out trying to integrate themselves into the prevailing delusional system. To the extent that, writing and living, they aim at autonomy" (*Cassandra*, 259).[9]

Wolf's essays and narrative re-place at least one woman, Kassandra, within the cultural record by giving her the voice she was deprived of in the literary and historical patriarchal tradition of the Trojan War.[10] Kassandra gains a literary voice (in Aeschylus's *The Oresteia* and Euripides' *The Trojan Women*) only after the war ends. The bulk of Wolf's text, however, focuses on Kassandra's actions during those war years in which she is largely missing from the literary record.[11] One of Wolf's major revisions of the Kassandra figure is to restore her as a speaking—and protesting—subject in the history of war, in which she has too often been only an object. This revision provides a unique perspective on Klytemnestra as well.

Like Euripides, Wolf narrates from the point of view of the vanquished and suffering survivors of war. And like Dares and Dictys, she depicts Achilles as an archetypal hero who is anything but the complex, musically and medically gifted, appealing Achilles of Homer.[12] Wolf's novel begins with Kassandra waiting before Agamemnon's gates in Mycenae. Her interior monologue as she awaits her imminent death takes her back to her childhood in Troy, to the peaceful times when she would sit at her father Priam's feet as he and her mother, Hekuba, discussed politics. Those scenes give Kassandra a glimpse of society at a moment of balance between the matriarchal and patriarchal traditions. Wolf is attracted to the Kassandra story partly by this fleeting moment of political and gender balance in Trojan history.

But Kassandra also remembers the destruction of that delicate balance between matriarchy and patriarchy. This shift will eventually lead into the larger displacement of Mother Right seen in Klytemnestra's story. It begins with Hekuba's alienation and ends with the war. Hekuba's close ties to Priam and to political power weaken when Priam feels compelled to destroy Paris because he fears the loss of his throne and his patriarchal powers to his son. This cruelty hardens Hekuba and alienates her from her husband and the male power structure. Matriarchal and patriarchal concerns are thus pitted against one another in Troy through Paris. The struggle between the two social systems will finally be decided at the farthest reaches of the repercussions of the Trojan War, when Orestes is acquitted of Klytemnestra's murder as Aeschylus's *Oresteia* closes. Father Right, the right of law and reason, will eventually win out over Mother Right, the right of blood and emotion. Hekuba's alienation thus symbolizes the alienation of the entire matriarchal social structure and its displacement by patriarchy. In this sense, Hekuba is closely aligned with that other alienated mother, Klytemnestra.

Wolf reveals more about her view of Klytemnestra in her Frankfurt lectures on poetics, in which she recounts her 1980 trip to Greece during which she explored materials for *Kassandra*. In the first person, Wolf recalls the trip and her simultaneous reading of Aeschylus's *Oresteia*, which helped trigger her writing of *Kassandra*. By speaking directly, she adds her own experiences as Wolf (rather than as the narrator of a fiction)—as well as those of the Greeks, Americans, and Germans she meets in her travels—to the body of communal memories that make up her text as a whole and help to shape her vision of Klytemnestra. Wolf refuses to be bound by any genre definition (either of "novel" or "formal lecture" or "travel literature"); this refusal to be contained in a categorization contributes to Wolf's revision of the tradition she must confront.

In reconsidering Aeschylus's *Oresteia*, Wolf focuses on Kassandra, but her revision also affects Klytemnestra. In Kassandra's narrating of her visions of the House of Atreus and its horrors in Aeschylus's *Agamemnon*, she rises to the intensity of madness. Her words produce isolated images of horror, of children slain and served to their unwitting fathers, of bonds broken and oaths violated. The old men of Argos begin to fear the truth of her visions. Unlike the Trojans, the men of Argos recognize Kassandra as a true seer. They cannot, however, bring themselves to envision that a woman, Klytemnestra, could kill the king. In a powerful vision of sexual and political role reversal, Kassandra reveals Agamemnon reduced to a slaughtered animal:

> Ai, drag the great bull from the mate!—
> a thrash of robes, she traps him—
> writhing—
> black horn glints, twists—
> *she gores him through!*
> And now he buckles, look, the bath swirls red—
> (*Oresteia*, 154, *Agamemnon*, ll. 1127–32,
> emphasis in the original)

The woman, Klytemnestra, seizes power; hers is the act of penetration now perverted from an act of procreation to one of death.

After foretelling Agamemnon's death, Aeschylus's Kassandra throws off the regalia that marks her as Apollo's seer. She rejects, finally, Apollo's voice for her own and declares herself "free at last." Wolf reacts directly to this moment of freedom in her sympathy with Kassandra. Only at this point, after throwing off the god and gaining her *own* voice, can Wolf's Kassandra begin to narrate her story. Aeschylus's Kassandra, too, seems to take on a new clarity of vision about the future once she has escaped Apollo. Unfortunately, what Kassandra so clearly sees is the coming of Orestes and the eventual triumph of patriarchy as he is acquitted of Klytemnestra's murder.[13]

Wolf sees Orestes' acquittal as rationalization in the service of patriarchy— and woman, here Klytemnestra, must be made hateful to pull it off:

> The ancient law of blood revenge, in which Orestes becomes entangled: Never could the son lay violent hands on his mother. Woman was taboo. Aeschylus seems to anticipate that his male public, who have since come to exercise absolute dominance, will still feel disquieted by echoes of the sacred awe of woman. A chorus of women are given the task of branding woman as the greatest evil under the sun. . . . The process of redrawing once-inviolable woman as a monster already has a long history. The woman must be eliminated! . . . all the same . . . Orestes is no murderer. This verdict is meant to be hammered into the public; but the Greek playwright foundered in that task. . . . Despite thousands of years of patriarchal efforts, human consciousness still feels matricide to be a grislier crime than any other. The principle that the son is the son of his father alone could not be sustained. (*Cassandra*, 222)

Even after Orestes kills Klytemnestra, motherhood must be further attacked and eradicated as it is in Aeschylus's *Oresteia*. But this point seems the most equivocal of all the patriarchal claims in Klytemnestra's saga. Wolf feels that even the classical audience (and Aeschylus himself) must have doubted it.

A similar skepticism is voiced by contemporary American writer Carol Lynn Pearson in *Mother Wove the Morning* (1992).[14] In this one-woman play, Pearson depicts an ancient Greek woman, Io, watching Aeschylus's *Eumenides* and reflecting on Klytemnestra's fate and Athena's collusion with the male. Io views as ludicrous Apollo's argument that "The mother is no parent of that which is called her child. She is only nurse to the new planted seed that grows, whose true parent is the male" (47). She is dumbfounded that the audience is prepared to accept this remarkable assertion: "They had just been told that the sun above them, . . . was really the moon. And they sat there unblinking!" (47). But she knows that the propaganda needed to displace maternal rights in favor of patriarchy has been relentless and that despite that everyone knows "who has been born of whom," they are silenced by the lesson of "what happens to a woman who dares to rebel as Klytemnestra rebelled" (49). Io leaves the theater knowing that women "perform" their part of supporting the male position, but they know the truth and wink to one another from behind the masks they wear for men.

Wolf associates the triumph of Orestes and patriarchy over the claims of Klytemnestra with the general suppression of women. Orestes declares in the *Eumenides* that he has suffered into truth (l. 274); Wolf takes this policy as typically male as she echoes Horkheimer and Adorno's *Dialektik der Aufklä-rung* (1947) (*Dialectics of the Enlightenment*):

> "To learn through suffering"—this seems to be the law of the new gods, and likewise the way of masculine thought. This way does not seek to love Mother Nature but to fathom her secrets in order to dominate her, and to erect the astounding structure of a world of mind remote from nature, from which women are henceforth excluded. Indeed, women are actually to be feared, perhaps because, unbeknown to the thinking, suffering, sleeping man, they are co-originators of that anxiety of conscience which pounds his heart awake. Wisdom against one's will. The gain of culture by the loss of nature. Progress through pain. The formulae which underlie Western culture, spelled out four hundred years before our era. (*Cassandra*, 216)

Wolf obviously believes that this strategy of suffering into knowledge—at the expense of women—is a mistake on Aeschylus's part, a mistake that structures all of Western culture and that leads us to the edge of our own annihilation in the nuclear age.

Wolf suggests that Aeschylus makes two other "mistakes" as well, both of which affect her reading of Klytemnestra. The first is to think that Kassandra would mourn for Agamemnon: "Never would she have said this: 'Indoors as well as outdoors I can / Mourn Agamemnon's fate.' Agamemnon—the last in the series of men who have done her violence (the first was Apollo, the god)—mourn for him? Not if I knew her as well as I thought" (*Cassandra*, 150). Wolf's Kassandra knows Agamemnon for the weak and abusive man that he is. This knowledge increases Kassandra's (and the reader's) sympathy for Klytaimnestra and her mariticide. Wolf makes clear, for example, that Agamemnon sacrifices Iphigenia not because he believes the gods demand it, but to pacify the other Greek princes who are jealous of his position as commander (*Cassandra*, 53). His pitiful actions provide another indictment of the hero and the husband, since Agamemnon is both a king and the military leader of the Trojan expedition—as well as an obviously callous father. Kassandra's shock at and disdain for Agamemnon give the reader additional insights into Klytaimnestra who, like Kassandra, has been abused by him.

The second mistake Wolf thinks Aeschylus makes is having Kassandra and Klytemnestra detest one another;[15] she takes this as a mark of his prejudice against Mother Right (*Cassandra*, 179). Kassandra and Klytemnestra would, perhaps, have been too terrifying as allies. Even though she will fall to Klytaimnestra's axe, Wolf's Kassandra sympathizes with Klytaimnestra, who she realizes must kill her husband or return to a repressed condition when he comes back. Kassandra knows that Klytaimnestra could not share the throne with the despicable Agamemnon. Kassandra can see in Klytaimnestra a seething hatred for a man who probably treated her vilely when he controlled her and a determination not to be controlled again. Kassandra discerns that Klytaimnestra bears her no personal hatred, but that as queen she must adjust to the political realities, which require eliminating Agamemnon and his paramour. Kassandra understands that she and Klytaimnestra could have been compatriots or sisters if their worlds were different; she also knows that Klytaimnestra has no choice in the logic of power but to kill her. Identical repressed smiles reveal to Kassandra and Klytaimnestra that they are both chagrined that fate has not placed them on the same political side. They recognize much in one another; they share thoughts and knowing looks; they even notice that they wear identical necklaces—each purchased by Agamemnon and bestowed on both "his" women out of guilt over the daughter he has slain. This mutual understanding between Kassandra and Klytaimnestra strengthens their bond but makes more painful the final murder. Kassandra perceives a highly intelligent Klytaimnestra who is insightful enough to know that power will eventually blind her so that she will be incapable of seeing the signs that foretell the fall of her house.

Having predicted Orestes' coming, Aeschylus's Kassandra accepts her fate and goes to her death. Wolf's Kassandra, too, accepts death when she has finished the tale that echoes with the realities of our century as well as hers. Only in telling her own tale does Kassandra regain her voice. Wolf's narrative restores to Kassandra what war and "duty" have robbed her of. That she tells her tale at all is an act of revolt against the heroic tradition. Kassandra fantasizes about begging Klytaimnestra to give her a slave girl who might remember her tale and pass on her voice through generations of women, thus instituting a new female narrative for culture: "'Clytemnestra, . . . I implore you: Send me . . . a young slave woman with a keen memory and a powerful voice. Ordain that she may repeat to her daughter what she hears from me. That the daughter in turn may pass it on to her daughter, and so on. So that alongside the river of heroic songs this tiny rivulet, too, may reach those far-away . . . people who will live in times to come'" (*Cassandra,* 81). The hope of creating an alternative to the heroic tradition, a society built not on war but on community and love and passed down through a matriarchal oral tradition, fires Kassandra's imagination. She envisions a new voice in history, a female counterpoint to the heroic code. She has, however, seen too much reality to become a utopian thinker. Her imagined plea is followed immediately by the lines: "And could I believe that, even for one day? Slay me, Clytemnestra. Kill me. Hurry." Ironically, it is Klytaimnestra who could help build a new female tradition, but it is also Klytaimnestra who will extinguish it as she murders Kassandra. This equivocal position will make it difficult to rehabilitate Klytaimnestra as a "feminist" heroine.

It is precisely as a "feminist," however, that Klytaimnestra is first introduced in Wolf's first "travel report" on her Greek journey. In a discussion with a male friend who is translating the classical *Oresteia* into modern Greek, Wolf asserts that Kassandra was the first professional working woman in literature, whose only occupation could have been seeress. The friend, Valtinos, asserts that in that case, "Clytemnestra was the first feminist" (*Cassandra,* 176). Valtinos argues that Klytaimnestra ruled alone for ten years; she endured the sacrifice of her child; she took a man who pleased her. How could she possibly go crawling back to her domestic duties after such a life? This is a telling—male—view of what constitutes a feminist—a view on which Wolf makes no further comment. Being "feminist" in Valtinos's mind entails having power and control, sexual freedom, and being forced to witness the destruction of one's children—or having one's maternal and nurturing impulses cauterized.

This modern male view of a "feminist" reveals some of the same traits that caused Klytemnestra to be denounced in the ancient tradition and allows Wolf to demonstrate through Valtinos that some gender assumptions have not changed. Taking political power, demanding the right to choose a mate, and ignoring the patriarchal rules also earned the classical Klytemnestra condemnation. But Valtinos also shows himself sensitive to Klytaimnestra's intelligence. He points out that in the ancient Greek of the *Oresteia*, when Klytemnestra spreads the purple carpet on Agamemnon's return and invokes *Dikē*, the translators have missed the ambivalence of the gesture: "*Dikē*, the goddess of justice, is being invoked as protectress of a murder. The death the woman plans for the man is just in her eyes. Thus, the 'purple way' could also be translated as the 'path of justice'" (*Cassandra*, 177). This reading makes the apparently hypocritical Klytemnestra seem much more cleverly open to those perceptive enough to read her meaning.[16] She sees her vengeance as serving justice and upholding Mother Right. Her prowess in defense of female rights marks Klytemnestra as a feminist of a deeper kind.

Wolf also ponders the issues of hypocrisy and ambiguity in the act of revision itself. For example, in repossessing her own voice, Wolf's Kassandra is also forced to speak the word that she hates most—*Achilles*. Her fondest wish is to eradicate the name of Achilles from all human records, but she cannot even utter the wish without recalling his name to the text. In a similar way, in revising the figure of Klytemnestra, Wolf is forced to recall her bloodthirsty patriarchal reputation in order to understand her motives. Wolf does this from the point of view of Kassandra, a victim of Klytemnestra's violence. Since Klytaimnestra has no voice of her own in Wolf's text, and since we see her in the harshest possible light, we would expect her to be roundly condemned. That she is not forces readers to rethink issues of gender, power, and violence.

Like Kassandra, the contemporary woman writer who would rewrite or unwrite the earlier historical and literary tradition is required to repeat it in order to change it. She experiences a kind of forced collusion even in the attempt at revision. Unless she wants to step entirely outside the tradition and overthrow it wholesale, as Monique Wittig tries to do in *Les guérillères*, the modern woman author must confront the tradition that suppresses her. But even Wittig draws on earlier myths and tales in *Les guérillères*. The ideal of an entirely new tradition is illusion. Wolf's Kassandra knows that she cannot eradicate Achilles' name—nor can she pretend that Klytaimnestra is not a murderess; both stories have been inscribed too long on the roles of the heroic tradition. She can, however, redefine Achilles' name to be synonymous with all the monstrosity and perversion of war; if Wolf's Kassandra cannot erase Achilles' name, at least she blackens it. In Klytaimnestra's case, Wolf can provide a sense of the intelligence, power, and motivation that drives Klytaimnestra's violence.

Wolf's *Kassandra* presents a number of traditional female roles: the mother as exemplified in Hekuba, Kassandra herself, and Klytaimnestra; the nurturing woman as depicted in Oenone or Arisbe; and the woman as sexual victim and war trophy as presented in Polyxena and Kassandra. But Wolf also depicts several less common female roles: the woman of power exemplified in both Klytaimnestra and, for a time, in Hekuba; the woman of true understanding represented by Kassandra; and the rebellious woman warrior epitomized in Penthesilea.

Let me focus on the role that most concerns us here, the familiar female role of mother. Both of Wolf's primary mother figures—Hekuba and Klytaimnestra—participate in the power structure that controls the war. They are among the ruling elite. Klytaimnestra loses a child to the war but not through her own foolishness or passivity. Her loss is due to the cowardly action of her irresolute husband, who sacrifices Iphigenia without even believing in the gods who apparently demand her death. But Klytaimnestra is also empowered by male absence; she rules Mycenae while her husband is away at war. Hekuba, who loses dozens of children to the war, is also of the ruling class. Wolf makes it clear that her husband Priam is not suited to the intellectual demands of ruling any more than Agamemnon is, and that only Hekuba's talents make it possible for him to remain king of Troy.

Both Klytaimnestra and Hekuba fulfill dual roles of mothers and professional women. Klytaimnestra will let her political profession of ruler replace her motherly role, causing further alienation of or loss of children. Hekuba, when barred from the political sphere because her cool logic threatens to undermine the effort to launch and sustain the egotistical and unnecessary war, turns to the growing alternative society represented by the group of women assembled around Aeneas's father, Anchises. Their unifying focus is the goddess Kybele (a figure who will become very popular as "The Goddess" in several 1990s texts).[17] A pre-Olympian and prepatriarchal earth goddess, one of whose names is "the Great Mother," Kybele and her devotees in Wolf's text symbolize a return to a communal social structure based on mutual cooperation and mutual needs rather than on competition and goal orientation. When excluded from the male-dominated power structure, Hekuba and Kassandra turn to this alternative society for comfort and redefinition of their lives. In this social configuration and the matriarchal figures such as Arisbe who compose it, Wolf offers her own version of the positive, nurturing mother figure. Wolf is careful, however, not to provide an easy utopia. While her alternative society is attractive, history tells us that it will eventually be swallowed up along with Aeneas in the founding of the next major military patriarchy—Rome. This alternative, nurturing world loses to the "heroic" narrative of history. Klytaimnestra, too, is forced to reinscribe violence in order to maintain power; she must slay rather than nurture—and both men and women fall to her axe. Wolf implies that even Kassandra's twin children will be slain by Klytaimnestra.

Relentlessly honest, Wolf does not give her characters all the necessary knowledge or answers. Questions of future solutions and lasting alternatives to the unacceptable social and political structure Wolf depicts are reserved for the reader's reflection. In this respect, Wolf sees her text as related to those of Brecht. In a 1983 interview, Wolf links her strategy in *Kassandra* directly with that of Brecht in *Mutter Courage* by suggesting that in both cases it is ultimately the viewer or reader who must achieve the understanding impossible for the character within the text (Wolf, "Gespräch über *Kassandra*," 108).

Understanding is crucial to Wolf, however. Wolf's revision of the Kassandra story is most powerful as it transforms the tale into a relentless search for self-knowledge and honesty.[18] Among her peers, Kassandra stands out as she who is not only able but also *willing* to see political realities—in this, she is indeed sister to Klytaimnestra. Kassandra is also willing to voice her knowledge. This voice carries to the listener/reader the problems of political and sexual power and of women's place in the patriarchal tradition. Wolf's fusion of the twentieth-century narrator with Kassandra's first-person narrative as the text opens and closes helps to meld the narrator, character, and reader into a unified experiential whole. Given that the narrative follows immediately upon Wolf's ruminations on Kassandra in her four "Poetik-Vorlesungen," the narrative voice closely resembles Wolf herself, and thus adds the author to the amalgam of narrator, character, and reader.

Wolf refuses to adopt the stance of godlike impartiality that Joyce's Stephen Dedalus espouses, and she refuses to abide by generic definitions. Her "Lectures on Poetics" combine the normally discrete genres of travel narration, work diary, letter,[19] and the narrative of *Kassandra* itself into a single text. This fusion denies the separation of the personal and the public, emotion and intellect, low and high literature.[20] Wolf insists on using these "personal" genres in which women have historically expressed themselves along with her narrative as part of her denial of a traditional, patriarchal "poetics." Wolf thus participates actively in the feminist attempt to question the hierarchical arrangement of "acceptable" literary genres and modes of knowledge in order to introduce *all* of human understanding into literature.[21] Wolf asserts diversity within the whole of literary experience. She refuses to be bound by traditional Western thought that has excluded the female and the subjective. She attempts in her "Poetik-Vorlesungen," *including* in the narrative *Kassandra,* to find the whole of experience once again. The fact that she could not have her text published as a single volume in West Germany and that the American publishers felt obliged to put the narrative first (presumably as the "most important" section) suggests the resistance to Wolf's attempt.

In her article "Vom Sehen zur Seherin: Christa Wolfs Umdeutung des Mythos und die Spur der Bachmann-Rezeption in ihrer Literatur," Sigrid Weigel sees Wolf's *Voraussetzungen einer Erzählung: Kassandra* as consistent with Wolf's attempt to convey the whole of human experience. Weigel feels, however, that the narrative *Kassandra* itself is forced to replicate too closely the heroic narratives to which it objects. But, as Anna Kuhn points out (*Christa Wolf's Utopian Vision*, 190–91), this conclusion can only be reached if the narrative is separated from the genre-challenging whole of the "Poetik-Vorlesungen." Wolf's narrative struggles against the heroic epic rather than simply adding another text to it.

Wolf herself analyzes the way in which the heroic epic comes into being and how closely tied it is to conflict:

> Only people with conflicts have stories to tell. . . . Only the advent of property, hierarchy, and patriarchy extracts a blood-red thread from the fabric of human life, which the three ancient crones, the Moirae, had in hand; and this thread is amplified at the expense of the web as a whole, at the expense of its uniformity. The blood-red thread is the narrative of the struggle and victory of the heroes, or their doom. The plot is born. The epic, born of the struggles for patriarchy, becomes *by its structure* an instrument by which to elaborate and fortify the patriarchy. The hero is made to serve as a model, and still does so down to the present day. The chorus of female speakers has vanished, swallowed up by the earth. The woman can now become the object of masculine narrative, in the role of heroine. (*Cassandra*, 296–97, emphasis in the original)

Wolf's discussion recalls Kristeva's comments on the epic and its monologic and hierarchical structure in "Word, Dialogue, and Novel." Wolf's own dialogic structure that includes competing attitudes, voices, and even genres, aligns itself with Kristeva's carnivalesque. Like the carnivalesque, Wolf's text "challenges God [or perhaps gods], authority and social law; in so far as it is dialogical, it is rebellious" (79). In being multivalent and multivocal, in demanding more than the rational as a basis for understanding the world, Wolf's text—like the carnivalesque—challenges the epic and monologic and its demands for hierarchy.

Wolf attempts to return women to the position of subjects rather than objects in her narrative, to make them tellers, singers, and seers rather than characters in a male plot. She is faced, however, with the problem that we no longer live the "undifferentiated whole"; patriarchy has dominated for thousands of years and defined narrative in its wake. If Wolf is to narrate at all, she must do so within a tradition determined by patriarchy. To some extent she is trapped, like her Kassandra who must utter Achilles' name in order to curse him, in having to invoke that which she would like to eradicate. But

Wolf does not simply repeat the tradition, she challenges its rules and underpinnings. By reasserting the female and the undifferentiated whole that has been denied and suppressed, she dialogizes Western culture. Wolf remakes thousands of years of the literary tradition by displacing the hero from its center, by making in it a place for women. She demystifies myth by laying bare its rationalizing pragmatism. Wolf does not simply want to inscribe new female myths; she wants human intelligence and clear-sightedness (like Kassandra's) to replace the need for myth. Wolf, with her highly critical revaluations of the past and of the roots of Western male-dominated civilization, presents a reinterpretation of history and of cultural tradition.[22]

Wolf's Klytaimnestra remains an executioner, but she is also a kindred spirit to both Kassandra and Hekuba.[23] She is forced to destroy that kinship when the need to retain power forces her to adopt violence. She must kill Kassandra, the one person in the narrative who is her equal in strength and perceptiveness. Wolf's Klytaimnestra cannot help Kassandra to generate a new, female narrative; Klytaimnestra is too firmly ensnared in the web of patriarchal tradition and the birth of Western culture. Her violence becomes patriarchy's excuse for subjugating Mother Right to Father Right, blood relationships to legal ones, nature to polis. And in this way, Wolf's Klytaimnestra is forced to remain a part of the "blood-red thread" that weaves the patriarchal epic. The threads that made up the "purple way of justice" for Aeschylus's Klytemnestra and the red scarf/net for Martha Graham's character all become entwined with the threads of the epic tradition itself as the net that ensnares Wolf's figure. Wolf's Klytaimnestra is more fully depicted as a powerful but wronged woman, but (like Brückner's character) she remains unrecuperated for any new female tradition.

Her Story Rewoven: Marie Cardinal's *Le passé empiété*

Marie Cardinal's 1983 novel *Le passé empiété* (Backstitch; or, The Past Reappropriated), like the works of Reinig and Maraini, is set in the late twentieth century. Like Brückner's and Bogen's characters, Cardinal's Clytemnestre loves gardens and nurturing; like Maraini's Clitennestra, Cardinal's unnamed first-person narrator works with textiles, although in Cardinal's case it is with exquisite and famous embroidery rather than basic weaving. But the most interesting aspect of Cardinal's novel is the gender and character merging that resembles the fusions that mark Reinig's ending. Cardinal, however, takes the gender and identity confusions and intermixing further than Reinig does. Not until we are two-thirds of the way through the novel do we begin to understand the many fusions that occur.

Born in Algeria in 1929 to a wealthy French colonial family, Cardinal often uses her birthplace in her works. She was repatriated during the Algerian war and became part of the French literary scene of the 1960s.[24] Given her dual cultural affiliations to Arabic Algeria and to France, she often focuses on issues of multiculturalism. The political events in France in 1968 encouraged Cardinal to emphasize exploitation of all kinds in her work. In 1975 her highly successful volume *Les mots pour le dire* (*The Words to Say It*, 1983), a semiautobiographical work that explores the experience of psychoanalysis,[25] made Cardinal a recognized literary figure in several countries.[26] Cardinal's publications examine women at moments of crisis, and she is closely aligned with women's issues. A few years after writing her Clytemnestre, Cadinal published her translation *La Médée d'Euripide* (1987; The *Medea* of Euripides). In the early 1980s, Cardinal moved to Montreal and became a Canadian citizen. She died in May 2001.

Cardinal's *Le passé empiété* begins with the first-person voice of a fifty-year-old woman who is trying to find herself after ten years of caring for her two children, who were seriously injured in a motorcycle accident when they were teenagers. The narrator provided them with the motorcycle and suffers from the guilt of that gift. She reveals that she desired the motorcycle and its image of freedom more than her children did. She also finds herself guilty of loving her work as a world-famous embroideress more than she loves her husband. Jacques, the husband, views her work as women's foolishness rather than "real" work. He resents the fact that she is dedicated to it rather than to him; he also resents being outearned by his highly successful wife. He eventually leaves her for a younger woman who sees him as the center of her universe.[27]

The embroidering is related to the weaving of nets, cloths, and plots at which the classical Klytemnestra excels.[28] For the narrator, embroidery represents freedom, creativity, and fulfillment—as both the net and the plot that trap Agamemnon do for the classical figure. Embroidery allows Cardinal's narrator to express her real self as nothing else in her life can do. She becomes obsessed with her work rather than with the riches it provides. She feels guilty about her wealth, thinking that if she had not been so rich, she could not have bought the motorcycle that proved so disastrous to her children. After their near-fatal accident, they became her obsession. Once they are well enough to be in a permanent care institution, the narrator again finds the desire to embroider and to find her true self in that work. She wants to begin anew by rethinking her life in the solitude of a trip to the seashore.

Unlike her classical counterpart, this female protagonist is very concerned with self-analysis—both psychological and physical. She examines her aging body in detail, comparing it to the landscape that surrounds the villa in which she is staying. She recalls giving birth to her daughter as well as experiencing menopause; she lives in a world of great physical awareness and detail. All of these physical perceptions feed into her embroidery designs, which we begin to understand as the unfinished patterns of her shifting life. The embroidery, which is identified as specifically women's work, is both an expression of her self, an essence that existed in her long before marriage and children, and a means of articulating without words her deepest feelings. She invests herself so thoroughly in it that life outside of the work becomes a distraction.

This absorption in personal work, in something other than husband and family, becomes an inexcusable transgression. The narrator comes to understand that she has violated gender and cultural rules by her actions: "I am guilty of having disobeyed the people, their rules, their laws, their culture, their morality, that which they call the 'eternal feminine,' and the astronomical price of this disobedience is the lives of my two children. . . . It's too much, you understand me? It is too much!" (47). This indeed sounds like the plight of Klytemnestra. Not subservient to her husband or to the cultural, moral, and gender rules of her society, Cardinal's narrator must be punished and brought back into line. As in the texts of Reinig and Maraini, this modern woman does not actually kill her husband, she simply sends him packing. She does not need his protection, and her ability to outearn him represents a modern form of castration, or desecration of the male, which was prominent in the texts by Reinig, Bogen, Brückner, and Maraini. Cardinal's female narrator, not overtly aggressive in any martial sense, is guilty of not needing the protection of men and therefore of not remaining in her proper place. This creates her disaster (48).

In Cardinal's text, the narrator's punishment is exercised through rather than by the children. Their crippling and the guilt that results from it is the Fury that pursues the narrator. The family configuration is also familiar to us. The husband has been removed from the house (although here not by death but by living with another woman); the family consists of the wealthy and powerful mother and a son and daughter. Although the narrator remains unnamed, we feel in the first section of the novel that she must be our Klytemnestra.

This now familiar pattern is disrupted, however, when the narrator declares that she does need one man, "du premier homme" (the first man), her father, Jean-Maurice. She wants to understand the father she did not know. Conceived in the middle of a divorce after her parents no longer lived together, the narrator feels her birth was the result of a momentary doubt or chance—or hypocrisy. Since she never lived with her father and he dies when she is seventeen, he becomes a myth, a legend in her imagination. Suddenly, we as readers are shifted from identifying the narrator as Klytemnestra to identifying her as the daughter, Electra. So that we might not miss the association, Cardinal has the narrator recall the classical Electra in her ruminations about her father, "I also thought of Electra arranging offerings on the tomb of Agamemnon, her assassinated father . . ." (51).

This melding of Klytemnestra and Electra in the narrator creates a unique problem for the reader. Usually pitted against one another, the mother and daughter here share feelings and experiences. They not only interact, but they also merge. Rather than making the female roles of mother and daughter antagonistic, Cardinal consolidates them in a single character. This fusing generates new insights and a new dynamic for the classical plot. Like Graham reconciling mother and son, Cardinal reconciles the consciousnesses of Klytemnestra and Electra.

To complicate matters further, the narrator, who subsumes Klytemnestra as well as Electra, also takes on the being of Agamemnon, thus crossing gender lines as well. The narrator can only become herself through her father. She contemplates returning to her embroidery work where she will be not the mother of her children or the wife of "X" or the girlfriend of "Y," but herself entirely. This is accomplished only in conjunction with her father: "Me, with my father, this new comer, this unknown. Me entire [or complete]" (52). The narrator realizes that she is as much her father as she is her mother, and that it is he who has inspired her. Her father expresses himself in her work.

Incorporating the father within the narrator who is both mother and daughter makes problematic any battle of the sexes between the male and the female. We must either all win together, or all lose. As Reinig does at the end of her novel, Cardinal, at the beginning of hers, complicates gender lines and gender antagonisms. She redraws the battle lines—or better, she blurs them. The struggle is no longer Mother Right versus Father Right; the same female character incorporates both—and she spends more than half of the book (188 of 372 pages) recapturing the father she did not know but who forms a part of her essence.

The narrator remembers becoming aware of herself as a young woman when she was with her father. She grows from a child and the daughter of her mother to a young woman conscious of her own sexuality and that her father is a man. But she goes well beyond her own memories in seeking her father's—and therefore her own—essence. She reincorporates her father not only by remembering him but by becoming him. She contemplates the difficulty of understanding a boy when she has never been one. But she feels that girls are more unknown to themselves than boys are. A girl's body holds more mysteries than a boy's. A boy, she notes, can ejaculate at two years old. He has his adult body and capabilities in miniature. A girl, on the other hand, must imagine breasts and periods; her body holds secrets that will only be disclosed in time. The narrator remembers her own attraction to nude African sculpture and its comfort with the body as opposed to classical pieces that she found more repressed and hypocritical. Male or female, one must make peace with the body in this text. But the female narrator will need to explore the male body in order to become her father. The world of male work dominates the book for most of its central section.

Speaking in another first-person voice, the female narrator enters the consciousness of her father beginning in his early childhood. S/he reexperiences his thoughts and feelings, his love of the family business and his expectations of becoming its director. S/he recounts the desires of a fifteen-year-old to command men, to be in charge of an army of workers, to be famous. These desires call up a young Agamemnon preparing to lead the Greek armies to Troy to build his fame. This is a capable young man of determination and strong will. S/he moves into adolescence and relives the euphoria of first orgasms. And, in a peculiarly acute case of gender merging, the female narrator, as a fifty-year-old woman, offers her father her hand—which is also his own hand because of their merging—in order to understand the other side of sex, the female experience as well as the male. They become a kind of joint Tiresias. This psychological-physical merger allows the father and daughter to give birth to one another. Addressing her fifteen-year-old father, she urges, "Listen, sweet daddy, my youthful daddy, my adolescent daddy, my daddy in the making. Listen, take my hand. . . . My hand is your hand. Take the hand of a fifty-year-old woman. . . . Take it, it is your hand, it is a woman's hand, it is the hand of your daughter. . . . For once, let us achieve orgasm together. You and me together. Equal. The father and the daughter alike, innocent, pure, free. Let us mutually engender ourselves, let us give birth to ourselves" (89).

This radical offer of mutual male/female engendering and birth provides a startling alternative to the battle lines drawn in the *Oresteia*. Even the House of Atreus and its infamous incest and exploitation of daughters and sons seems capable of redemption if Cardinal can turn physical incest into liberating mutual psychological rebirth. Literally experiencing the other (both the other man and the other woman) allows this woman to become both mother and father without usurping either and without excluding the other sex. Apollo's appropriation of motherhood for the male in the *Eumenides* is not simply reversed here by Cardinal; it is rejected as the wrong strategy. Inclusion rather than exclusion is what this narrator works to achieve. The mutual orgasm that this merging accomplishes is a brief moment of perfection and fulfillment that envelops all of existence.

This moment is short-lived, however, as the narrator's father finds himself displaced in his inheritance and expectations by a usurping brother-in-law and an aging father who fears being replaced by his son. We follow the father through his own recreation of himself by his own creative and manual labor in the building industry. We come to understand Jean-Maurice's complicated relationship to his own father, Théodule, who himself becomes an Agamemnon figure with a mistress named Cassandra—thus making his wife, Ernestine, yet another fleeting Klytemnestra figure. In this way, Cardinal constantly multiplies the modern characters who partake of the ancient archetypes. Cardinal thus demonstrates how culture constantly repeats ancient patterns throughout its history. But, like Reinig, Cardinal also reveals that the modern world is too fragmented for a single identity to embody the ancient figures entirely. Agamemnon's characteristics migrate through several modern identities just as Klytemnestra's do. This diffusion makes it more difficult to see any modern figure as an embodiment of a particular moral, social, or political stance. All the modern characters in Cardinal's novel struggle with many identities and occupy many positions from the ancient myths. Each of Cardinal's figures becomes a Proteus shifting from one position to another. Condemning or lauding anyone becomes a difficult task that we soon abandon in favor of simply trying to understand each character's complex motivations.

Through the female narrator now in the first-person consciousness of her father, Jean-Maurice, the reader experiences his traumas of being gassed in World War I and of contracting tuberculosis in an army hospital. Jean-Maurice eventually settles in Algiers and marries a wealthy younger woman, Mimi, the narrator's mother. Because he fears losing her and being cast out by society, he does not tell Mimi of his tuberculosis. His attempts to hide this secret lead him to be unnecessarily brutal on their wedding night and to change Mimi from a romantic adolescent into a cynical adult woman. Their first child, Odette, who is ardently loved by her mother, contracts tuberculosis as an infant. Her death reveals the father's secret and forever alienates Mimi, who would like to see Jean-Maurice dead.

At this point, we have another Klytemnestra character, the betrayed mother, Mimi, who loses a child because of the father/Agamemnon's unhealthy heritage. This Klytemnestra, the female first-person narrator's mother, kills her husband with language rather than with a sword, and she takes many years to do it. She constantly plants the image of him as a diseased, evil wanderer in the minds of her children. The female narrator feels guilty toward her

mother in her allegiance to her father and in her compassionate understanding of his complex life. But the narrator also feels forced to sympathize with
her mother and her dead infant sister when she imagines them. As a mother
herself, she cannot but experience her own mother's pain at the death of her
firstborn daughter. Although the narrator sympathizes with her father and his
intense love for her mother, she cannot remain in his consciousness; she shifts
to her mother's consciousness. In visceral empathy with her mother, the narrator shifts perspectives and first-person minds: "For me, it happens in the
belly, it is visceral. I can not remain on the embankment with him, I am on
the bridge, with her, I am 21 years old. I clasp my little daughter in my arms . . ."
(234). Again, the normally sharp dividing lines drawn between father, mother, and child in the ancient texts are blurred here as an empathetic female
center of consciousness moves among her own family members.[29]

The final third of the novel introduces yet another complication for analysis of the revisionary impulse. The text becomes literally dialogic as the classical Clytemnestre appears to the female narrator to inspire her most crucial work of embroidery—the story of Clytemnestre herself. Having worked
many months in her studio remembering her father in her embroidery, the
female narrator finally sets aside her passionate and hermaphroditic love for
him. Having moved beyond her children's motorcycle accident and her father's consciousness, she discovers that her dead infant sister, Odette, is the
image that haunts her. Odette will lead her to Clytemnestre. She remembers
Odette from a photo in which her mother had posed her as a tiny, infant
coquette, already being initiated by Mimi into the ironic war of submission
that women struggle with their whole lives.

In remembering Odette, the narrator also remembers her mother's hate
and her sense of vengeance when Jean-Maurice dies. At her father's grave,
the narrator realizes that she is passing from adolescence into adult womanhood; it is a tortured passage propelled by her mother's sense of subdued
rage at the inescapable position of women. The mother, Mimi, formed her
own sense of love and relationships as a young girl by reading romances.
When her husband's clumsy and inhibited attempts to make love on their
wedding night without giving away his secret of tuberculosis leads to brutal
and unromantic sex, Mimi resigns herself stoically to the role of submissive
wife. She learns that women have no choice in marriage. This coupled with
the hate she feels at Odette's death creates a mother of rage and vengeance
whose inability to kill directly results in a life of suppressed wrath—which
makes Mimi sister to Maraini's Clitennestra. Mimi attempts to pass on to the
narrator her sense of the battle of the sexes, the perverse tactics of sexuality,
the politics of patience, and the dialectic of lies that makes up a marriage.

At her father's graveside, the narrator knows from the terrible pressure of her mother's hand on her shoulder that she is meant to hate her father, to see him as the vanquished enemy. The narrator, however, has come to love and understand her father; she cannot hate him. The narrator also understands that her mother's hand would force her into the same role of submissive hate and repressed fury that her mother feels all women must play out when they become wives. The narrator, however, escapes Mimi's grasp and sidesteps her role, thus radically isolating herself. Remembering the *Iphigénie* that she is studying in school, the narrator thinks in regard to her vengeful mother, "She had only to act like Clytemnestre. As for me, I would prefer murder to vengeance" (256). This statement presents a crucial choice for the narrator; she finds Clytemnestre's assertive murder to be preferable to her mother's patient, submissive wrath. Better to act than to live the life her mother envisions, fulfilling the expected social role but hating it and the man who would marry her.

In remembering this moment as a fifty-year-old woman, the narrator wonders why she has repressed Clytemnestre for so long. She wonders who this woman and her daughter Iphigénie really are and whether she fears to emulate the "wicked" queen. The narrator comes to comprehend that she has issued from all her female examples—Odette, Clytemnestre, Iphigénie, and Mimi—and that she must understand their histories in order to decipher her own. These women of dreams, of memory, and of cultural myth occupy the narrator more than living beings. (Her two children slip away from home in single-line asides amid the more engrossing psychological narrative.) Clytemnestre gives the narrator a model for rebelling against the life Mimi has laid out. The narrator researches the figure of Clytemnestre but finds that all the documents and myths do not reveal the real woman. Clytemnestre has been lost in obscurity. The more the narrator seeks to understand Clytemnestre, the closer she feels to her, until the ancient Clytemnestre actually appears to the embroideress in her dreams. Whether this is delusion or diachronic miracle, by the time Clytemnestre shows up in person in the twentieth century, we, like the narrator, are anxious to speak to her.

Cardinal, then, merges not only characters, identities, and genders, but she also merges myths and historical periods even more directly than Reinig or Wolf. The ancient Greek figure and the contemporary French narrator literally carry on a dialogue that allows the contemporary writer to interrogate her female role model directly. This dialogue supplements those narrative dialogues that have been taking place among the narrator and her family members. Clytemnestre first reminds the narrator of her mother, Mimi; however, the narrator rapidly decides that this figure is not like her mother but rather like herself—her equal.

As the two speak, Clytemnestre occupies various roles for the narrator—mother, equal, daughter. Their lives intertwine particularly when they speak of their children. As Clytemnestre remembers her own son and daughter and their vengeance, the narrator imagines her son and daughter on their motorcycle but this time safely reaching the seashore and bathing there. The narrator and Clytemnestre occupy one another's consciousnesses; Clytemnestre takes form in the narrator's body. In the embroideress's studio, where the narrator is most herself, Clytemnestre tells of Iphigénie's death and of her frantic attempts to get her daughter to resist her father or to convince the father not to carry out his sacrifice. Because she is the only one resisting the decreed fate of her daughter and the fortunes of Greece, because she protects blood rights and the female, Clytemnestre is seen as ignoble and currish, the "queen of the dogs." Her attempt to offer herself in place of her daughter is rejected by a proud and regal Iphigénie. Clytemnestre feels excluded and degraded by her daughter's dedication to patriarchy. Even her hate for Agamemnon seems churlish to her countrymen when compared to Iphigénie's majestic acceptance of her sacrifice. Clytemnestre is cast aside, not consulted about the sacrifice of her daughter, which is seen as a "matter of state" and therefore not her concern. She is isolated and excluded, disgusted by her daughter's submission, jealous of her admired state, and driven mad by all of these emotions. Clytemnestre is faced with the impossible choice of remaining silent or ceasing to exist. She remains silent, like thousands of obedient women, including the narrator's mother. In speaking to the narrator (with the familiar pronoun), Clytemnestre breaks her ancient silence so that a new story might be told.

Clytemnestre feels that her degraded condition is perpetuated in myth, but she demands to know who chooses the myth, who gets to truncate or stretch history and inscribe it through time. Indeed, this is one of the questions that all the female revisionists must ask when they themselves appropriate the past in order to create a new narrative. Cardinal's narrator can only answer "'Les hommes, le Pouvoir, le roi'" ("Men, Power, the king") (266). But the narrator is not satisfied with this response; she knows it is too simple. She decides that she herself will recast Clytemnestre in her embroidery; she will change the depiction, rework the myth. She thus becomes a revisionary artist within a revisionary text.

The narrator's "passé empiété" is both the backstitch embroidery that marks her work and the capacity to appropriate the past in order to change its trajectory into the future. As she puts it in describing her embroidery, "on empiète dans le passé pour se lancer dans l'avenir. Le passé empiété" (one appropriates [or impinges upon] the past in order to throw oneself into the future. Le passé empiété [The backstitch or the reappropriated past]) (249). The very act of stitching here is a revision of the past.[30] This revision in cloth is matched by a second revision enacted by the text itself. Clytemnestre's story is retold, rethought, and relived by the narrator with an overlay that will change it and throw it into the future in a new form. This produces a double revision to match the many doublings of characters and identities that shape the book as a whole.

The revisions for Cardinal have to do with understanding the situation of women and their relationship to men. They include epiphanies about love, including the comprehension that the greatest love is incest, since a woman must always become either a man's child or his mother in order to be loved by him (270). This suggestion recalls the metaphoric incest that the narrator experiences with her father at his first sexual encounter. Clytemnestre and the narrator also mutually understand that the ultimate sacrifice is in giving birth, that this suffering is truly joy. Cardinal's Clytemnestre comes to accept the death of her daughter by seeing her reincorporated into the cyclical rebirth in nature in the garden that becomes her refuge. She cannot, however, accept Agamemnon's role in the murder. She feels that he reduced the death of his daughter to a family duty without ever understanding that he was only an insect in the service of universal regeneration, a worker bee contributing to a larger cosmic order. Clytemnestre's disdain for her uncomprehending husband eventually kills her love for him.

Although the narrator is quite interested in Egisthe and is determined to embroider him in his splendid youth, Clytemnestre sees him only as a distraction, an admiring boy who serves as a diversion. It is clear that she does not kill her husband and king in order to be with Egisthe. She also does not slay by chance or in a frenzy; like both Aeschylus's and Graham's Klytemnestras, her killing is decisive and conscious. She makes no attempt to disavow or mitigate her actions. Clytemnestre herself wields the knife and stabs her husband while he is tangled in the net that Egisthe has thrown. But, unlike her namesakes in Aeschylus and Graham, she also affectionately recalls every detail of the body she once loved. This Clytemnestre climbs into the bath to embrace the body of her dying husband as a mother might, creating a strange pietà in which all the relationships of sacrifice are redefined. Clytemnestra becomes profoundly aware of the enormity of her crime; she has killed her husband and her king, she has committed mariticide and regicide. She reminds us, however, that she has not performed a blood-killing, not slain a child or parent—as Agamemnon did. This is her only brief self-defense. It is coupled with Cardinal's choice to eliminate the murder of Cassandra from her narrative. Cardinal's Clytemnestre is thus not guilty of killing another woman; this omission makes her more sympathetic for feminist purposes and allows for more solidarity among women than the other late-twentieth-century revisions envision.

In listening to Clytemnestre's story, the narrator feels compelled to defend her own actions; she asserts her own ideas about the tale and insists on her individual creativity and power. The narrator wants to mitigate Clytemnestre's murder and regicide so that her own life will somehow be justified; Clytemnestre, however, believes her crime to be indefensible. She kills out of an instinct to preserve herself—to escape the erasure that has been imposed on her, but she does not wish to speak in order to justify herself. Silence remains for her a female survival tactic. She resents the narrator's cajoling her into speaking. Like the narrator, however, Clytemnestre invokes her father for consolation. In introducing Clytemnestre's need for the father, Cardinal offers a unique revision not found in any of the other texts, either classical or modern. Cardinal makes the divine Zeus rather than the human Tyndareos the father of Clytemnestre. This gesture raises the need for one's father to a divine level, but it also displaces the strong feminist identification of Clytemnestre with her mother, Leda. Known as the daughter of Leda rather than of Zeus, the ancient Klytemnestra descends from a strongly female line, as does her sister, Helen.

Feminists could be annoyed at Cardinal's imposition of yet another father—just as we are confused by the narrator's desire for her father in the beginning of the text. But Cardinal depicts equally compelling sympathies for maternal figures in her revision. I believe that her reclaiming of the fathers is not to be read as a return to patriarchal power but rather as an attempt to recover wholeness, to reestablish the entire human cycle and perpetuate the race without having to opt exclusively for either Mother Right or Father Right. Cardinal balances Clytemnestre's need to murder the human patriarch, husband, and king with her need to reestablish a relationship with a divine father. Perhaps coming to understand the father—for both the narrator and Clytemnestre—will forestall the need endlessly to reenact the murder of the husband. Perhaps reincorporating the male and female principles within a new configuration in which genders and roles are thoroughly blended will end the cycle of violence that has plagued the figure of Klytemnestra from the beginning.

This reincorporation takes place on the level of the narrator/embroideress. It is really she who has lived the father and the male, literally incorporated him into her self. The ancient Clytemnestre realizes that she has killed her husband to save her self, to escape her submission, to be free of the male domination that clearly persists into Mimi's time. But she comprehends too late that in her version of the myth there is always another male to fill the place of authority. The once weak and boyish Egisthe arises to replace Agamemnon. A much less worthy authority, Egisthe makes Clytemnestre's bid for selfhood and self-determination a vain act. She must again don her tragic mask and play out her own death scene. She cannot escape the mask in order to confront her children with her human needs and reasons. She can only speak through the mask and the role that myth has imposed on her. In reenacting her own death, she even makes herself more obscene and guilty in order to encourage her son, Oreste, to kill her. Clytemnestre begs the embroideress not to attempt to justify her mariticide and regicide but rather to depict her own death, the punishment that her act demanded.

Clytemnestre's real transgression, however, is not the murder but her act of will: "That day, I understood what had been the harmony of my life, and I understood also that I had just committed an act which had pulverized this harmony. Pulverized! Not because I had committed a crime, no. Because I had done something, myself, by myself, and for myself. A woman must never do that, never!" (315). Mimi's vision of the role of women returns once more to grip the narrator and attempt to make her accept women's lot by the negative example of the one woman who tries to escape it—Clytemnestre.

The narrator, however, also seeks to escape this mythic, cultural grasp in order to find a new possibility of freedom and a new self; she wants to paint Clytemnestre's story in a different light in order to find a new path for women. She listens as Clytemnestre describes the innate estrangement and isolation of men, their need to create laws and rules in order to reassure themselves, and the need for women to understand and accept this fact. This reminds the reader of Aeschylus's version of the movement from blood right to a legal system in order to found Western civilization. But the narrator feels that she must stop listening to Clytemnestre's own interpretation of her story; Clytemnestre has been too deeply mired in her own myth to react as a woman without the tragic mask or to see a new interpretation of her story. The narrator comes to understand that Clytemnestre's fear and despair need not be her own. She can embroider a different narrative for herself.

The narrator accompanies Clytemnestre to her death knowing that their final separation will allow the modern narrator to be free. The embroideress needed to justify Clytemnestre's murder in order to end her own torturous guilt. By making Clytemnestre's actions comprehensible and sympathetic, the narrator exorcises her own demons and is liberated to invent a new future for herself and, by extension, for all women who see her work and rethink their founding moment in Clytemnestre's action. In her final parting from the tragic Clytemnestre, the narrator knows that she will be absolutely alone, without any mythic model, resisting the temptation to take refuge in the lesson of history that teaches that women can find peace by conforming. She must disentangle herself from Clytemnestre as she did from Mimi. Clytemnestre will be turned back into the icon that culture and myth have created of her. She is petrified in her role.

The narrator in her dream returns to her own children, who are seen bathing and being reborn into a new future. She awakens determined to find a new studio in which she will produce work such as no one has yet seen, so astonishing as to be irresistible. Finally she has found hope. By reliving Clytemnestre's story as she has that of her father and mother, the narrator is freed to find a new future.

By having her narrator take her final leave of Clytemnestre, Cardinal implies that we must leave the old myths behind. We need not be bound by ancient models that put women in an inevitably submissive role. This is a message of hope and liberation. I would argue, however, that Cardinal herself does not really abandon the myth of Klytemnestra but rather reinvigorates it. Much like Wolf, who realizes that she cannot obliterate the name of Achilles without uttering it again and inscribing it again in cultural memory, Cardinal must recall Clytemnestre and rethink her story before she can progress beyond it. The past myths of gender roles must be revisited in order to be changed—this is precisely the project of the women revisionists.

Cardinal must redraw Clytemnestre in order to backstitch so that she can move the total picture in a new direction. By blurring gender lines, roles, and identities, Cardinal changes the legend of Klytemnestra from a battle over Mother Right versus Father Right, blood versus law, women versus men, to a complex psychological understanding of individuals for one another. She generates sympathies not possible with starkly drawn divisions. Her narrator occupies not only Klytemnestra's position but Agamemnon's and Electra's as well. She becomes male and female; she experiences everyone's pains and needs. She is truly a self constantly in process. This unifying incorporation forces us out of single-figure positions into a more dialogic and multivalent narrative world. The underpinnings of the ancient story of Klytemnestra provide Cardinal with the multiple mythic and cultural resonances necessary to accomplish this alchemy.

Is Electra or Iphigenia Klytemnestra's True Offspring?: Séverine Auffret's *Nous, Clytemnestre*

Séverine Auffret's 1984 *Nous, Clytemnestre: Du tragique et des masques*[31] (We, Clytemnestre: Of the Tragic and of the Masks) is difficult to categorize. The paperback cover implies that the 230-page text is an *essai*, although it has many passages of imaginative lyrical description as well as quotations from and analyses of earlier texts. While many modern French thinkers incorporate personal responses in their works, this text presents a purposeful mosaic of theoretical analysis, literary criticism, and personal lyric designed to make us cross boundaries of thought and academic discipline. It participates strongly in the feminist impulse to include a personal voice within academic analysis. The piece was awarded the 1985 Prix Marcelle Blum de l'Académie des Sciences Morales et Politiques, which leads new readers to expect a work of moral philosophy or political science rather than one of literary analysis. Auffret's thoughts on Clytemnestre are all of these. Much more than a useful reference work on the topic (such as Sally MacEwen's very fine collection of essays *Views of Clytemnestra, Ancient and Modern*),[32] Auffret's study is a genuine revision of Klytemnestra, a rethinking of her role and her being. Part fiction and part critical analysis, Auffret's text is most akin to Wolf's multigenre "lectures," which include her narrative of *Kassandra.*

A professor of philosophy in Paris, Auffret is closely aligned with women's issues in France. In her 1982 volume *Des couteaux contre des femmes* (Knives against Women), she campaigned against female genital mutilation in Africa. She has studied women in philosophy and history[33] and in her critical editions.[34] Most crucially here, Auffret also contributed to the 1994 volume *Conceptualización de lo femenino en la filosofía antigua* (Conceptualization of the Feminine in the Philosophy of Antiquity).

Nous, Clytemnestre is a personal reflection by Auffret as well as a recognition that all of us—male and female—in the Western tradition are Clytemnestre. The volume is dedicated to four women, including Auffret's mother, but Auffret clearly feels that the issues generated by Clytemnestre's story are crucial to both men and women. While the *nous* of the title might indicate the "royal we" of Clytemnestre the queen as well as a non-gender-specific modern humanity, it also triggers in late-twentieth- and early-twenty-first-century women an identification and self-recognition—particularly in those aspects of Clytemnestre's story that touch on women's roles and motherhood. Auffret focuses on the mother-daughter affiliation in great detail, finding that the Clytemnestre-Electre relationship has its origin in the one between Clytemnestre and Iphigénie. Concentration on Clytemnestre's very different connection to her two daughters continues very strongly into the 1990s, a shift that Auffret anticipates in her study.

The *nous* of Auffret's title also recalls the Greek word *nous* (or, more commonly, *nóos*) meaning mind, intelligence, spirit, or soul. This sense of the word would imply that Auffret will explore Clytemnestre's very soul, the spirit and intelligence that prompt her to slay Agamemnon in retribution. Whether or not Auffret had the Greek in mind, she does indeed explore those aspects of Clytemnestre that make her a powerful individual spirit. Auffret also investigates just what kind of "intelligence" or "reason" comes into play in judging the ties of blood and motherhood versus those of marriage and law. She assists us in inhabiting Clytemnestre's mind, in seeing through her eyes, and in understanding her thoughts and motivations.

In the course of her analysis, Auffret points out some curious details about Klytemnestra and her story; among these is the fact that no ancient Greek tragedy is named for her, although eponymous plays abound for Electra, Iphigenia, and even Agamemnon and Orestes. Despite the fact that Klytemnestra is the central figure in the resolution of the curse on the House of Atreus and that she is crucial to the action of all the other characters in her troubled immediate family, she is never accorded the honor of an eponymous play among the extant Greek tragedies or those that are known to have been lost. Auffret traces this tendency to exclude Clytemnestre from the title among later French classical and French and German Romantic writers[35] as well as among modernist writers such as Eugene O'Neill (all male examples). She notes only one exception among modern writers, Maraini and her play *I sogni di Clitennestra.* Clearly, Auffret's own text should also count, as well as Bogen's *Klytaimnestra Who Stayed at Home* and Graham's ballet. Late-twentieth-century women, it seems, are willing to give Klytemnestra top billing. A male and female joint venture by Daniel Foley and Risako Ataka at the 1998 Edinburgh Festival Fringe also reworks Aeschylus's *Agamemnon;* this production focuses intensely on Klytemnestra and even renames the play *Clytemnestra.* As the last millennium and the twentieth century drew to a close, Klytemnestra was finally given center stage and title billing—particularly among female artists.

Auffret, like her sister writers, acknowledges the complexity of Klytemnestra's story—its dark and light sides, its timeless appeal, its relentlessly tragic nature. She feels that Klytemnestra's history must be played out theatrically in an exchange of words (or gestures in Graham's case), whether these be inscribed in opera, theater, or cinema. The fact that none of the Klytemnestras we have examined exists as a lyric poem (in contrast to many revisions of Helen) underlines Auffret's point. Auffret also explores the fact that the tragic and the heroic seem to be at odds. She argues that Clytemnestre is more tragic, whereas her daughter Iphigénie (who dies in the cause of war) is more heroic. Tragedy reveals social restrictions and conflicts that need to be worked out in drama to be evident and to be available for social judgments. For Auffret, Clytemnestre provides a particularly crucial case of

An ancient Klytaimestra. (Antikensammlung, Staatliche Museen zu Berlin—Preussischer Kulturbesitz)

social necessity at odds with family loyalties and thus a compelling instance for interrogating "the tragic." We see Auffret's larger theoretical concerns (announced in her subtitle, "Of the Tragic and of the Masks") worked out through her contemplation of Clytemnestre.

Auffret's approach is multimethodological, involving literary as well as historical analysis and the study of myth and culture. She reviews the "history" of Clytemnestre and her family—by which she means all the versions of Klytemnestra's story, since each telling of a myth forms part of its totality. She must know the composite of all available texts in order to begin to rethink Clytemnestre with "virginité de la pensée" (virginity of thought) (22). (This is a curious turn of phrase given Auffret's concentration on Clytemnestre as mother as well as woman and daughter. It more fittingly applies to Electra, whose name implies "unbedded" or unwed, and Iphigénie, who remains the virgin priestess.) In this unity of works and multiplicity of creators, Clytemnestre becomes *nous*, we—all of us who grew up in the Western tradition. She is part of the heritage of the West, and the continuity of her history traced to its origins becomes more than one woman's re-creation; it becomes a part of the whole of this myth. As T. S. Eliot sees each new work shifting and redefining the canon of literature, Auffret suggests that each retelling of Klytemnestra realigns the myths that underpin Western culture as a whole. The title must be *Nous, Clytemnestre* because we are all involved and implicated in the rethinking and reevaluation of this crucial figure's actions and motivations.

The contradictory demands of state, family, and fate in Clytemnestre's story generate the violence, as well as the tragic *souffrance*, that indelibly marks her. Auffret notes that this conflict is exterior, played out in the public space, in ancient Greece. It pits two mythic universes against one another: the male heroic world of divine glory versus the female world of darkness and anguish. In modern times, the conflict will be interiorized, displaced into reflection and subjective guilt. But Auffret wants to trace the tragic back to its ancient origins. She will largely bypass Homer, who she feels leaves out too much of Klytemnestra's personal story, to move to the Greek tragedians of fifth century B.C. Athens. These authors (Aeschylus, Sophocles, Euripides) themselves refer to larger legends of the House of Atreus that in turn form part of a more vast mythology still.

Auffret thus uses Clytemnestre as a conduit to the foundations of Western culture. Clytemnestre's heritage, her connections to family, line, or "House," creates her tragic fate and allows us to see what violence is generated in the struggle between polis and *oikos*, public social construction and blood relationships. It also reveals what is at stake for the female in the founding of Western society. The Athenian tragedian must find a precarious balance that creates good out of the terrifying daughters of the night while acknowledging that society must constantly propitiate them. This balance between repression and preservation (or redefinition) of the female principles also continues to haunt modern dramatists such as Giraudoux and Sartre. Auffret indicates that the Erinyes survive in the twentieth century as a destructive power to haunt men with "l'inquiétante étrangeté" (disquieting strangeness) or what Freud will call "das Unheimlich" (the uncanny), which Freud ties to female genitalia and the mother's body. Consequently, the body of the mother is at stake in repressing but not eliminating the Erinyes. In the same way, Klytemnestra's own life, body, and Furies are the contested objects that must be both repressed and preserved by the Athenian law court in order to found Western society. Klytemnestra's story is, therefore, more than personal or even familial; it underpins the founding of Western culture as a whole. Of all the revisions we have examined, Auffret's is clearest in announcing the cultural weight of Klytemnestra's role.

Auffret insists, however, on also remembering the personal, maternal Clytemnestre. Auffret intersperses lyrical passages in which she imagines Clytemnestre's thoughts as a loving mother who watches her cherished Iphigénie as a young girl. This mother lingers over the details of the radiant appearance of her daughter; she inscribes on her own heart her child's every feeling; she breathes through Iphigénie's soul. Clytemnestre clearly loves this child above all her children as she dreams of a kind of "Sophie's choice" in which she does not hesitate to offer the infant Chrysothémis as a sacrifice in place of Iphigénie. Addressing Iphigénie, Clytemnestre narrates: "I had a horrible dream. Barbarians had laid siege to the palace. They raped, pillaged, abducted. They seized you. Chrysothémis was in my arms, small soft form, poor absent look. I quickly let her go, you wrenched yourself free from your ravishers, I seized you, my arms welded to you. The baby cried. You shivered, I saw your eyes big with terror. I cried: Take the baby, the baby!" (98).

The intensity of Clytemnestre's love and pain is underlined by Auffret's horrific depiction of the violence enacted against her when Agamemnon tears her first child from her breast: "Clytemnestre was at first married to the son of Thyeste, who was named *Tantale,* as his first ancestor. Agamemnon killed Tantale and the children of Clytemnestre, including a son still at her breast, whom he smashed on the ground" (31–32). Mixed among more scholarly passages that discuss the nature of tragedy and quote Kierkegaard and Marx as well as scholars of literature, history, and myth, these lyrical musings draw the reader into Clytemnestre's personal, maternal world. We see her as loving, devoted, attentive, and violently abused before we are asked to understand the violence she herself enacts.

Much like Wolf in her opening of the *Kassandra* narrative, Auffret herself occupies the space and ruins of Mycenae at several points in her text. She is seized by the spirit of the place and experiences what Clytemnestre must have felt long ago (35–37). But Auffret also remains very much in her own time as well: "Peregrination of the other world gathered in this *place* of origin; all the potential brought together in one point. Cinematic effect of a puzzle that builds itself and animates itself. The multiplicity of images converge into a single fluid image. It is at once my time and Time, my memory and Memory which concentrate themselves" (37). This merging of the modern writer with her ancient counterpart, as well as with readers who can feel the same inspiration, allows us to occupy Clytemnestre's consciousness, to understand and sympathize with her lyrical memories as Auffret intersperses them among her analyses. As it does in Wolf's *Kassandra,* such a merging also allows us to understand the implications of Clytemnestre's story for our own times; it facilitates a revision and retelling of her role in Western culture. This amalgamation allows us to reexamine the foundations of the culture that women in the West still occupy. Auffret's narrative helps to create "*Nous,* Clytemnestre."

Perhaps even more than Wolf, Auffret produces a generic hybrid that combines personal musings, narration, scholarly analysis, and lyrical interpolations.[36] Auffret's text defies categorization. Clearly more than an academic treatment, Auffret's text is an imaginative reconstruction of Klytemnestra that goes beyond simply presenting the classical variants to imagine Clytemnestre's emotional response to the killings of her children. Like Wolf, Auffret refuses to bar any area of human experience—whether logical or emotional, analytic or affective—from the pursuit of understanding. Her text includes many possible forms of knowledge, both rational and intuitive. By creating such a generic mix, Auffret undermines canonical and hierarchical categorizations of ways of knowing. Her kaleidoscopic presentation situates her text between academic literary criticism and creative writing. This allows Auffret to contribute to both cultural and personal understanding of Klytemnestra as well as to challenge generic boundaries of all types.

After examining several male authors' treatments of Klytemnestra, in which Electra (who sides strongly with Athena's judgments and with the father) is often the center of consciousness and which inevitably leave out much of the history of hate that fuels Klytemnestra's rage, Auffret wonders how women would read Klytemnestra. Auffret analyzes Cardinal's Clytemnestre to reveal that here, too, children identify with the father and feel they must resist their mother's sorcery. According to Auffret, then, a female author does not guarantee a mother-centered perspective. Auffret seems unaware of Yourcenar's earlier Clytemnestre monologue and of Zeitlin's essay on the *Oresteia*. Either of them might have taken her analysis in a different direction. Had Auffret also been exploring the German or American women writers discussed earlier, she would have seen a more varied treatment of Klytemnestra by women artists. But Auffret also underestimates the multiple embodiments of Klytemnestra in Cardinal's text as well as her complex gender and identity mixing. Cardinal balances a sympathy for the father and mother, for male and female positions, but she also has very much a mother-conscious and mother-centered position.

Looking more deeply into ancient traditions, Auffret explores the Homeric "Hymn to Demeter" as a foundation for Clytemnestre's story. Taking us back to Crete and a matrilinear kin system and matrilocal marriage (which Auffret is careful to distinguish from matriarchy[37]), Auffret stresses the importance of the myth that valorizes the mother and female love, a valorization that Greek tragedy must forget as the Olympian gods of light replace the older gods of night. In this myth, the daughter must be taken from her mother by the husband in order to create new life. To marry the beloved daughter to Hades (and the underworld) perverts this function and prevents the daughter from ever becoming a mother in her turn. In Clytemnestre's case, Iphigénie is "married" to death as well, but this perversion only enables more death in the Trojan War. The mother-daughter bond is torn not to produce new life but to perpetuate death. This represents a violation of both the mother's love and the daughter's role of future mother. According to Auffret, it violates women's most privileged functions, again allowing Auffret to stress the every-woman role of Clytemnestre and the universalization of the violence enacted against her. While contemporary feminists might well question the identification of woman's function with motherhood, finding it a relic of patriarchy, Auffret's point about the universalization of violence aimed at women even on the reproductive front is a compelling one.

To underline this crucial connection of the mother's body to broader sexual issues, Auffret explores the associations the name Clytemnestre calls up. Some of her associations are based on sound rather than etymology—Clytemnestre and clitoris, for example. Auffret does not insist upon these too vehemently, protesting that her Greek is not strong enough to do so, but her stating them inscribes them indelibly in the readers' minds as subliminal associations that override the need for scholarly support. Auffret recalls that first exploring Clytemnestre's world as a child of eleven, she did not consciously think of the connection of Clytemnestre to *kleitoris* or clitoris, but she feels nonetheless that a subconscious intuition links them and creates a productive confusion as a result. Toying with the variant spellings of Klytemnestra/Klytemestra, Auffret suggests a variant of her own, deleting the *s* rather than the *n* to arrive at *mētra,* or womb—and thus ultimately, mother. While she acknowledges that the name is never spelled by the Greeks without the *s,* Auffret insists that they could not have ignored the *mētra* inscribed within Clytemnestre. Given Clytemnestre's choice of (female) child over (male) husband and king, Auffret may well have a point. Exploring the sounds of words, a technique familiar to readers of poetry, thus comes to provide a new insight into Clytemnestre's *nóos.*

Auffret stresses the importance of names (including their sound, alliteration with other words, and etymology) to the Greeks, who multiply and combine names to create a multilayered history of variants that form a complex whole. For the ancient Greeks, names create overlapping layers of legends rather than a simple chronology; thus many interpretations of any event or figure are possible simultaneously. Within Clytemnestre's name, Auffret finds traces of verbs indicating "to remember," "to plot or weave," and reminders of "womb" and "mother." These come together as the mother who remembers and who plots. While Auffret's ruminations differ from those we explored in the scholarship on the classical Klytemnestra, they do capture the essence of the figure she contemplates. Clytemnestre is the mother who remembers the violent wrong done to her and her daughter and who weaves a plot to avenge it.

Having scrutinized Clytemnestre's essence as a central female actor, Auffret turns to the question of whether women also served as audience for Greek tragedy (Wolf assumes they did not). She compares the nineteenth-century restrictive theory that women were excluded from theater to later twentieth-century assumptions that although women could not act on stage (all parts were played by men), they must have been admitted as audience. Since playwrights like Euripides are so intent on presenting the proper behavior of women—usually espoused by women figures themselves[38] (for example, Iphigenia's defense of her self-sacrifice, Electra's speeches on modesty and humility to her offending mother, etc.)—Auffret reasons that women must have been present to receive the instruction. Despite Euripides' moralistic streak, however, Auffret does not see him as the misogynist he is often taken to be—even in his own time. She reminds us that many of the most interesting female figures are Euripides' and that his *Iphigenia in Aulis* presents us with the most sympathetic Klytemnestra we have. I agree. While Euripides has speeches of moral instruction, he also allows some violent female characters such as Medea miraculously to escape from human condemnation, leaving judgments about male and female transgressions to the gods—and to Euripides' audience. Like Brecht (also accused of misogyny), Euripides seems to me to inspire uncomfortable questioning in the audience rather than purging of emotions.

While Auffret may seem sidetracked in her ruminations by inquiring into the status of women as audience, she touches on an issue that becomes crucial. Can tragedy succeed in indoctrinating all the members of the society (male and female) into accepting the dominance of law and male control and the repression of the female, or at least in rendering the female incapable of wielding power that threatens the new social order? If women are present during the *Oresteia,* how convinced are they by Apollo's male usurpation of birth itself? How do they react to the father-birthed Athena? And how are they to understand marriage and its relationship to the sacrifices and sacrificing of women?

This last issue becomes vital for Auffret as she examines the relationship between marriage and sacrifice—particularly in the case of Iphigenia in Euripides' *Iphigenia in Aulis.* For Auffret, this play acts out the myths and rites of marriage but with a twist. The young bride who normally sacrifices to Artemis to insure a good marriage is instead herself sacrificed to Artemis. As both the German Reinig and the Italian Maraini do in their modernized revisions, Auffret investigates the identification of marriage with sacrifice and violence in the classical tradition. When Maraini's Agamenonne condemns Ifigenia to marriage, he slays her as surely as his classical counterpart did. Reinig strongly agrees in her depiction of women in marriage. Auffret examines this violent conjunction of marriage and death in the classical texts themselves.

Auffret provides a powerful reading of Iphigénie's sacrifice as a ritual necessary to restore patriarchal right by reasserting the legal claims of marriage. Iphigénie must die so that Helen can be returned to Greece and to her husband. But we might well ask, as Clytemnestre herself does, why Helen's daughter, Hermione, is not required as the sacrifice for Helen's transgressions. Helen will become divine, of course, and must be reconciled to Greece later. But Auffret argues that Iphigénie is chosen to bring to a head the conflict between Mother Right and Father Right. Iphigénie must die so her mother Clytemnestra can be made to submit to patriarchal needs and rules. Unlike her twin, Helen, who chooses her husband—who must then come to live in her land and who becomes king of Sparta only by virtue of possessing Helen—Clytemnestre is forced to marry Agamemnon. She must go to live in his land and by his (patriarchal) rules. That is, Clytemnestre must be forcibly moved from a mother-centered power base to a patriarchal one, from daughter of Leda to wife of Agamemnon. Clytemnestre's marriage to Agamemnon represents that collision between a world of Mother Right and inheriting of the female name and a world of Father Right and inheriting of the male name—the daughters of Leda versus the House of Atreus. Sacrificing the firstborn daughter, Iphigénie, for the glory of patriarchy and the restoration of the rights of the husband makes clear who is destined to win the conflict.

When Agamemnon is no longer present to enforce his patriarchal prerogatives, Clytemnestre chooses her own lover, Egisthe, who lives in her palace. She reverts to the system from which she came, she becomes again the "daughter of Leda." Clearly, Clytemnestre represents a matrilineal system that must be eliminated to preserve patriarchy. Auffret demonstrates that patriarchal marriage is based on conquest and control of the woman and of her offspring, on making her submit to male inheritance and law. Clytemnestre exemplifies the dangerous "enemy within" that represents both a threat to society and, as the mother figure, a threat to male dominance. Killing her denies maternal power and maternal legal rights.

Clytemnestre's tragedy thus plays out a battle of the sexes as well as a battle of mother-centered versus father-centered cultures and myths. According to Auffret, Oreste's personal guilt over slaying his mother becomes social in the *Oresteia*. His story becomes a new social myth that cures his personal torment.[39] Oreste's killing of the mother also slays the female maternal principle, disposing of the intractable female in favor of benevolent females who protect the male social order of Athenian citizenship. Auffret points out that Oreste is not alone among Clytemnestre's children in supporting the patriarchal order. Electre passionately sides with her father and his power structure, but so, ironically, does Iphigénie, who accepts her role as virgin sacrifice in order to promote the patriarchal project. These two daughters, then, are closer than one might guess. Auffret suggests that Electre's almost universally depicted hysteria may stem from her close identification with her sacrificed sister. Electre dies as Iphigénie, the mother's child, in order to be reborn as her father's daughter. Enacting Freud's model of first identification with the mother and later alignment with the father, Electre's personal story, like her brother's, figures larger psychological, social, and cultural evolution.

In closing her study, Auffret dwells on how and when myths die and are reborn. When they become powerful enough to speak to a new generation, ancient stories find new shapes and new tellers. Clearly, Auffret's own study, as well as the several Klytemnestras of the 1980s whom we have examined, marks this late decade of the twentieth century as a time when the issues at stake in Klytemnestra's story speak most urgently. The works of women writers of the late twentieth century become a site of rebirth for a myth that figures crucially in defining the distribution of social and cultural power at the roots of Western culture. Klytemnestra is reborn in the 1980s, but, as Auffret correctly predicts, her two daughters will find new life in the 1990s. We will follow the remaining traces of Klytemnestra herself in the 1990s in the next chapter.

A Community Effort: *The Fabulous Furies reVue*

In 1988[40] at the University of Texas at Dallas, Judith Piper, a professor of art and performance, and her colleague Nancy Tuana,[41] a professor of historical studies, in collaboration with a number of their students (both male and female) conceived and presented a performance work that recasts Aeschylus's *Oresteia* in the guise of American popular culture of the 1950s.[42] That decade shares with the ancient story a focus on the plight of women when their men return from war. The stated intention of the creators of this performance piece was to "disrupt and displace our inherited discourses of aesthetic, historical and philosophical understanding"[43] in order to make possible new understandings of Western cultural tradition. The piece grew out of a graduate seminar on feminist epistemologies, and it enabled students to use the creative process to test and extend the theories they had explored.

Using the technique of collage (including film and television tapes running in the background of many scenes) and focusing on issues of style in clothes, home, and culture, *The Fabulous Furies reVue* explores a number of male and female characters, including Athena, Clytemnaestra, Agamemnon, and Zeus. The piece is made up of loosely related units that form a commentary on ancient culture, the 1950s, and the late 1980s. This structure allows the collaborators to explore aspects of culture by appropriating fragments of texts and songs from a wide variety of sources. At times, they quote directly from Aeschylus's *Oresteia,* but within their newly created context, Aeschylus's words take on different meanings—often more ominous for women. (*The Fabulous Furies reVue* shares this technique with Reinig, Maraini, and Auffret, among others.) This 1988 revision thus introduces conflicting voices that enlist the classical material in a resolutely dialogic new format. Alongside Aeschylus, Piper and her students place sections of a bowler's manual to describe Zeus in a mock-heroic posture that undercuts both the idea of the hero and the image of Zeus's sexual prowess. By juxtaposing texts from such different realms, the fabulous "reVue" creates a running critique in which each part of modern and ancient culture comments on the other. The roles of women in this new assembly are pointedly highlighted.

Athena, for example, like her ancient counterpart, clearly aligns herself with patriarchy and the male order, but she also reveals male secrets. In both a younger and a more mature persona, Athena examines the high heel as a complex symbol that helps to fetishize women. Young Athena points out: "the support for the foot is drastically reduced so that the ankle and the whole leg adopt a wobbling or quivering or teetering action. However, these imbalances are positive gestures—they appeal to a supporting arm, to the promise of imminent fall, to the likelihood of surrender. The high-heeled woman, set to action, becomes a tantalizing object of the chase" (Piper script, "The Fetish," 10).[44] The more mature Athena persona then engages the younger in discussion:

> She is both aggressive and submissive, both predator and prey. The stiletto heel (Vogue 1952) accomplishes this aim. A thin, long, heel, reinforced with a steel core.
>
> YOUNG ATHENA: It is sometimes called by other names—the saber, the spike, the rapier. It is known that men are attracted to the stiletto. I know, for when I wear a 5–inch pair, delicate and refined, he is captured by the look. Is it because these peculiar shackles are self-imposed? I wonder.
>
> ATHENA: Or is it the fantasy of physical subjection, the possibility that his body may be trodden upon by the goddess before whom he secretly wishes to abase himself?
>
> YOUNG ATHENA: It is no wonder that smart women buy the highest and slenderest stiletto.
>
> ATHENA: I give you the illusion of woman. You come here to be satisfied. (Piper script, "The Fetish," 10–11)

Piper and her students here reveal the multilayered problem of style and the fetishization of women that the 1950s and 1980s share. Piper's Athenas are complicit with the male but also revealing to the female. As Piper puts it, "Athena is both co-opter and spy, androcentric and other" (Piper, "(Re)-Dressing the Canon," 7). This 1980s revision creates a multivalent female symbol that makes us reconsider both Athena's position and that of late-twentieth-century women in the West.

Other sections of *The Fabulous Furies reVue* explore stereotypes of women's roles, such as the courtesan, daddy's girl, wife/secretary, and femme fatale. The performance also investigates women's invisibility in a patriarchal culture. Ironically reminding the viewer of the *reVue*'s own genesis as a revision of Klytemnestra's fate, an invisible voice suggests the status of women in drama and society: "You know, it's always necessary for the women to die before the play begins. That's right, it's only when she has disappeared that the curtain can go up, that the story can begin" (Piper script, "Detective," 1). This comment reminds us also of the necessary suppression of the female, embodied in the Furies, in order for Western democratic culture to begin.

The invisible status of women explored in this performance through the concept of style and male projections of the perfect woman from the 1950s onward also makes us think back to the initial creation of that invisibility at the founding moment of Western culture. This brings us to the Furies of the piece's title. The chorus of Furies occupies the stage for the entire performance; each carries a colorfully painted cutout of a well-decorated 1950s home. Early on, they dance with cutouts of home appliances, emphasizing the forced return of women from the work world to the home environment after World War II. But the issue of women and the home is of ongoing concern for women throughout history. Revolting against their status as home objects, the 1980s Furies reappropriate their ancient voices of anger and rage "stolen from them in the *Oresteia*" (Piper, "(Re)Dressing the Canon," 18). But Athena, reciting Aeschylus's lines from the *Eumenides,* persuades the Furies to relinquish their anger and have dominion over the prosperity of households. All the conveniences of the well-furnished home will be at their command. The late-twentieth-century Furies are again lured into the enclosed repressed space that is the perfect household. To support the patriarchal order, the female is enticed once again from the public to the private space.

The performance lays bare the violence against women who inhabit that perfect home by staging Zeus's swallowing of Athena's mother, Metis—an episode avoided by Aeschylus. The famous birth of Athena from her father's head is accompanied in this staging by Apollo's speech from the *Eumenides,* which claims that the mother is no parent, that only "he who mounts" can claim parenthood. Athena herself becomes proof of this claim. Zeus's violence against women is further emphasized by performers recalling his many rapes (of Europa, Asterie, and Leda, among others). Athena's alignment with her father makes her complicit in this violence against women. But Athena's own position as child of her father also puts her in the way of secret violence. As performers echo the line, "From the gods who sit in grandeur, grace comes somehow violent," an elder woman reads from a child's storybook. We think of the child Athena with her father, Zeus. The story, however, turns out to be a scene in which the father makes his four-year-old daughter masturbate him and then warns her not to tell her mother. This view of Athena as female victim gives her loyalty to her father a new twist.

The concentration of violence against women finally calls onto stage the sisters, Helen and Clytemnaestra. In this version of the story, Clytemnaestra, who studies martial arts despite the fact that it may give her muscles, discovers that her often-married sister, Helen, is being beaten by her current husband. Clytemnaestra sees this violence as reducing her sister to muteness and robbing her of her self. Clytemnaestra, however, grows in strength. She muses that, "maybe she [Helen] made a connection between those things, and hoped her lost self was going into me" (Piper script, "Radtke-Tong," 3). Clytemnaestra's growing strength allows her to exert violence in turn when the battering husband threatens the sisters. (The husband must now, according to the ancient story, be Agamemnon rather than Helen's husband, Menelaus—but perhaps the play's point is that it could be any husband.) In a narrative of extreme violence, Clytemnaestra, in order to save her sister, chokes her husband despite having her own ribs broken in the fray.

This scene revises the original story in a number of ways. Clytemnaestra here kills not to avenge a dead daughter but to protect a living sister. Female solidarity is reintroduced into Clytemnaestra's world. Her strength makes her fearless; her determination saves her and her sister's lives. However, the female can still be saved only by the violent elimination of the male. The binary oppositions between male and female are still operative in the 1988 revision of the ancient tale and in the 1950s. Women haven't escaped from an old order or conceived of a new one. Like the other 1980s texts, the *reVue* is a piercing critique of the gender order that still exists in Western culture. The piece is a protest that demonstrates that women can assemble bits of Western cultural traditions from many historical periods, but the collage we create still reveals the same gender issues, the same violence inherent in them. Clytemnaestra is still forced to exert violence to defend herself and the female.

In another binary reversal of power, Clytemnaestra becomes a martial arts instructor taking the apprentice Agamemnon through his exercises. Again, the audience realizes that Clytemnaestra can only survive and exert her own will if she becomes a master of brutality. This scene runs simultaneously with the young Athena struggling to get into her first girdle and high heels for the prom. This attempt to conform represents the only other way to survive and fit into the male order. Neither option seems very appealing to those in the audience caught between tragedy and comedy. Women can either be complicit in perpetuating violence or they can be complicit in their own physical deformity and fetishization.

The *reVue* strongly implies that history is a record of perpetually repeated violence that helps to repress or destroy women but that also deforms and devastates men. Agamemnon in this script confronts his own masculine and feminine self. Through Agamemnon, heroism is revealed to be posturing that conceals a different war. Piper suggests, "the war the hero wages is a war against the self as hero. The fear of woman is expressed as the fear of self" (Piper, "(Re)Dressing the Canon," 32). The male, too, is torn apart by his need to suppress the feminine; this Agamemnon ends in self-annihilation. Binary gender oppositions that Western culture has constructed do neither sex much good.

As the 1980s end, *The Fabulous Furies reVue* issues a final critical protest that implies that the world of women has not progressed as far as we might have hoped since the days of the classical Klytemnestra. The 1950s and the 1980s bear eerie and striking resemblances to the social issues explored in the *Ores-*

teia. This postmodern reinscription of various particles of Western history and culture within a new performance piece forces us to see different meanings inherent in those fragments. The collage of high and low cultural artifacts creates new juxtapositions and new contexts, which relativize cultural assumptions and reinforce a dialogic view of the twentieth-century Western world and its gender hierarchies. This *reVue* helps us to understand and criticize the male-created female self as stylized object; it forces us to contemplate how we might generate a new sense of the female. It also reinstates Clytemnaestra as a powerful female presence but one who (like Wolf's figure) is trapped in a cycle of violence she seems unable to escape. In the 1990s her escape may again render her invisible, as the next chapters will reveal.

Comparisons and Contrasts

Like their colleagues earlier in the 1980s, Wolf, Cardinal, Auffret, and the *re-Vue* all depict the repressive nature of marriage for women—but Wolf and Cardinal also suggest other possibilities. The *Fabulous Furies reVue* is most critical in its depiction of marriage as a trap that catches women with the bait of the happy home and a comfortably applianced personal space. Piper, Tuana, and their students show women's status as diminished by the happy housewife role that men seduce them into. They reveal the fetishized nature of men's vision of women, and they focus on the battering husband from whom Clytemnaestra must defend herself and her sisters. Auffret also explores the repressive nature of marriage by examining Klytemnestra's punishment as the transgressive wife as well as Iphigenia's ritual sacrifice to restore patriarchal rights and the legal claims of marriage. In Auffret's version of the story, marriage is the central issue at stake. Iphigénie's murder brings the conflict between Mother Right and Father Right to its conclusion. It forces Clytemnestre to choose blood over legal arrangements, child over marriage. And it allows society to punish her for her choice, thus instating the rule of law in Western culture.

Both Wolf and Cardinal have a more varied view of marriage. Although Wolf's Kassandra understands that Klytaimnestra must slay her abusive and cowardly husband, she has also seen other examples of marriage. In the beginning, Kassandra's own parents, Hekuba and Priam, share an equality in marriage. They embody—if only briefly—a gender balance in the family. Their tranquility is admittedly destroyed by the relentless martial history of Western civilization, but it is presented as a utopian possibility. Kassandra and Aeneas's love also presents an alternate model based on equality and mutual caring. Aeneas accepts Kassandra's twin children as his own. He creates a family of choice rather than of blood. This unifying bond based on love rather than law provides a new basis for "marriage" and family.

Cardinal depicts a number of marriages in which women are repressed or diminished, including Clytemnestre's, Mimi's, and the narrator's own. But the narrator resists seeing this as the ineluctable fate of women in marriage. She opposes her mother's attempt to make her hate men and the submissive state of women in marriage. She also resists Clytemnestre's demand that she believe in the justice of punishing transgressive wives by defamation and death. Even though the narrator's own marriage ends with her husband's leaving and even though we do not see a "happy marriage" in the text itself, Cardinal nonetheless implies that there are other options for women. There is no outline of what those options may be, but they do imply women not trapped by repressive marriages.

While abortion does not surface in these later revisions, the threat of losing one's children does. Auffret focuses on Clytemnestre's real loss of Iphigénie to Agamemnon's patriarchal knife. But she also depicts a Clytemnestre whose maternal consciousness is haunted by the threat of that loss. Auffret's Clytemnestre can envision sacrificing her infant female, Chrysothémis, to save her firstborn daughter, Iphigénie. But this dream-sacrifice is still exacted by brutalizing males, who keep demanding the destruction of female children.

However, children in texts by Wolf and Cardinal are lost in very different ways from those in the other revisionary texts. Cardinal's narrator almost loses her two children to a motorcycle accident. The narrator feels responsible since her success allows her to buy the nearly fatal machine. But she also argues that this "accident" is a punishment for her insisting on being independent and creative. Like Klytemnestra, the narrator is "acting like a man" and must suffer the consequences. Patriarchy is still demanding child sacrifice, but it does so much more indirectly than in the other texts. Mimi's loss of Odette is also indirect. Her husband's tuberculosis infects the child, but he himself is infected because of the war.

Wolf's Kassandra also loses her twins to the struggle for political control of Mycenae—but she loses them to Klytaimnestra! In this case, Klytaimnestra is forced by the logic of political control to kill both Kassandra and her offspring. Wolf's Klytaimnestra has been pushed even further in "acting like a man"—and acting like a male ruler. Klytaimnestra's sense of motherhood is swamped by her need to control a patriarchal society. Her slaying of Kassandra's twins undermines the justification for her revenge against Agamemnon. Maternal love does not extend to the children of others. In the end, Wolf's Klytaimnestra, like Bogen's and Brückner's, is not a female to be emulated, but she does demonstrate how patriarchal political logic can lead women to destroy other women and children.

Tellingly, the motif of castration, so prevalent in the earlier texts, disappears in the later 1980s, or at least it becomes sublimated. Cardinal's narrator may "castrate" her husband by earning more than he does and by being more famous, but she does not imagine castrating him literally. In fact, Cardinal's narrator herself experiences male sexuality when she merges with her adolescent father to experience his first sexual encounters. Rather than trying to destroy an essentialist symbol of the male, Wolf and Cardinal attempt to understand the male and to find the positive in both genders. Wolf's Aeneas and Anchises as well as Cardinal's Jean-Maurice are loving males who suffer under the pressures of patriarchy as much as the women.

Violence, however, remains central to the concerns of all the revisionary texts. *The Fabulous Furies reVue* depicts many scenes of violence—both against and by women. Its Clytemnaestra has learned martial arts and can take Agamemnon in a physical fight. She is not so physically and psychologically abused as Reinig's or Maraini's modern figures are. She is, however, still caught in the binary oppositions that pit her against the male and the patriarchal order. Women in this piece have learned to use violence more efficiently, but that they must still fight remains the problem. While this performance creates brief gender role reversals, it ends in a repression (or consumer-oriented social buy-off) of the Furies and the female principles they represent. Violence perpetually recurs in slightly varying patterns; Clytemnaestra is still caught in the web she helps to weave. *Fabulous Furies reVue* reinscribes violence in new postmodern fragments that form an intense critique, but it does not escape the cycle. Auffret also remembers violent moments—both inscribed in ancient texts and imagined by Auffret's narrator. Auffret insightfully connects these moments to larger social, psychological, and cultural issues. But neither the *Fabulous Furies reVue* nor Auffret's text offers a way to escape the cycle.

Like Reinig, Wolf selects contemporary events against which to weigh the violence in Klytemnestra's and Kassandra's story. In the Kassandra essays, Wolf contemplates being a European woman in the no-man's-land where East and West dream of fighting a "limited" nuclear war. She reflects on the assassination attempt on Ronald Reagan by a delusional young man trying to impress an actress and on conflicts in the Middle East. She examines pictures of Americans liberating Dachau and films of Hiroshima. In short, Wolf recalls all of the nonheroic aspects of the Western military tradition, of institutionalized male violence. Her Kassandra struggles against that heroic code; she values human beings (male and female) more than propaganda and political rhetoric. For a brief moment, she finds an alternate society in the caves outside Troy, but these people vanish into history as they follow Aeneas to Rome to found a new "heroic" culture. Kassandra understands the violence Klytaimnestra will have to wield in order to avenge her daughter and retain political power. But that same violence ends Kassandra's life and her vision of an alternative female narrative in history. Wolf, who passionately advocates an antiwar stance, understands that violence will not free women—or men. Her critique of both false "heroic" roles and violence is rigorous. She can imagine an alternative gender-neutral nonviolent world, but she must acknowledge that history has not produced it. Kassandra goes to her death knowing that Klytaimnestra will soon go to her own. Violence does not save either woman.

Violence in Cardinal's text is often more gratuitous than in Wolf's. Accident nearly takes the narrator's children; disease takes her sister and father. Clytemnestre does exert violence, and she feels she must be violently punished for doing so. In the end, Cardinal's narrator comprehends that she must step outside the cycle of violence in order to find any new reality. The violence of the past can be contained and changed in works of art—both the embroidery and the literary text—into something new. It can be pushed in a new direction that might allow the kind of reconciliation that Graham envisioned at the beginning of this study.

One other similarity links the works of Wolf, Cardinal, Auffret, and Piper and Tuana. All of them use the strategy of disrupting boundaries of all kinds—generic as well as cultural. Auffret and Cardinal both represent a multicultural and transnational experience. Cardinal's novel is a geographic as well as temporal hybrid. Its characters move between France and Algeria as well as between the 1980s and ancient Greece to create a culturally relativized point of view. Cardinal, a Canadian citizen who was raised in Algeria and France and who translated Euripides' *Medea,* sees herself as "Mediterranean" in a broad sense (as does her first-person woman narrator in *Le passé empiété*). Auffret, a campaigner on women's issues in Africa, crosses generic and temporal as well as national boundaries in her communal vision of Klytemnestra. Her text is a hybrid composed of lyric, essay, and diary. Like Auffret, Wolf refuses to observe traditonal genre divisions in her "Frankfurter Lectures." She includes travel journal, diary, and letters with her narrative. And, like Cardinal, she moves between modern and ancient times and fuses the consciousness of her modern narrator and her ancient Kassandra. Finally, the *Fabulous Furies reVue* melds high and low rhetoric and culture, mixes drama, dance, and film techniques, and transgresses temporal boundaries of all kinds to move among ancient times, the 1950s, and the 1980s.

All of these transgressions of spatial, temporal, and genre boundaries allow the women writers to reject hierarchy of all kinds. They draw no distinctions between high and low culture (between "high art" and embroidery, for example, or between speeches from Aeschylus and bowling manuals). This enables them to reject the relegation of genres in which women have traditionally been active (diary, letters, travel writing) to the category of "trivial literature." These women insist on merging "women's art" and "women's writing" with classical tragedy. Genre disruption itself becomes an act of rebellion against a patriarchal, hierarchical order inscribed in literary culture in the West. The symbolic act of destroying hierarchical arrangements for genre carry over to a similar dismantling of gender hierarchies.

Like Reinig, Cardinal crosses gender boundaries to purposefully confuse gender roles in her text, thus making the battle of the sexes a more vexed issue. By the time she completes her narrative, we have several Klytemnestras and Agamemnons; Cardinal has many characters, particularly the unnamed female narrator, experience multiple ancient roles. This constant migration of identities functions to shift our concern from gender wars to complex individual psychologies and experiences. After conversing with the ancient Clytemnestre in her dreams, Cardinal's narrator finally turns away from the Greek queen and her family in order to seek a new world in which women would not be constantly combating an inescapably submissive role, a world in which women could find a flexible self always in process. Cardinal's female creative artist seeks ultimately to weave a new narrative (perhaps the one Wolf's Kassandra could not create) not constrained by past types—either personal or cultural—or by gender roles and hierarchies. We do not see these new works within the borders of Cardinal's novel, but at least her narrator can envision the possibility of creating them.

Like Wolf merging consciousnesses with her Kassandra, both Cardinal (through her narrator) and Auffret (through her own occupying of the ancient figure's mind even more extensively than in Wolf's *Kassandra*) converse directly with the classical Klytemnestra. They both seek to interrogate the classical figure, to reexperience and understand those factors in Klytemnestra's story that shape her and continue to influence women through generations. Auffret looks to women writers such as Maraini to transpose Klytemnestra's experiences from their ancient setting to the late twentieth century. And Maraini does precisely this. It is really Cardinal, however, who moves beyond what Auffret envisions. Cardinal's narrator seeks to stabilize the story of Klytemnestra, to fix it in embroidery so that she may move into a future differently imagined than the past. She must retrieve the past, reappropriate it so that she can stitch it into place in order to move on. This movement made by Cardinal's embroideress may be the most optimistic moment in any of the 1980s texts. Unlike the shrill lament that closes Maraini's work or the wistful hope of Auffret's, Cardinal's ending takes us beyond the ancient archetype to create at least the beginnings of a less submissive, more independent, and assertive identity.

Given the extensive genre disruption of these texts, we can see how thoroughly they relativize many cultural assumptions and call into question the underlying principles of Western art and culture. The many pieces of the *reVue,* the many consciousnesses in Cardinal's novel, the many genres of Auffret and Wolf, all contribute to a cacophony of voices that leave few social or cultural institutions unquestioned. In *Le passé empiété* the dialogue of many female voices produces for Cardinal a new conversation among women who will live a new future. By challenging the definitions and interpretations of crucial female figures, they will create a new reality and a new narrative. This dialogization relativizes and de-privileges the patriarchal version of Klytemnestra's story as well as the gender prescriptions inherent in it. These women writers make us aware of competing definitions in Western cultural assumptions. They thus escape the roles of their own mothers as well as of the symbolic mothers of Western culture.

Notes

1. Wolf recounts those years in her novel *Kindheitsmuster* (1976; *A Model Childhood,* 1980). See Kuhn's *Christa Wolf's Utopian Vision* for an analysis of Wolf's life and works up to 1988.

2. For example, see *Nachdenken über Christa T.* (1968; *The Quest for Christa T.,* 1970).

3. Witness, for example, her novella, *Störfall* (1987; *Accident: A Day's News,* 1989), about the Chernobyl nuclear accident.

4. Wolf recounts this period in her short piece *Was bleibt* (1990; *What Remains and Other Stories,* 1993). See Stephan's *Christa Wolf* for a discussion of Wolf's life and work in the late 1980s and early 1990s. For an analysis of Wolf's literary and political reputation after the fall of the Berlin Wall in 1989, see Mittman and Kuhn, "Rewriting GDR History."

5. "Voraussetzungen einer Erzählung: Kassandra" (Conditions of a Narrative) and the Kassandra narrative itself were published as a single volume in East Germany in 1983. When marketed in West Germany, the narrative was sold separately as an expensive hardback. Van Heurck's 1984 English translation rejoins essays and narrative under the title *Cassandra* but ironically places the "Voraussetzungen einer Erzählung" (which implies *Pre-*suppositions of a Narrative) after the narrative.

The Luchterhand *Voraussetzungen einer Erzählung: Kassandra* ends with a bibliography (156–60) that includes a list of ancient literature in German translation as well as a list of secondary literature and a brief list of German-speaking authors cited (including

Ingeborg Bachmann, Annette von Droste-Hülshoff, Marie Luise Fleißer, Goethe, Sarah Kirsch, Robert Musil, and Schiller). Unfortunately, this list, which lends insight into texts that Wolf consulted, does not appear in the English version.

6. The 1980s and 1990s are rich in revisions of classical materials by German-speaking writers (both male and female), particularly in Austria. See, for example, Schrott, *Finis terrae;* Ransmayr, *Die letzte Welt;* Köhlmeier, *Telemach* and *Kalypso;* and Merkel, *Odysseus und Penelope: Eine ganz gewöhnliche Ehe.* A special issue of *Modern Austrian Literature* (vol. 31, nos. 3–4) treats several of these authors.

7. This is not unprecedented, of course, since Euripides also provides a view from the perspective of the defeated women (including Kassandra) in his *Trojan Women.*

8. Kuhn sees this focus as part of Wolf's transition from Marxism to feminism.

9. For more extended discussions in English of Wolf and her relationship to "women's writing," see Love; Pickle; and Komar, "The Communal Self" and "Paradigm Change." Kuhn's *Christa Wolf's Utopian Vision* is currently the only full-length study of Wolf in English.

For more extended discussions in German of Wolf and her relationship to "women's writing," see Emmerich; Lennox; Stephan; Fehervary; Hilzinger; Adams; Cramer; Jurgensen; McPherson; Sprigath; and Meyer-Gosau.

10. Kassandra is almost totally absent from *The Iliad,* for example. She is mentioned only twice: once as a promised wife to be given in return for military service [*Iliad* 13, 363–68] and once when she summons the Trojans to mourn for Hektor's returning corpse [*Iliad* 24, 699–708]. See Homer, *The Iliad,* trans. Richmond Lattimore (1951), 281, 493–94.

11. Wagner (87) notes that Lycophron's *Alexandra* also gives Cassandra center stage in a long narrative monologue. Lycophron's text is notoriously obscure and complex, with passages referring to the glories of Rome that cast doubt as to the authorship and date of the poem. Although Wolf does not refer to Lycophron or the *Alexandra* directly in her *Literaturnachweise* (list of reference literature) at the close of *Voraussetzungen einer Erzählung: Kassandra,* it is possible that she may have known the text.

For an extended discussion of the figure of Cassandra in classical literature, see also Davreux and Jentgens.

12. For a thorough and insightful discussion of Achilles' progression through various classical texts, see King.

13. In their astute and moving introductory essay to *The Oresteia,* Fagles and Stanford argue that a balance between male and female, the Olympian gods and the Furies, is achieved to produce a new Athenian democracy built on law (1–99). While I would prefer their reading, the more feminist reading informs Wolf's text. And even in the *Oresteia,* I must admit that the female, though indispensable, does not seem to me to exist on equal footing with the male.

14. This is a one-woman play that Pearson began performing in 1989. Klytemnestra does not actually have her own monologue here (as she does in Brückner and Yourcenar), rather she is discussed within the monologue "Io, the Greek," 46–49.

15. While it is clear in Aeschylus's *Oresteia* that Kassandra finds Klytemnestra and her actions horrifying (ll. 1241–46 of Fagles's *Agamemnon* translation, in which Kassandra calls Klytemnestra a "sea-witch," "viper," "monster of Greece," and "raging mother of death"), Klytemnestra's feelings are masked in her multivalent language. She certainly invites Kas-

sandra to her own sacrificial altar where Klytemnestra herself has prepared for the sacrifice. Klytemnestra, however, seems only to advise Kassandra to bend to her fate; she does not accuse her directly of any evil or demonstrate an effusive hate (see *Agamemnon* ll. 1032–68).

16. Fagles's *Oresteia* translation makes this point clear to English readers, 142. Goldhill's discussion of Klytemnestra's multivalent use of language underscores the same point.

17. Kybele and her worship would eventually follow Aeneas to Rome. Stone points out: "The discovery of several tablets . . . in 1608 A.D., by workmen repairing St. Peter's Church, raises the possibility that the Kybele temple was not far from, possibly beneath, where the Basilica of St. Peter's stands today" (*Ancient Mirrors*, 186). If Wolf's matriarchal society centered around Kybele survived the trip to Rome with Aeneas, it would eventually be overrun by the later Christian tradition.

Wolf's use of the names and details of the age of matriarchal myth are largely accurate. Her use of "Myrine" for one of the Amazons, for example, reflects the Amazon sisters/queens Myrina and Mitylene, who engineered a series of conquests. See Stone, *Ancient Mirrors*, 186.

18. For an analysis of the steps in Kassandra's progress toward self-knowledge, see Pickle, "Scratching Away the Male Tradition."

19. Herrmann discusses the use of the letter as a literary form and its dialogic implications for women. She comments specifically on Wolf's *Cassandra* on 50–54.

20. Vogelsang's "Killa's Tertium" discusses Wolf's attempt to develop a nonbinary, nonhierarchical form of narration that defies genre definition.

21. See Robinson, "Treason Our Text," and Baym for two examples among many of feminist analyses of genre hierarchies and how they display gender bias. Ironically, in "Canon Fathers and Myth Universe," Robinson suggests that some traditional stories do not appeal to women, who feel like outsiders with regard to them: "Women writers, for instance, do not compulsively retell the history of the Trojan War and its aftermath, not even adapting the myth to fit female conditions" (29). Writing in the mid-1980s, Robinson may not have been aware that precisely this women's retelling—centered on Klytemnestra—was taking place with great intensity.

22. See Porter, "Resisting Aesthetics."

23. Gilpin sees Klytaimnestra as akin to Aeneas (353–54), but I think her alignment with the female characters is more compelling.

24. For a more detailed biography of Cardinal, see Hall, *Marie Cardinal*. For a discussion of "Roots and Alienation" in Cardinal's work, see Cairns.

25. For a broader discussion of the use of autobiographical material in Cardinal's work, see Hall, "'*She* is more than *I*,'" and Lionnet.

26. In 1972 Cardinal published *La clé sur la porte* (1972; The Key in the Door); in 1973 she collaborated with activist Gisèle Halimi in writing *La cause des femmes* (*The Right to Choose*, 1977) and in 1976 with Annie Leclerc in the volume *Autrement dit* (*In Other Words*, 1995).

27. For more on Cardinal's depiction of men, see Cairns, "Passion and Paranoia."

28. Weaving might also call to mind Klytemnestra's foil Penelope, but the two problematic children and the husband removed by a powerful wife in Cardinal's text is closer to Klytemnestra. Weaving also figures prominently in Maraini's text; however, it is linked not to freedom but to the fact that women and their labor are owned by the husband.

29. The discussion of the relationship to the mother is a lively one in Cardinal criticism. See Haigh; Roch; Le Clézio; and Elliot. See also Powrie on the womb as metaphor and Minh-ha, "L'innécriture," on problems of gender in language in Cardinal.

30. For a discussion of female creative practice and the use of weaving, knitting, and embroidery to figure the narrative act, see Durham, *Contexture,* particularly 49–56.

31. The French edition ends with a bibliography (similar to that appended to Wolf's *Voraussetzungen einer Erzählung: Kassandra*), which includes French translations of Greek texts as well as a number of modern texts (including some by Goethe and O'Neill among others) and a list of films and secondary materials.

32. *Views of Clytemnestra, Ancient and Modern* (1990) is an enlightening collection of essays. The volume focuses primarily on male renderings of Klytemnestra's story—both classical texts and modern revivals. While actors' dramatic interpretations of Klytemnestra are discussed, only Freiert discusses a female revision of the story as a whole, Graham's ballet.

33. See her volume *Mélanippe la philosophe* (1988; Mélanippe the [Female] Philosopher).

34. See her editions of *Traité de la morale et de la politique, 1693: La liberté* (Treatise on Morality and Politics, 1693: Liberty) and *Du célibat volontaire, ou, La vie sans engagement, 1700* (Voluntary Celibacy; or, Life without Engagement, 1700).

35. Auffret acknowledges four eponymous tragedies by lesser-known authors between 1806 and 1822 in France. These texts show a brief shift of opinion in favor of Clytemnestre, but they also insist on showing her as repentant and seduced by an evil Egisthe. Thus Clytemnestre is acceptable if she is depicted as weak and given to the flesh and sensation—as women are wont to be. These authors also focus on the love triangle pitting lover against husband rather than on the battle between female and male rights. Since these Clytemnestres are nicer women, Orestes must kill his mother either by accident or by denying her motherhood as his classical counterpart does.

36. Auffret's *Mélanippe la philosophe* uses a similar genre mixture; this "trilogy" is composed of a scholarly essay on the origins of philosophy, a translation (with commentary) of fragments of Euripides, and a fictional work.

37. Auffret explains that matriarchy implies female political control and parallels patriarchy. She is indicating rather the institution of the "droit maternel" (maternal rights), which concerns the organization of the family in a society that remains politically controlled by men. Women are mediatrixes of power and wealth but do not themselves possess them. Women's role in producing children is acknowledged in a valorization not of women generally but of the mother. See Auffret, *Nous, Clytemnestre,* 53 n. I.

38. We must also keep in mind in this already baroque line of reasoning that the female figures were all played by men in women's clothing. A female character, played by a man, lectures to women in female monologues composed by a male playwright.

39. We must acknowlege that he is not entirely cured, however, since he is depicted in other tragedies (such as Euripides' *Iphigenia in Tauris*) as still haunted by the Furies even after his acquittal. Slaying one's mother is not easily expiated even—or perhaps especially—when it is necessary to found a new social order. The internalized Furies continue to inhabit twentieth-century versions of Orestes.

40. There is one other intervening Western European piece, Ragué i Arias's 1987 play *Clitemnestra.* Since the play is written in Catalan (to which I do not have access) and has

not been either staged or published in any other language, I have not treated it here. See Cavallaro's dissertation for an extensive discussion of this play.

41. Tuana is currently a professor at Pennsylvania State University's philosophy department; she also directs the Rock Ethics Institute. She is researching the relationship between attitudes toward women's sexuality and gender politics.

42. I obtained a copy of the script from Piper, who was kind enough also to send her videotape of the production. Page references are to the script, which remains unpublished. The pagination is by section, so the numbers do not run consecutively but rather repeat in each section.

43. Quoted from a paper by Piper, "(Re)Dressing the Canon," proposed to the American Comparative Literature Association for its national conference in 1990.

44. The script does not make clear that these lines are an interchange between a younger and an older Athena, but the videotape implies this dialogue.

4. The Fate of Klytemnestra in the 1990s: Upstaged by Her Daughters

Following Klytemnestra into the last decade of the twentieth century, we are faced with a curious fact: the House of Atreus became big business in the late 1990s. After early development at the Donmar Warehouse in London and a 1998 run at the McCarter Theater in Princeton, New Jersey, Frank McGuinness's adaptation of Sophocles' *Electra* under the direction of David Leveaux ran successfully on Broadway and was nominated for several Tony Awards (including a nomination for Zoe Wannamaker as Electra). The two main female roles, Electra (played by Wannamaker), and Clytemnestra (played by Claire Bloom), impressed audiences with the power and timeliness of the ancient tale. At Princeton, Leveaux used footage of the carnage in Sarajevo and Bosnia to underscore the endless repetition of violence and war in the story.

German-speaking playrights used a similar technique when reviving Euripides' plays. Jürg Amann's 1998 *Iphigenie oder Operation Meereswind* (Iphigenia or Operation Ocean Storm) uses a television broadcaster in the style of those who reported Operation Desert Storm to update Euripides' *Iphigenia in Aulis* and to draw parallels between the ancient tragedy and political events of 1991. A strongly antiwar piece, Amann's play uses Euripides' work to comment on war in the late twentieth century.

Many of the reviews of the New York *Electra* production cite Bloom's dignity, power, and splendidly imperial quality as Clytemnestra as well as her convincing maternal ambivalence. The play, which debuted at the Ethel Barrymore Theater on west Forty-seventh Street in December 1998 and was to have run until January 17, 1999, was extended for several months due to overwhelming demand for tickets. And all this after several years of musicals dominating Broadway! What was afoot in the cultural unconsciousness of the West? Were the concerns of the more esoteric 1980s women writers becoming mainstream in Western society at the end of the millennium?

In the 1990s, the House of Atreus was being revived in multicultural, multinational ways and in varied artistic media. Garrett Fisher's opera *Agamemnon*—which uses Taiko drummers as well as dance (choreographed by Christy Fisher, the composer's sister) and masks—played in Seattle's Nippon Kan Theater in June 1998. Aeschylus's *Agamemnon*, reworked by Daniel Foley and Risako Ataka, ran at the Edinburgh Festival Fringe in August 1998. Euripides' *Orestes* was revived in April and May 1998 at the Franklin College Theater in Indiana. The playwright Ellen McLaughlin staged *Iphigenia and Other Daughters* at New York's Classic Stage Company in 1995, and Ruth Margraff presented an opera, *The Elektra Fugues,* in New York's HERE Theater in 1997, which was later done as a play in Culver City, California, in 1999. *The Greeks,* an adaptation by Kenneth Cavander based on Euripides, Aeschylus, and Sophocles and commissioned by the Royal Shakespeare Company in 1980, ran in Los Angeles in a six-hour production in September 1999.

Perhaps even more unexpected than the stage performances is the plethora of Web sites dedicated to various members of the House of Atreus in the late 1990s, including <http://www.Electra.com>, <http://www.Iphigenia.com>, and <http://www.Orestes.com>.[1] The site <http://www.Agamemnon.com> was available to be purchased from a Web site designer group when I first checked in 1999. By June 2000 the site had become Agamemnon Film, owned (appropriately, I think) by Charlton Heston and his son Fraser. Even <http://www.Atreus.com> appears as a Web page design company.

Orestes' Web site gives some indication of the attraction that the names from the House of Atreus still possess. <http://www.Orestes.com> was the homepage for a Finnish media agency that designs Web sites for other companies. When I asked the Web master, Tapio Nissilä, how the name Orestes was chosen, he responded (in an e-mail message of July 23, 1999) that the Finnish company needed an "international" name (that is, not identifiably Finnish) and Orestes "sounded attractive." Orestes' name still carries cultural weight, even though the Finnish group was clearly unaware of his actual story. Because I inquired, the company researched Orestes' story. Mr. Nissilä then expressed the hope that "our name is not any kind of offence to you or any other person interested in ancient mythology" (e-mail message, July 23, 1999). I assured him that I was fascinated rather than offended since the Web site began with a handsome, well-dressed young man who looks like he is in charge of a business. I felt (along with Maraini perhaps) that this might be an appropriate late-twentieth-century Orestes—a new kind of economic king for a rising group of young entrepreneurs in a stock market gone wild at the end of the millennium. The Finnish group did, however, change its name to "Identia.com" in May 2000.

Like the multicultural, multimedia performances of the story of the House of Atreus, these Web sites take the notorius family away from single nations and into the "world-wide" space of the Internet. These sites move the House of Atreus from the printed page (or what cybercritics refer to as the "codex book") into cyberspace itself. This ancient family makes a surprising jump into an entirely new medium at the end of the twentieth century, thus ensuring its continued cultural and symbolic importance. Resurrections of this family line, then, are unexpectedly frequent. However, these 1990s revisions and revivals took a very different turn from the direction of the 1980s—a turn away from Klytemnestra.

During the 1990s, Klytemnestra's progeny displaced her from center stage. Rather than texts or performances that feature Klytemnestra as their main actor, 1990s women's revisions of the story of Troy and the House of Atreus have a Klytemnestra who is still present but no longer the dominant force. Women writers turn to Klytemnestra's daughters, particularly Iphigenia and Electra, to follow her story to new conclusions.[2] Finally, both Electra and Iphigenia appeared online at their eponymous dot-com addresses (which Klytemnestra lacked) as the millennium neared its end in 1999. In texts by women, Klytemnestra is upstaged by her daughters.

Rather than follow Klytemnestra's daughters, I will examine the only eponymous piece I found by a woman writer in the 1990s,[3] the American poet Laura Kennelly's 1993 poem "Clytemnestra Junior in Detroit," as well as a cyberspace "embodiment" entitled "The People versus Cltyemnestra," and finally a photo from Greece, in order to catch a glimpse of Klytemnestra at the end of the twentieth century.

A Dysfunctional Nonqueen as Avaricious Cutthroat: Laura Kennelly's "Clytemnestra Junior in Detroit"

Laura Kennelly, a Texas writer who edited the volume *A Certain Attitude: Poems by Seven Texas Women*,[4] often uses earlier literary texts (such as *Hamlet*, *Dr. Zhivago*, the Bible, and classical texts) to create her poems. Kennelly's interest in Klytemnestra and her family (as well as in Wallace Stevens's work) is evident also in her poem "Helen with Insomnia, at the Clavier" (*A Certain Attitude*, 60–61) in which Helen makes clear that Klytemnestra's husband, Agamemnon, also made love to Helen.

However, the incident that triggers Kennelly's Klytemnestra poem is not ancient but occurs in the late twentieth century. A quotation from *USA To-*

day, (March 27, 1991) describes the murder of patriot missile crewman An-
thony Riggs upon his return from the Gulf War of 1991 (Kennelly, *A Certain
Attitude,* 62). Riggs's wife, Toni Cato Riggs, and her brother Michael Cato
were charged with first-degree murder; their motive was receiving insurance
money. Kennelly takes this opportunity to recall another husband returning
from war and being slain by his wife. But the circumstances are much reduced
in their grandeur and significance. "Clytemnestra Junior" is a weak echo of
her ancient counterpart; this 1990s Clytemnestra's murder of her husband
will not enable her to rule the kingdom—or even her own household.

The poem begins by recalling a sentiment familiar from the 1980s revisions.
An editorial voice announces, "Bad news is always the same, only a few
changes in a few thousand years" (62). The story of Agamemnon and Klytemnestra is repeated endlessly over the millennia. In Detroit in 1991, however, every role has been diminished: "He wasn't a king. / She's not a queen."
And the story is no longer shocking or so crucial as it once was. The news-
paper comments, "'New twist is no surprise to family, friends.'" Murders have
become commonplace in the violent modern world of "this spectral city."

What has changed, however, is the number of different voices that comment on the event, each assigning it a different value and a different meaning. An editorial voice points out the degraded conditions of postmodern
urban poverty and the instant communication of unhappy news ("Fiberop-
tics, satellites spread the tidings"). This editorial voice merges with the community that surrounds the event, a "we" that forms a chorus of suspicion and
blame. ("When the police questioned us, we said: / 'Start with the wife. She's
the only one who has a motive.'" "We weren't surprised: 'Start with the wife.
She'll be a rich widow'" [62–63].) This chorus of community judges is jux-
taposed to a more colloquial voice, with a Midwestern African American
accent. ("She live by herself, she say. / Girl, you believe that?") This colloquial narrative traces the actions of Clytemnestra Junior, who, alerted by the
newscasts of her husband's homecoming, prepares "the happy / homecoming." Three sets of voices, the editorial, the community chorus of shocked
bystanders, the colloquial chorus that understands the circumstances of
poverty, all carry on a dialogue about the event. Where we expect the dialogic, however, we will eventually find surprising agreement.

Clytemnestra Junior, Toni Cato Riggs, is excited when her husband goes
to war. It is difficult to tell, however, if she will miss her man or if she is re-
lieved to have him gone. Not driven by the ancient Klytemnestra's desire to
avenge a wrong, or to defend Mother Right, Clytemnestra Junior hatches her
murder plan for lesser reasons. She is compared to an older Clytemnestra,

still not her ancient forebear; the second Clytemnestra, described in exaggerated dialect, is

> Ole Clytemnestra, down on Elm Street,
> her man, he gone ten
> years; when he get back,
> he come down dead sure. (63)

Klytemnestra's story of the slain returning husband has played itself out in Detroit's recent past. It is not clear that "Ole Clytemnestra's" husband was off at war; perhaps he had simply deserted his wife for ten years. Whatever the reason for his absence, the deadly homecoming is the same.

There are, however, other changes in the plot. The most recent Agamemnon is seen by the colloquial chorus as a good man and faithful husband:

> Anthony Riggs. He a good man.
> Didn't tote no hussy home
> no wall-eyed Cassie gal
> talking silly to herself
> like the dead Agamemnon
> over yonder on Elm Street. (63)

Clytemnestra Junior, unlike her recent and ancient counterparts, does not have the justification of an unfaithful husband who brings home his new conquest. Since the poem also has no mention of a daughter sacrificed by her father, Clytemnestra Junior has neither psychological justification nor even sheer jealousy to explain her mariticide. This degraded, modern Clytemnestra Junior is simply after the cash:

> she empty
> his bank account, wreck his
> car in four months. Then she start
> talking to her brother. (63)

Neither kingdom nor Mother Right nor personal pride are at stake in postmodern Detroit—only money.

During the explanation of the colloquial chorus, the second, well-spoken chorus of shocked bystanders comments, "'I just hope it wasn't true.'" This weak hope is followed by an extremely ironic editorial comment that sounds as though it is quoted from a women's self-help handbook that could have been written in the late 1960s or in the 1990s. "Women have become self-actualizing when spouses absent themselves. We applaud opportunities for personal development" (63). What must originally have been a positive self-actualization here is realized in murder; personal development proceeds out of the dead husband's bank account. Women's liberation gets degraded to violently preying on the money of a murdered husband. This 1990s Clytemnestra Junior does not fight for blood rights or for any female principle; she kills only for her own benefit. Klytemnestra's story has descended to personal economic gain. The "tragic" moment here consists of the commercial fact that "Car dealers say she'll get no sympathy car now." The cultural weight and importance of the ancient story is lost.

To underline the trivial nature of the event, the well-spoken chorus produces extreme litotes in the comment, "Events such as this do tend to disillusion" (63). But why are we disillusioned with this recurrent event? Because the wife fails to honor the returning war hero? Because the poor, too, can do heinous acts? Our sense of the "hero" and of heroic honor is debased. (And in this, Kennelly agrees with her 1980s sister writers.) Any romantic notion we might have about faithful wives waiting anxiously at home during the war years is demolished. The act itself cannot be construed as a feminist protest of any kind. We are faced with a reality that has no redeeming social or cultural value. We have reached bottom, where, ironically, the dialogic collapses into a single moment of common disillusion. There are no competing interpretations left.

As the poem closes, a hopelessly idealistic voice laments, "I just hope it isn't true. I hope that life hasn't come to mean nothing at all." But readers, as well as the other internal voices in the poem, know that it *is* true, that life has come to mean very little. Clytemnestra Junior and her Agamemnon, as well as the "Ole Clytemnestra" down on Elm street and her Agamemnon, have all lost any capacity to signify larger social or cultural issues. Their actions now constitute often repeated news items rather than a struggle between male and female rights and roles. Clytemnestra Junior ends (as does Maraini's Clitennestra and Reinig's characters) in psychoanalysis. But there seems little hope that such counseling can address the social deterioration that has produced Clytemnestra Junior, who reduces the ancient Klytemnestra's struggle to a uniquely late-twentieth-century moment: "She / say all families dysfunctional at one time / or another." The original struggle of the female against the male has been tamed into psychojargon. Mariticide becomes simply a dysfunctional moment in any family. Any cultural weight that the ancient Klytemnestra's story carried vanishes.

Although Clytemnestra is still the central character in this eponymous poem, she has been thoroughly emptied of any meaningful content. Her story is no longer a well motivated act of vengeance or valiant defense of the female. The act of mariticide no longer inspires horror but rather chagrin. This view of Klytemnestra's story typifies the 1990s treatments. If Klytemnestra survives in the story at all, she loses her unique cultural status as well as her stature. Clytemnestra Junior and the female violence she exercises are neither complex nor problematic. In a world reduced to bits of cultural jargon tossed together in the popular press, Klytemnestra seems to have lost her value as the powerful archetype we traced in the 1980s.

This 1990s piece does not look back more than fleetingly to the Greek cultural materials. It is not seeking origin, but rather using the Greek texts and myths as shards of a cultural tradition to be reshuffled into a new postmodern arrangement. The late-1980s performance piece *The Fabulous Furies re-Vue* already begins to advance in this direction. By the time we get to Kennelly's "Clytemnestra Junior in Detroit," Klytemnestra's story is no longer simply being revised; it is atomized and reassembled with a strong admixture of popular culture at its most banal. While pieces of Klytemnestra's story persist in this poem as well as in the revisionary novels and plays that focus on Klytemnestra's daughters or on Helen, and while 1990s women can recognize fragments of themselves in those pieces, Klytemnestra's original gender battle as depicted in these literary texts from the 1990s does not have the same cultural weight or determinacy that it had for women writing in the 1980s.

Klytemnestra's Case Retried on the World Wide Web

Curiously, while Klytemnestra's daughters, Electra and Iphigenia, each have an Internet address, as does her son, Orestes, Klytemnestra herself lacked an electronic address in the 1990s. (When I checked in July 2000, a site named <http://www.Klytemnestra.com> was supposedly under construction but has not actually materialized as of the time of this writing.) Although Klytemnestra does not have her own Internet address, one of the most fascinating and confusing revisions of her story can be visited at <http://www.members.tripod.com/NWO_2/index.html>.[5] At this site, a new World Wide Web of connections envelops Klytemnestra. Technology and popular culture collide with high literature and some of the founding mythical texts of the Western tradition. And investigating gender issues becomes much more complex in this context in which the gender of the "author" (or Web master or mistress) proved impossible to determine.

The mock-legal site, entitled "The People vs. Clytemnestra," stages the trial not of Orestes but of his mother. In this late-twentieth-century retrial in cyberspace, Clytemnestra is prosecuted by Plato and defended by Socrates. The Web site encourages its visitors to read both the "legal" testimony and the unredacted testimony to see if our judgment would change. The home page ends by underlining the gravity of the reader's responsibility by cautioning, "The fate of Clytemnestra lies in your hands." Or rather the home page almost ends with this line. Immediately beneath it is a picture of Jerry Springer, the popular talk-show host who specializes in having as guests those who are sexually perverse, confused, or unfaithful. A "shock-jock" who was once mayor of Cincinnati, Springer stops short of having murderers as guests, but he certainly thrives on sexual betrayal—often within immediate families. Springer encourages audience participation and judgment of his "guests," and he always closes with a moral evaluation of the episode meant to edify his audience. This last touch can only seem hypocritical given Springer's exploitation of his guests' and his audience's most perverse sexual and voyeuristic impulses. Startlingly, "The People vs. Clytemnestra" is dedicated to "our mentor and hero, Jerry Springer." While this dedication might attract a larger popular audience, it immediately gives the serious literary critic more than slight pause. The Web site visitor begins to expect the screaming confrontations, hair-pulling, and fist-swinging characteristic of Springer's show.

What we find instead is a serious and balanced presentation of Klytemnestra's story with links to legitimate classical reference materials, fictitious witnesses drawn from the history and religion departments at Harvard, and testimony culled largely from the Greek literary classics (including the plays of Aeschylus, Sophocles, and Euripides). In a postmodern mélange, popular culture, serious scholarship, and a campy sense of the comic collide and merge on this site. For example, the pop celebrity Carmen Electra is pictured as an example of a "modern day portrayal" alongside the classical Electra. Bits of historically displaced culture are atomized and reassembled into a site that makes us rethink the concepts of high and low culture as well as of gendered judgments about Klytemnestra. We gain no clue as to whether the mind behind this site is pro- or anti-Klytemnestra—or whether we are dealing with a Web master or Web mistress. The site could have been constructed by feminists with a sense of humor or by Jerry Springer fans with a sense of irony. Since I found it impossible to trace the Web master of this site, I cannot determine whether it was mounted by men or by women—or both.

To further complicate matters, the site is credited to the "N.W.O." I hoped that these initials might conceal the National Organization for Women with its letters transposed. What I found, however, was variously identified as the "Nesson World Order" or the "New World Order," which led me to a home page that is self-proclaimed as belonging to "wrestling's greatest fringe group," with pictures of wrestling figures such as Hulk Hogan. I began to wonder if among the eight wrestlers listed on the NWO home page a classical scholar

INDEX

Opening
Statement

Prosecution's
Witnesses

Defendant's
Witnesses

Closing
Arguments

Full, unredacted
testimonies

o are
N.W.O.

Links

Home Page

The People vs. Clytemnestra

THE STATE WILL PROSECUTE
CLYTEMNESTRA FOR THE MURDER
OF HER HUSBAND, AGAMEMNON...

You, the jury, must decide whether
she is guilty or not guilty of this
charge. Before you decide her guilt or
innocence, Judge Smails has advised
you to read the opening statements,
the testimony transcripts, and the
closing arguments.

After making your decision, read the
unredacted testimonies, and see if
your decision would have been different had you seen the excluded evidence.

The fate of Clytemnestra lies in your
hands...

This webpage is dedicated to our
mentor and hero, Jerry Springer.

Clytemnestra on the World Wide Web. (<http://www.members.tripod.com/NWO_2/>)

secretly lurked. I was entertained by the irony of the situation but somewhat discomfited by the possibly fascist overtones of the "New World Order" title. The only way I could make sense of the House of Atreus coupled with the World Wrestling Federation was to recognize wrestling's ritual quality for 1990s crowds. Group participation in a ritual battle in which cunning and physical power are tested and in which a ruler receives the group's adulation and allows the group to vent emotions may not be so far from the self-devouring House of Atreus worked out in the ritual of tragedy.

With Jerry Springer on one side and the World Wrestling Federation on the other, one embarks on Clytemnestra's trial with some trepidation. However, the site provides a serious presentation of the facts and issues in Clytemnestra's case. I can only guess that the site was constructed by a classics graduate student (who might also be a professional wrestler) with some legal training. The prosecutor, Plato, argues that Clytemnestra is guilty of the murder of her husband and that Agamemnon's murder of Iphigenia does not change that. He adds that Clytemnestra is an adulteress who is cruel to her remaining children. Plato thus presents the classical world's condemnation of Clytemnestra. Socrates defends her as a woman who kills to avenge her daughter and who was extremely abused by Agamemnon, who also killed her first husband and child. The parameters are familiar from the classical tragedies and tales.

The testimony of the classical figures (Clytemnestra, Chrysothemis, Electra, and Sophocles' Pedagogus, the old servant who looked after Orestes) comes largely from the plays of Aeschylus, Sophocles, and Euripides with some embellishment from the Internet characters. Clytemnestra's own testimony draws upon her story as presented in the classical materials. In the unredacted version of her statement, she adds the argument that Agamemnon could have chosen not to sacrifice Iphigenia (thus rejecting the classical Greek argument that he was fated to do so and had to obey the gods) but that he clearly valued his own reputation more than his daughter's life. Electra stresses her mother's adultery and mistreatment of her remaining daughters and son. Chrysothemis is torn between her living and dead sisters. Pedagogus is called as witness to Clytemnestra's reaction upon hearing the untrue tale that her son had been killed. An informed reader of Klytemnestra's story as told in the classical Greek texts is conversant with all of this material.

What the NWO adds is testimony from fictional (but quite plausible) academics—two Harvard scholars: Edward Wilson, a specialist in Greek history, and Francine Bell, an expert in the history of religion—and the feminist "Gloria Stonehem."[6] The testimony presented by these three contains legitimate academic positions substantiated by actual scholarly reference material. Although the names have been fictionalized, the positions could easily represent established critical attitudes regarding our evaluation of Clytemnestra. The Greek historian argues that Agamemnon was instructed to sacrifice Iphigenia by the gods and that, given his beliefs, he had to obey. Socrates retorts that Agamemnon's own arrogance was the cause of the gods' demands in the first place. The expert in religion (whose testimony is suppressed and appears only in the unredacted version) argues that fulfilling a demand by a god can be a righteous act. Like Kierkegaard, the religious expert Bell compares the actions of Agamemnon to those of Abraham in his willingness to sacrifice Isaac. Bell does not, however, experience Kierkegaard's fear and trembling at Abraham's example but rather suggests that it helps to justify Agamemnon. Socrates points out that Agamemnon's own arrogance caused the god to demand sacrifice in the first place; Abraham did not share this characteristic.

To offset the scholarly testimony that seems to support Agamemnon's position and Clytemnestra's guilt, Socrates calls Gloria Stonehem, who in this version is also a classics scholar and an expert on feminist issues in ancient Greek society. Merging Gloria Steinem and her sister feminists who have studied ancient women, the Web master or mistress produces a very feminist perspective on Clytemnestra's actions. Stonehem points out the hypocrisy in the ancient Greeks' demanding that women be faithful but allowing men to be adulterous with no repercussions. Stonehem also emphasizes Agamemnon's killing of Clytemnestra's first husband and their child. Stonehem argues that if Clytemnestra were a man, her murder of an adulterous spouse would not be objected to. Plato points out that the woman in Greek society was supposed to be the moral center of the family and that men's respect followed from that female duty. Plato's response does nothing to overturn the hierarchical position of the man, which is Stonehem's point.

Stonehem's view receives backing from other Web sites as well. In discussions mounted on several university Web sites, undergraduate female students express sentiments similar to the fictional Stonehem's. In an entry entitled "What I think about Clytemnestra," "Daydreamer XX" from the MIT classics Web site argues:

> It seems that some people agree that Clytemnestra is a villain. I really disagree. . . . Clytemnestra saw her daughter getting killed and that's the point. I think that Agamemnon is just power-mad that he kills his own daughter. . . . And if we say Clytemnestra is unfaithful, how about Agamemnon? First he tries to keep the girl Chryseis at Troy, and then he takes away Achilles' price [*sic*] Briseis. And . . . brings Cassandra home. . . . Such a sexist society of the Greeks [*sic*], when the guys are allowed as many girls as they like and women suppose [*sic*] to be "loyal, fidel, and faithful." Ugh—I think Clytemnestra did a great

deed, challenging the ancient idea by killing her husband, who is just as great a villain as anybody else. . . . I don't find any, or just a wee bit, guilt on [*sic*] the women. It's all the men's fault.[7]

At least some female college students, then, agree with Stonehem's assessment of the imbalance in gender relationships in the ancient story. Clytemnestra's cyberspace trial reveals guilt in many directions and does not simply reinforce Athena's original judgment by siding with the male.

The NWO's trial of Clytemnestra presents a balanced depiction that is sympathetic to both interpretations of Klytemnestra. It becomes difficult to judge her culpability. We regain a more complex view of this infamous woman and her actions. The Web site does not, however, challenge the hierarchy of which Klytemnestra's death is the foundation. In reevaluating Klytemnestra's actions and asking a late-twentieth-century audience to judge them, those who constructed "The People vs. Clytemnestra" make a curious choice. They do not restage the famous trial of Orestes in Athens, but rather they try Klytemnestra for a deed that has already brought her ample punishment. We are not asked to reconsider the son's vengeance against the mother but only to rethink the wife's vengeance against her husband. What at first held the promise of creating a radical challenge to gender roles in a new technological context begins to reinforce assumptions about gender and hierarchy. Whether mounted by a man or a woman, this Web site does not undermine the founding of gender role distribution in the classical texts.

Even if we were to acquit Clytemnestra of murder, the acquittal does not change the founding of the Western patriarchal tradition since Orestes' actions remain unchallenged. The Web site might help us to understand better the actions of the woman, but it does not displace the man from his position atop the power structure. And as modern jurists, we would be hard put to acquit Clytemnestra entirely. The fact that she slays Agamemnon remains undisputed. We can only find her "less" guilty on the basis of a kind of justifiable homicide. The woman remains guilty; the degree of her guilt depends on how we evaluate the male whom she kills.

This retelling of Klytemnestra's story helps us to rethink her actions, to reconsider the values established in ancient times and modern attitudes toward those values. It does not go so far as to challenge the Western, patriarchal social structure itself. In fact, by presenting legal proceedings, the Web site operates within one of the major social institutions that grows from Klytemnestra's final displacement by Orestes. By the legal rules as they are established at the founding of the Western tradition, the wife cannot really be judged "not guilty" in the killing of her husband and king. Like Athena, Western culture as it is constituted cannot set more store by the female than the male. Orestes' acquittal is not questioned here; Klytemnestra's guilt is revisited.

What I had secretly hoped would be a radical cyberspace gender challenge turned out to be a more traditional narrative retelling than I had expected. While cyberspace puts various categories into question—the identity and gender of the "author" or Web master, and the historical context, the time and place, of the text's composition, for example—and provides a multiperspectival version of the story, this particular cybertext at least does not really shift either our interpretive strategies or our gender paradigms.

That Klytemnestra appears in such a montage of popular and ancient culture reveals that the issues at stake remained crucial as the last millennium closed. These very odd components of this interdisciplinary and, indeed, cross-cultural montage bear witness to the fact that changing media do not leave behind Western culture's founding myths. They may be more interactive and visually available on the Web, but these myths do not morph into new paradigms. *The Matrix* does not entirely displace *The Oresteia*.[8] New technology and popular culture bring new pressures to bear on Klytemnestra's story, but they do not change its essential elements. That Clytemnestra is still on trial while Orestes is not suggests that underlying cultural values have not shifted as drastically as Ms. Stonehem might hope. Moving into cyberspace does not shake the foundations of Western culture but rather reaffirms them by inviting us to participate in the legal and narrative structures they spawn.

Klitemnistra: ROOMS with Bath

The last electronic entry from the 1990s is the Web screen labeled "A Photo from Dr. J's Illustrated Aeschylus's *Oresteia*."[9] This photo is in some ways the perfect postmodern ending to the twentieth century's visions of Klytemnestra; it brings her back to her place of origin—but with a distinctly modern architectural touch and ironic sensibility. The picture, which was taken by a female tourist on a trip to Greece, reinscribes Klytemnestra as the name of a late-twentieth-century motel—Klitemnistra—appropriately and menacingly offering rooms "with bath." The ironic viewer who catches this moment is included within the frame of the photo. While the gender of the photographer is difficult to tell in the photo itself, the photograph is copyrighted by Kathleen Lewis. A relatively run-down reality, with Klytemnestra remaining both homemaker and potential murderess, is captured by a technology that writes itself into the picture (both as the rearview mirror of a car and as the camera's eye). The photo presents an updated and deflated version of Klytemnestra. And the modern woman revisionist is incorporated into Klytemnestra's world in order to force us to see it differently. Here the visual itself is dialogized without the assistance of any narrative voice whatever. We can

Klitemnistra: Rooms—with Bath. (Photo by Kathleen Lewis and Janice Siegel. Mycenae, Greece, 1998)

only wonder if the owner of "Klitemnistra" is also a female—with a sense of humor or irony or anger.

This devaluing of Klytemnestra in the 1990s creates an odd effect for female readers. They come to occupy the role of unrecovered trauma victims who see Klytemnestra cut down, and with her any possibility of a culture built on a foundation other than that of the suppression of the female. Women— even contemporary women—have not found a way to escape the trauma of subjugation that occurred in the founding moment of Western culture. They can loudly protest it, as most of the 1980s authors do, but neither the 1980s nor the 1990s women actually rewrite the traumatic script. There are, however, a few hopeful gestures in the final decades of the twentieth century. Cardinal's narrator manages to recover from both her personal trauma and that imposed on her by Klytemnestra's example and to envision a different future; Reinig succeeds in scrambling the gender roles entirely to create a new potential for change. Not even these authors, however, actually produce in their texts the new narrative that they project as a possibility.

This inability to revise the traumatic script at the close of the last millennium has two possible effects. First, some women are forced constantly to replay the original traumatic event and are thus doomed never to escape the violence exerted against and by women in the original story. A quick perusal of 1990s news items reveals wives still violently disposing of abusive husbands and paying the social—and legal—price for doing so. The *labrys* may have turned to kitchen knife or pistol, but the violence it figures is still ominously present. This impulse to relive the story might also explain the surprising plethora of restagings of the *Oresteia* as the 1990s ended and the twenty-first century began. Second, the incapacity to rewrite the traumatic narrative may force some women to repress it, thus leaving them suppressed and forced back into the subterranean caves of Western culture like the benevolent spirits, the Eumenides, who are literally but not figuratively underfoot. In a world of pop culture and diminished roles, Klytemnestra and her Furies are vanquished once again. Klytemnestra slips from center stage to the wings as her daughters, Electra and Iphigenia—and their determinedly paternal allegiances—come into sharper focus as the millennium ends.

Notes

1. Curiously, all these Web sites were folded into larger sites by the end of 2001. The site <http://www.Iphigenia.com> still existed as an address but was being reconstructed as part of a larger site; <http://www.Electra.com> was folded into its mother site, <http://www.Oxygen.com> (run by the media mogul Gerry Laybourne); <http://www.Orestes.com> is discussed below.

2. For examples of American revisionary texts by women writers in the 1990s, see Cargill's 1991 novel *To Follow the Goddess* (which focuses on Helen); Kennelly's 1993 poem "Clytemnestra Junior in Detroit,"; McLaughlin's 1995 play *Iphigenia and Other Daughters;* Margraff's 1997 punk rock opera *The Elektra Fugues* (revised as a play in 1999); and Concannon's 1998 novel *Helen's Passage.*

3. A colleague in Slavics alerted me to the fact that the Ukrainian philosopher, translator, and poet Oksana Zabuzhko also penned a "Clytemnestra" poem as part of her 1994 collection *Avtostop.* Unfortunately, I cannot treat the Slavic materials here.

4. An English teacher at the University of North Texas, Kennelly also edits *Grasslands Review.* Norton Coker Press published her chapbook, *The Passage of Mrs. Jung,* in 1990.

5. I discovered this site during my many attempts to trace Klytemnestra and her offspring on the Internet. I visited the site several times during late August and early September 1999. All references are to these visits (the content of the site did not vary during that time and has not changed as of January 2002). I could not trace the links to a specific Web master or mistress, nor could I determine the exact date when the Web site was constructed. The various links within the site (e.g., to classical reference materials) had dates from 1998.

6. The pun on Gloria Steinem's name implies the toughness of this particular woman when it comes to feminist issues.

7. See <http://www.classics.mit.edu/cgi-bin/comment.cgi?935255442.2219>. I visited this site on August 23, 1999.

8. *The Matrix* was a popular 1999 film that won an Academy Award for special effects. The film is a modern cautionary tale about our relationship to cyberspace and "virtual reality."

9. Photo displayed on the Web site <http://www.nimbus.temple.edu/-jsiegel/texts/ oresteia/0017.htm>. Dr. J is Janice Siegel, a classics scholar at Temple University, who, with her colleague Kathleen Lewis, kindly gave me permission to use this photo, taken on one of their trips to Greece. Siegel's entire Web site is a remarkable resource for her students and colleagues. It couples scholarship with a sense of humor.

Conclusion

The Issues for Women Revisionists—
Trauma, Violence, and a New Gender Dialogic for
Klytemnestra at the End of the Millennium

Gendered Commonalities

Looking back at the Klytemnestra texts at the close of the last millennium, we find that these culturally and linguistically diverse women writers display a wide range of common ground. Despite their differing national origins and some very specific local detail, the texts agree on several points: the centrality of violence against women, marriage as control by the male and ultimately as sacrifice, the difficulty women have making themselves heard and escaping a submissive role. Some of these women writers (Bogen, Maraini, Brückner, and Kennelly) lament that Western culture has not progressed as much as women might have hoped in improving our lot since 500–400 B.C., when the Athenian tragedians wrote. For these later writers, Western women seem to have lost both stature and the capability to exert real violence in their own defense. Not only have women not regained the world of Mother Right that Orestes' acquittal ended, women in the West cannot even exert enough economic or political pressure to force the confrontation between maternal and paternal rights. As the twentieth century closed, women in many nations (including in this study Germany, Italy, France, Canada, and the United States) shared feelings of being repressed (as Klytemnestra and her Furies are) in a still strongly patriarchal society. The use of a powerful archetype such as Klytemnestra helps to make this fact evident.

However, versions of Klytemnestra presented by women writers of the 1970s and 1980s do form a new vision of the complexity of her motivations, the strength of her character, and the reasons for her violence. While Reinig, Brückner, and Maraini cannot restore the potency of Klytemnestra's *labrys* in destroying male authority, they do recuperate her strength, passion, and dignity. Bogen adds to this Klytemnestra's tenderness, compassion, and nurturing qualities. Cardinal and Auffret provide an extensive psychological and emotional reevaluation of Klytemnestra both in her own time and in the authors' time. Graham creates a powerful Klytemnestra of ultimate reconciliation while the "Fabulous Furies" doubt that possibility. Because of her revision by these women artists, Klytemnestra becomes again a powerful symbol of resistance to male suppression of the female. Her power lies, however, not so much in the weapon she wields as in the internal strength that she calls upon to resist a world she cannot conquer. The 1980s women's revisions of Klytemnestra make readers reconsider her as one of their foremothers. These writers turn Klytemnestra's ancient fate into a passionate twentieth-century protest. They challenge the conceptual foundations that relegate her to the role of abused wife and social victim.

Double Visions of a Female Self in the 1980s

Rethinkings of Klytemnestra by women in the 1980s strongly recall Weigel's notion of "double vision" in which women must see the patriarchal image painted of them while at the same time envisioning the self that they want to be. Virtually all of the Klytemnestras display this capacity. Bogen's and Brückner's heroines both lament the mariticide that they have been forced to become by patriarchal society while arguing that they should have been allowed to develop their nurturing, loving selves. Maraini's Clitennestra sees her self as pregnant and nurturing but is forced to behold the mad woman and property that patriarchy defines her as. Reinig has a group of women— and even a man, Kyra, who sees himself as female—who are categorized and controlled by a patriarchal society while knowing that they are more and different. We witness several literally doubled female characters (particularly Clytemnaestra and Athena) in the *Fabulous Furies;* and Wolf's Kassandra knows that Klytaimnestra would be a person with whom she could bond if it were not for the social and political deformation both women undergo. And in *Nous, Clytemnestre,* Auffret enters her character's perspective to provide the human, mothering emotions left out of the patriarchal picture of her. In these cases, the self that the female characters seek to become is inundated by the self that patriarchal society demands that women be.

Graham presents a more triumphant Clytemnestra who analyzes the self that patriarchy portrays and her own actions to find that her understanding of her self is the more powerful. She has acted justly despite her total divergence from the image of wife and queen that her society stipulates. It may be this insistence on a self of her own design that allows Graham's Clytemnestra to reconcile with her son and to leave the stage with a coherent and fulfilled sense of self. And finally, Cardinal creates a female narrator who comes to understand not only her own doubled self but the doubling of many of the characters who surround her. The narrator comprehends her mother, Mimi, who has absorbed too well the self that patriarchy paints and who allows her loving self to be perverted into endless hate for the men who control her life. But the narrator also empathizes with her father, who is just as trapped by the patriarchal demands of war and work placed on him and who has a loving side that has been submerged. The narrator also comes to understand Clytemnestre's doubled self through their conversations. Cardinal's narrator has a clarity of vision about her own identity and self as well as those of the other characters that allows her to revise everyone's story—including her own—into a more hopeful future and to foresee a time when her doubled selves might be resolved into a coherent and sympathetic new self.

The Klytemnestra revisions by women writers also focus on the social alienation and/or suppression of women by looking at aspects of the Klytemnestra story that differ from those stressed in the tradition of most classical male authors. However, despite the extensive revisions of Klytemnestra by contemporary female writers, she remains separated from other women and pitted against them even in the 1980s. All of the 1980s revisions show her either as totally alone or as accompanied only by a more or less benevolent but weak Aegisthus. She cannot turn to other women for support despite the fact that she is the supreme champion of women's blood rights. She is barred from enlisting her children's help and invoking maternal allegiances since her remaining children sympathize only with their father.

Klytemnestra's isolation is reflected, to some extent, even in the genre in which some writers choose to embody her. Brückner in Germany as well as Yourcenar in France and Carol Lynn Pearson in America all realize the Klytemnestra character in a monologue that is part of a series of isolated monologues—usually by women (although Yourcenar includes male monologues as well). (Pearson's one-woman play has a monologue in which a female member of the ancient Greek audience, Io, comments on Klytemnestra and Athena at a performance of the *Oresteia*.) In the case of all three modern texts, the short narratives grouped together have the effect of separating the speakers from one another and making them discrete individuals. While this treatment focuses the spotlight on each speaker and emphasizes their importance, it also removes a communal context and leaves them adrift without companion or support. The women of these monologues are reacting to a culture that does not want to hear them. Brückner's title, *Wenn du geredet hättest,*

Desdemona (If You Had Spoken, Desdemona), underlines this by pointing out that her women were those who never got to speak for themselves in the cultural tradition—or who feel the need to defend themselves or justify their actions. If there is any community to be established, it must occur between the character and the reader/viewer; it does not exist within the character's own context.

Because of her isolation from both the male and the female community, Klytemnestra is not able to establish an "open" female self, a Kristevan self *en procès;* she is therefore an extremely difficult figure to fashion into any kind of modern model for women. Her direct attack on patriarchy (in the person of Agamemnon) and her refusal to yield to the male the prerogatives of ruling and killing made her unredeemable in the classical tradition; her isolation from other women and her murder of Kassandra as well as her alienation from her own children (both male and female) make her difficult to reclaim for the feminist tradition of the 1980s and the 1990s as well.

One female author, Marion Zimmer Bradley, in her 1988 Kassandra novel *The Firebrand,* deals in passing with the issue of Klytemnestra's murdering another woman by revising the plot so that Klytemnestra does not kill Kassandra. (Klytemnestra plays only a fleeting part in Bradley's novel, which has, therefore, not been treated at length here.) Bradley's Klytemnestra is a fierce but understanding woman who realizes that Kassandra does not choose to be Agamemnon's trophy. She allows Kassandra to live to old age in order to challenge the traditional narrations of the "heroic" Trojan War focused on kings and gods rather than on queens and goddesses. In allowing Kassandra to live, Bradley's Klytemnestra plays out the actions that Wolf's Kassandra contemplates requesting of her. Bradley's Klytemnestra allows Kassandra to survive to record a female counternarrative. Bradley's Kassandra admires Klytemnestra, who is feared by Agamemnon and described as favoring her daughters over her sons. But when Kassandra finally joyfully witnesses Agamemnon's slaughter, she also witnesses Klytemnestra's fearful strength and power. Klytemnestra defends the goddesses and women's rights, but Kassandra fears her capacity for destruction. Although she does not kill Kassandra, Bradley's Klytemnestra cannot form a bond with her.

Cardinal's narrator presents an exception—or perhaps better, a solution—to the isolation that surrounds Klytemnestra. Cardinal's embroideress has the capacity to create a community within her imagination by becoming her father, by occupying her mother's sorrow, by feeling Electra's mourning, and by sharing their experiences with great intensity. She also has a literal dialogue with her classical counterpart that allows her to understand that the ancient Klytemnestra, like the narrator's mother, Mimi, cannot change her own story. They wear a mask of female submission that they can rebel against or hate but that they cannot remove. It falls to the narrator finally to cast off the mask—as well as the archetype of female behavior modeled by Klytemnestra's story. Cardinal's exploration of the seclusion of many characters allows her narrator to find a path beyond isolation and submission.

Cardinal's literary text, however, is alone in overcoming Klytemnestra's enforced seclusion and striking out upon a new road. Klytemnestra's usual isolation from other women and even abuse and subjugation by other women (in Maraini's text, for example) foregrounds a very vexed issue for contemporary feminists. It challenges any easy visions of "sisterhood" or female solidarity, and it reflects the split between modern feminists and antifeminists—as well as splits within feminism itself. On a philosophical level, many women have come to embrace various psychological tenets (particularly those of Freud in their various modern incarnations) that define their subservient position as "normal" and therefore ultimately unchallengeable if one is to live a "healthy" psychological and social life in Western culture (as Maraini's psychoanalyst explains). These issues are embodied in the struggle of the modern Klytemnestras.

The contemporary revisions also stress, however, Klytemnestra's human needs to love and nurture—and to be sexually fulfilled—rather than her ability to swing the axe. Maraini's Clitennestra's desire to have a child with her lover underlines the fact that Clitennestra remains a mother or wishes to be a mother even amid the violence that envelops her. Bogen's Klytaimnestra also values nurturing, as does Cardinal's narrator. But it is Klytemnestra's status as mother that triggers the violence—either against her (or her children) or by her (in retribution for her children's deaths). This fact tends to complicate any discussion of the joys of motherhood or any idealization of its status. Being a mother in Klytemnestra's context implies a necessary connection between fierceness and nurturing. This union calls into question many of those cultural dualities that assign strength and brutality to men and softness and nurturing to women. One of woman's most basic biological roles demands that she be capable of brutality and defensive destruction even against the husband.

When she is seen as the nurturing mother but battered wife, Klytemnestra's acts of violence take on a new dimension as blows for freedom and for survival of the female in the face of male domination. The fact that Klytemnestra's rebellion and aggression is opposed by other women (in Maraini's text, for example, by psychoanalyst/Athena and Electra in particular) is used in the modern texts to demonstrate that "patriarchal" attitudes are not limited to men. Women impose subservient roles upon one another as well.

Indeed, in Cardinal's text, Clytemnestre herself tries as does her modern counterpart, Mimi, to convince the narrator that submission to the male is an inescapable part of being a woman. If a woman rejects this role, as Clytemnestre does in her slaying of Agamemnon, she must be destroyed in order not to serve as a model for rebellion. Cardinal's ancient Clytemnestre accepts this condemnation, thus finally supporting the founding of the patriarchal tradition; her modern embroideress does not.

But Klytemnestra also supplies the perfect incarnation of contemporary female anger and violent retaliation. She finally rebels against her status as victim and becomes the avenger. The 1980s female revisionists make Klytemnestra's suffering clear to the readers or viewers. This shift reveals a psychological motivation for Klytemnestra's violent acts that makes her killing of Agamemnon justifiable homicide—or even a valiant act of justice. Klytemnestra parallels the heroines of the slasher movies popular in the 1970s and 1980s,[1] in which the plot hinges on making the female victim of abuse sympathetic enough that we cheer when she kills her abuser. After having been physically and psychologically traumatized by men, the female slasher-movie victim becomes an active self-avenger; she employs that same physical violence (and often the same knives and chain saws) used by men to avenge herself against the males who have attacked her. In Klytemnestra's case, the violence is enacted against her blood in the person of her daughter as well as an earlier child. When the aggressor, Agamemnon, returns to take over Klytemnestra's world (domestic as well as political and sexual), Klytemnestra exacts vengeance with the same violence that Agamemnon employed. Seen as an abused woman finally liberating herself from her abuser, Klytemnestra becomes a more sympathetic character.

The ability and willingness to wield the axe in defense of her rights and those of sacrificed women make Klytemnestra particularly appealing. This feature of her story resurfaces in other effectively violent heroines in films of the same period such as the Aliens series, *Terminator 2,* and *Thelma and Louise,* and in popular television shows such as *Buffy the Vampire Slayer.* Klytemnestra thus remains alive and well in the last decades of the twentieth century—metamorphosed into other women violently asserting their rights. The ancient Klytemnestra displays an extraordinary physical and psychological strength often disallowed to women. Several of her modern counterparts (Brückner's character, for example, and Graham's as well as Piper's and Tuana's) share this strength and the capacity to use it.

Klytemnestra's story also reminds us, however, that women can exert violence against other women. Klytemnestra kills Kassandra as well as Agamemnon. In the modern texts, women can torment and abuse other women (the psychiatrist in Maraini's play, for example). In Wolf's *Kassandra,* Klytaimnestra's violence expands even farther as she slays Kassandra's children. Violence in Klytemnestra's world—whether ancient or modern—refuses to stay within familiar gender bounds. Once it is unleashed, violence is driven by the logic of power, by the need to maintain political control. Wolf's Kassandra understands this ineluctable spread of violence as she foresees both Klytaimnestra's violent end and Aeneas's movement into a new "heroic" sphere of violence. Women who revise Klytemnestra's story demand that we rethink the Western cultural conception of violence. Constructively disruptive, the 1970s and 1980s revisions call into question gender assumptions and role assignments as well as deconstructing the effects of violence on both men and women.

Violence Revisited

The issue of violence remains central to all of the revisions we have examined. The ancient Klytemnestra is most often viewed as a woman who exercises extreme violence. But the fact that she must witness the loss of a first husband and child to Agamemnon's own violence and then must endure the sacrifice of Iphigenia makes one reconsider casting her as the bloodthirsty mariticide. Given her background, Klytemnestra's story makes much more sense if she is read as a trauma survivor. But she is a survivor of a very special kind; her trauma has a strong gender component. She suffers the sacrifice of the child by and for the father and of the *female* child for the male enterprise. The domestic relationship (Iphigenia's supposed marriage to Achilles) is sacrificed to the public and military cause. Furthermore, Klytemnestra's ultimate destruction by her son is the founding moment of the Western patriarchal tradition.

Some residue of violence seems unavoidable in the women's revisions. Violence is lamented and openly opposed as a strategy to emulate (particularly by Brückner and Bogen). However, the texts that do not allow their female characters to exert physical violence end in insanity or imprisonment for the female (for example, Maraini and Reinig). In general, these writers seek some alternative to violence that would allow Western culture to rid itself of its endless cycle of self-destruction and find a path that does not require the suppression of the female. None of the writers examined here depicts that option within the boundaries of her text, but each looks toward it. Those texts that do not renounce the violence but insist on moving beyond it to a new conclusion (especially the texts of Graham and Cardinal) allow women to envision a different future in which male and female might be reconciled rather than pitted against one another in a forced competition to establish a gender hierarchy. We might conclude from reading these texts that violence in a just cause might be a necessary step—but not if it creates an infinite loop of endless destructiveness. These women writers suggest that we must work through the violence inherent in establishing Western gender roles in order to get beyond it. The ability to wield the *labrys* must be preserved while women work to eliminate the necessity of actually swinging it.

These women writers also seem fascinated with Klytemnestra's strategies for surviving—both physically and psychologically. The classical Klytemnestra eventually survives her trauma by reenacting the sacrifice and replacing the female sacrificial victim with the father/husband/male. In slaying her husband, she can finally lay the murder of the daughter to rest and restore (even if briefly) Mother Right. Klytemnestra pays a high price for her actions—not unlike the battered women in several countries sentenced to death in the 1970s and 1980s for killing their husbands/abusers. This doubled violence makes Klytemnestra a discomforting but exemplary standard-bearer for female rights.

Yet the violence in Klytemnestra's story is also doubled in another way; it resonates so strongly as a threat to all women that we are forced to share the trauma involved in vulnerability. If the queen cannot forestall abuse or protect herself or her female children, how can ordinary women expect to do so? If Western culture condemns her attempt to stand up for a maternal sense of justice, how will it treat less powerful women? Klytemnestra becomes an image of what Maria Root and Laura Brown refer to as "insidious trauma."[2] With this concept, Root refers to "the traumatogenic effects of oppression that are not necessarily overtly violent or threatening to bodily well-being at the given moment but that do violence to the soul and spirit" (Brown, 107). As an example, Brown explains that in a culture where rape or sexual assault is common, many women who have never been raped develop symptoms of rape trauma—they become hypervigilant, avoid situations of high risk, respond in fear to approaches from men who might actually be friendly. In short, cultural conditions can produce a secondhand trauma in larger populations that are subject to the same traumatic threats. Reexamining the fate of Klytemnestra produces this effect.

When women confront the inherent violence exercised against the female in Klytemnestra's story, we recognize our own vulnerable positions writ large and inscribed as both the founding moment of Western culture as a whole and the determining condition for later gender relations. The innocent female must be sacrificed; the powerful female must be eliminated; and the male must be exonerated from both crimes in order to found the patriarchal order of law. This shocking recognition strengthens the effect of "insidious trauma" in late-twentieth-century women since it makes clear that the traditional cultural order requires the suppression of the female in order to survive. This realization produces in women writers the compulsion to relive Klytemnestra's experience, much as the trauma victim herself is forced to reenact the original shock (in dreams, flashbacks, or actual physical repetition). Western women must recreate Klytemnestra's portentous ordeal until we can change it, create out of the traumatic memory a narrative memory, a story that helps to understand and cope with the trauma.

If trauma involves the inability to forget the past, to move beyond an acutely painful moment in one's personal history, then the works of these women writers embody a kind of cultural trauma that is simultaneously a personal trauma for each author, character, and reader who relives Klytemnestra's story. Those few texts (particularly those of Graham and Cardinal) that recast the story itself rather than simply reprise Klytemnestra's part in ancient or modern guise can make it possible for the reader to push beyond trauma into a new, less hurtful narrative. Those writers who cannot get beyond the past but rather reexperience it with no possible change (Brückner, Maraini, Bogen, and Kennelly) repeat the founding moment of trauma but cannot escape it. They may make us feel our problematic state more intensely, but they do not foresee a new state of gender and power relations. Texts such as "Clytemnestra Junior in Detroit" perpetuate the moment of trauma by reinscribing it endlessly in Western culture with no way to change the narrative.

Klytemnestra therefore continues to haunt late-twentieth-century texts by women. She literally haunts Cardinal's novel, but all the writers are "haunted" by Klytemnestra to the extent that they cannot avoid the fact that her life and narrative continue to leave a living trace in their lives. The overload of cultural affect generated by Klytemnestra's murder and condemnation in ancient Greece persists as trauma among modern women and as a haunting by the ghost of woman as suppressed by law and patriarchy at the very founding of the Western tradition.

Women writers at the end of the last millennium seem forced to relive this crucial cultural event until they can retell the story in a way that makes sense, in a way that women can live with. In the 1980s, Cardinal may come closest to accomplishing this task. Revising a story of such wide-ranging cultural importance and such strong gender implications makes the task particularly difficult. Many writers find that they are condemned to reexperience the story in anger without, finally, being able to reshape it in a way that allows women to survive without trauma. They can replay the violence of Klytemnestra's story but not eliminate or recast it in a way that lets us escape the brutality of Western cultural foundations. Graham is one of the few artists who see Klytemnestra as fully accepting of her actions, redeemed by her understanding of them, and reconciled with the male on a basis of equality.

In Search of Female Voices

Ironically, Graham's Clytemnestra does not need words or voice. She operates by gesture, by showing rather than telling. This realization leads us to a curious fact: the late-twentieth-century Klytemnestras seem to lack the voice and the ability to manipulate language exhibited by Aeschylus's figure. By "voice" I mean primarily the feminist sense of the expression of political power and authority connected to a personal identity that is publicly recognized. In this sense, the term comes into critical focus as a lack in relation to groups that are silenced in historical and political arenas—most often women, minorities, or marginalized peoples. However, I am also referring to "voice" in the narratological sense as the capacity to narrate, to act as a teller to whom some larger audience will listen. In trying to bridge this gap between feminist and narratological usage, I follow the path of critics such as Susan Lanser and Rachel Blau DuPlessis.[3] Both kinds of voice are crucial to the women writers whose work I am analyzing. But I also mean "voice" in a third sense tied to the rhetorical arena. In this case, "voice" indicates the capacity to wield language successfully to carry one's point—as in "the speaker finally found her true voice."

All three kinds of voice become problematic in the women writers analyzed here. Their Klytemnestras have difficulty coming to voice in any of these senses. Given the fact that these late-twentieth-century female characters are being created by women writers, their lack of the capacity to wield language as a weapon, to "have one's say" in announcing and explaining vengeance, seems highly ironic. One implication is surely that Western society throughout its history, and not just in the ancient world, suppresses women's voice—and some of these women writers imply that it does so more effectively as time goes on. Aeschylus's Klytemnestra mastered words in order to weave of them her net of vengeance. Her rhetorical power allowed her to tempt Agamemnon and accuse him—all under the guise of praising him. She could demand political and personal recognition through her speech, and she could certainly narrate her story and her motivation. The late-twentieth-century Klytemnestras no longer seem able to do this. Many of them have as little capacity to enact liberating violence in language as they do in physical reality. If they do articulate their fury, they tend to be blunted and suppressed by figures (the psychiatrist in Maraini, for example) who have come to represent the millennia-long success of male dominance. These figures (like

Maraini's psychiatrist) are not always themselves male; like the classical Athena or Electra, a woman often serves to preserve patriarchal order.

When these revised Klytemnestras do find a voice, it can sometimes only be used postmortem—after they have slain their husbands (Brückner)—and thus be addressed to a dead male auditor. (Although the female readers of these voices are certainly alive to hear their lament.) Or their voice is heard only among groups of women (Reinig) who have no public forum. Or the voice is a personal singular uttered only internally (Bogen and Wolf) and addressed to the self.[4] Or the female voice is vocalized after the woman has been incarcerated as insane (Maraini and Reinig) and thus dismissed as not having the capacity to speak, to "make sense" at all. The modern Klytemnestras cannot confront their adversary directly—often because they cannot even get his attention—a point Brückner makes forcefully. The female voice in the narrative texts is muted and confined to the personal and often to interior monologue. When an authorial voice is present in the narratives (in Reinig's work, for example) it is not clearly marked as female. Given this fact, these revised voices cannot generate any more positive interaction between men and women than the original story embodies.

The Klytemnestras who do find a voice (even if belatedly) in the modern revision usually are pictured in their original setting. Both Brückner and Bogen stage their revisions in ancient times. They go back to the founding moment in an attempt to shift its direction. But compared to Aeschylus's aggressively intelligent Klytemnestra, who is a master manipulator of words, these modern Klytemnestras display less linguistic power. They are forced into physical violence partly due to their lack of ability to control language and thus their social situations. The classical Klytemnestra displays an authority reinforced by both rhetorical and physical power. Her late-twentieth-century counterparts seem to have lost both. Most disturbingly, they have lost the authority established by the capacity to use language effectively and publicly.

As readers, we do become convinced, however, that this model must change. If modern Western women cannot rewrite the founding gesture, we must at least set about changing our position in our own time. But those writers who update the setting of their revisions (particularly Reinig and Maraini) paint an even bleaker picture. Their Klytemnestras are incarcerated even for minor violence (the vegetable-slicer attack in *Entmannung*) or declared insane for wanting to enact motherhood (Maraini). Their voices are effectively silenced again. Even when their voices rise to fury (as in Maraini), they remain ineffective. These modern Klytemnestras are defeated without any of the moral trauma that Aeschylus's society must wrestle with. Many of the late-twentieth-century women writers imply that once the patriarchal order has been successfully inscribed, a modern Klytemnestra figure cannot find a voice powerful enough to change it.

Nonetheless, as readers, we hear an unmistakable and powerful voice of protest in these texts. The female voice of protest and critique that rises in these texts is not that of Klytemnestra the character but rather that of each author herself. The rhetorical power to manipulate language so as to change social conditions switches from Klytemnestra to the author. These women writers paint a portrait of Klytemnestra that evokes her original crucial position at the moment of transition between a matriarchal (or at least matrilineal) world and a new patriarchal, legal order. But they paint in muted and dark tones. The visions they produce incite their readers/viewers to anger and indignation over the plight of the modern embodiments of Klytemnestra. Their texts as a whole, rather than Klytemnestra's own speeches, provide an eloquent protest over the situation of women. The voices of the female principles, of Klytemnestra and of the female Furies, have migrated from the character to the female writers—and they echo in female readers.

These acts of revision by women remind us of Kristeva's discussion in *Desire in Language* in which she points out, "The only way a writer can participate in history is by transgressing this abstraction [of linear history] through a process of reading-writing" (65). Kristeva stresses the importance of "le mot littéraire" to this endeavor: "The poetic word, polyvalent and multi-determined, adheres to a logic exceeding that of codified discourse and fully comes into being only in the margins of recognized culture. . . . Carnivalesque discourse breaks through the laws of language . . . and, at the same time, is a social and political protest" ("Word, Dialogue, and Novel," 65). Women revisionists reclaim their access to a place in history by occupying those margins of recognized culture and by wielding the poetic word in the service of social protest.

Many of the revisionary texts in this volume come very close to Kristeva's description of the carnivalesque:

> Carnivalesque structure is like the residue of a cosmogony that ignored substance, causality or identity outside its link to the whole, *which exists only in or through relationship.* This carnivalesque cosmogony has persisted in the form of an anti-theological (but not anti-mystical) . . . movement. It remains present as an often misunderstood and persecuted substratum of official Western culture throughout its entire history. . . . As composed of distances, relationships, analogies and non-exclusive oppositions, it is essentially dialogic. ("Word, Dialogue, and Novel," 78)

Although Kristeva is speaking here about popular forms such as folk games, fables, and anecdotes, the description of the structure that exists only in and through relationship, of the antitheological (but not antimystical) movement, of the persecuted but always present substratum of culture, of the use of nonexclusive oppositions, all also define the contemporary women's revisionary texts and mark them as clearly dialogic. (I am not arguing that the revisionist texts match precisely Kristeva's definitions of the carnivalesque. The contemporary women's texts are often less bawdy, erotic, scatological, or fantastic than one expects of the Rabelaisian carnivalesque. The women's texts, however, share many characteristics of the dialogic that make it rebellious and revisionary—particularly the suspension or inversion of norms.)

Despite the women authors' subversive use of language as protest, only Cardinal's theoretically nonverbal artist, her embroideress, actually succeeds in moving beyond the violence and suppressed rage of the Klytemnestra narrative. Cardinal's narrator envisions a world different from the eternal repetition of submission and hate experienced by her own mother and verified by Clytemnestre. She will weave a future not yet seen by women. But the embroideress's real talent is in her voice, in her role as teller, in her ability to experience empathy and to transmit that communal feeling in narrative. Cardinal's language seeks not powerful irony and manipulation of men but rather clarity and understanding. Because the embroideress can move her first-person voice from herself to her father to her mother to a convergence with the ancient Clytemnestre, she can use narrative technique and language itself as a unifying force. She creates what DuPlessis or Lanser might think of as a communal narrative in which both male and female characters find voice through this narrator's telling. (Wolf also posits such a communal voice, a "we" that might come to replace Cassandra's isolated "I." Wolf thematizes this possibility, however, whereas Cardinal creates it in the very narrative structure of her text.) In at least one late-twentieth-century, female-authored world, then, language rises to the importance, if not the grandeur, that it held for a woman and queen in classical times. And more important, the language wielded by a woman in Cardinal's text becomes a unifying force, a weaving tool rather than a *labrys;* it knits together rather than violently severing.

In the late twentieth century, women writers such as Cardinal catch glimpses of a new vision—not of Klytemnestra herself (whom Cardinal must leave behind), but of a still indistinct possibility generated by rethinking Klytemnestra's fate as a crucial cultural figure and symbol of gender organization in Western culture. Rather than recuperating the axe-wielding avenger for modern feminism (as, I must admit, I thought they would), these women writers seek to use her fate as a vehicle of protest. They sympathize with Klytemnestra, but they do not suggest that emulating her violence is a useful strategy. Although they are haunted by her destruction, these women writers do not transform Klytemnestra into a winner in the battle between female and male rights. At their most effective, these modern women writers redefine the struggle involved in Klytemnestra's narrative so that the battlefield becomes a meeting place. They recoup a female voice intent on escaping submission but most often heard in the shrill mode of protest.

None of these women writers rethinks the Western tradition itself by reversing the ancient plot and following cultural development from Klytemnestra's acquittal and Orestes' conviction. (Although perhaps Reinig's gender confusions move in this direction.) None of these women reconceptualizes Western society beginning from matriarchal social principles. None has emplotted the story as if Orestes had been executed and a daughter (Electra? Chrysothemis? an unnamed offspring of Klytemnestra and Aegisthus?) had inherited the kingdom. None asks where Western culture would be if Mother Right had prevailed[5]—or where Western women would be if ancient Greeks had not insisted on equating women with the irrational and with blood feuds, thereby necessitating women's suppression in order to form a democratic society.

A few of these women do, however, ask what is perhaps a more apt question: would it be possible to imagine a world in which neither men nor women had to be suppressed? This dream may be an impossible vision to conceptualize since Western culture has never yet attained it. Female utopias (Wittig's *Les guérillères,* for example) often cast women in the power roles of men without being able to envision a system that might have different roles entirely, roles not based on hierarchical domination (although Wittig gestures toward this in her text). Of the texts we have examined, a few do, in fact, attempt to rethink gender roles in a more radical way than a simple reversal of power structures. These texts call gender definitions themselves into question. They do this by leaving behind the ancient Klytemnestra in order to disrupt her role and challenge her narrative in the late twentieth century. Indeed, the power of Cardinal's message is that current and future worlds must occupy women's creativity; the old worlds and the founding gender battles must be revisited, but we cannot allow ourselves to be stranded in them and overwhelmed by them. Some women writers discover that they should not fixate on seeking origins but instead use the Greek texts and myths as analytic tools for conceiving a new social reality.

Gender Dialogized: Unity through Disruption

The issue of structure brings us full circle in this study and returns us to the dialogic as used by these women revisionists. As we have seen, the dialogic plays a crucial role in each of the texts I have examined; it is built into the very structure of the texts and allows for a constant questioning of the social dictates that continue to suppress women. Bogen and Brückner, for example, produce competing voices that protest cultural values; Wolf, Auffret, and the *reVue* disrupt literary hierarchy and generic expectations of narrative by melding multiple genres and high and low culture. Reinig's multistrand narrative that incorporates and redigests ancient drama as well as popular culture undermines both any claim to authority and any easy marking of gender within the text. Cardinal chooses a strategy of shifting gender as well as narrative perspective to relativize cultural values. While the surface and thematic development of the 1980s texts seem to present a depressing devolution of Klytemnestra and the female cause that she embodies into an increasingly powerless position, the structure of the texts engages in a generic disruption that allows for a voice of protest to be heard beneath the depressing silencing of the female protagonists.

A few of these women go farther, however; they create a structure in which gender itself is dialogized. In fact, Reinig and Cardinal produce what we might call a gender dialogic that challenges the authority that dictates gender roles themselves. These texts go to the heart of Klytemnestra's story in order to change the gender arrangement that her murder and condemnation set in motion. The gender dialogic in Reinig and Cardinal destabilizes the traditional structures in order to create a new space not defined by the past or by established power relationships. The texts of Reinig, Cardinal, and Graham become sites of possibility that do not define this new society within the bounds of the text but rather allow readers to imagine new social and gender relationships. Those texts that are a simpler retelling of Klytemnestra's story (Bogen, for example) create rather a lament over the inferior status of women and of inescapable gender role assignments.

Bogen's *Klytaimnestra Who Stayed at Home* is the most straightforward retelling of the texts I have examined, despite its dialogic use of many competing voices that call into question and relativize cultural assumptions and values. Her many first-person speakers do challenge traditional interpretations of categories such as heroism, but they do not move to undermine the idea of gender itself. As Bogen humanizes the main actors in the ancient myths, she tends to reinforce the traditional femaleness of her Klytaimnestra by associating her with nurturance, growing things (gardens and plants), gentleness, and a tender heterosexual relationship with Aigisthos. (Brückner's iconography of water as representing the female versus blade or flame as signifying the male produces a similar reinforcement by traditional gender imagery.) Bogen seems to regret that the gender roles do not produce the salutary social effects they are supposed to more than she wishes to destroy the roles themselves. This is perhaps the most conservative lament and the least gender-disruptive text of the group.

At the other end of the spectrum, both Reinig and Cardinal create narratives that disrupt not only the classical tale of Klytemnestra but also the clear delineation of gender itself. Being female becomes what Judith Butler would call a performative act in both authors' novels.[6] Otto Kyra, Reinig's debonair ladies' man, becomes a lady-man as he takes on the maternal role and eventually the clothing of his dead wife, Thea. He literally (and figuratively) performs the female (and man-hating) Valery Solanas in Reinig's restaging of the *Oresteia* as *Entmannung* ends. In this case, Reinig's competing textual voices clearly disturb more traditional assumptions about gender as well as about guilt and responsibility in Klytemnestra's story. This is not only a complex dialogue between a modern and ancient text but also a dialogic disruption of the values and gender assumptions that underpin that founding moment in Western culture.

Cardinal, too, creates a disruptively dialogic narrative that also depends partly on the performative as the narrator imagines herself as many other characters—her own mother or Electra, for example. But the narrator's most striking moment of self-projection is her merging with the consciousness of her father as he has his first sexual experience. In Cardinal's case, the performance is not a literal one but rather an imaginative projection of the female into the male—and in the case of the Klytemnestra story that the narrator weaves into her textile—of the literary into the visual. Cardinal is thus able to rupture gender divisions in order to re-member a unified male-female world not realized in her actual surroundings. Just as Reinig does, Cardinal uses narrative innovation and structural complexity to create a dialogic text that forces the rethinking of gender definitions and separations.

For both Reinig and Cardinal, Klytemnestra's story as well as her gender role assignment must be made multiple, multivocal, and more problematic. The interpenetration of voices, roles, and genders in these texts redefines the dilemma itself. Klytemnestra's story can no longer represent the bald displacement of a matriarchal sensibility by a patriarchal one, Mother Right by Father Right. In these texts, the two are inextricably entwined. Male and female shift from person to person and from situation to situation. We are forced as readers of Cardinal and Reinig to redefine the basic problem as one of balance (precisely the issue that attracts Wolf to Kassandra's story) rather than displacement of one political, ethical, and legal system by another.

This redefinition created by texts that institute a gender dialogic takes us back in the direction of the reconciliation that Graham's ballet anticipates at the beginning of this study. Graham creates a dialogic structure by resurrecting the "voice"—or at least the indomitable will—of Clytemnestra, who can then refashion her story so that her voice is not simply silenced but rather blended with that of her son in a reconciliation that again reunites genders (even if in a less direct way than in Reinig or Cardinal). This new multivocal unit reconfigures gender by disrupting the traditional divisions and hierarchical arrangements imposed on men and women.

Among the literary texts we have examined, then, Reinig and Cardinal create the most gender-disruptive narratives, and they do it by dialogizing gender itself. These two writers finally reject the double-bind choice inherent in Klytemnestra's story—that a society must choose either the male or the female as dominant and consider them as forever separate in order to found Western culture. Reinig and Cardinal, along with Graham, envision a different path, one created by their dialogic disruption of the category of gender and the power and role distribution that it institutionalizes.

The late-twentieth-century women writers and artists who rethink Klytemnestra trigger a complex exchange that is both intertextual and dialogic. They are in dialogue with their ancient counterparts, with the men and women of their own times, and with one another. Together, they create a chorus of different voices forming both a lament and a protest. These women have managed to "dialogize" Western culture, to "relativize and de-privilege" the traditional assignment of gender hierarchies and roles, to "make us aware of competing definitions" of crucial female figures such as Klytemnestra.[7] Women writers who remember Klytemnestra force us to face crucial issues that extend into many facets of life. If Western culture forces a response by female victims that reenacts the violence visited upon them,[8] we must end by questioning Western cultural values themselves. Certainly, we want to celebrate liberation from abuse and strike a blow for freedom and dignity. But late-twentieth-century women writers who rethink Klytemnestra's "triumph" also ask why women must keep wielding the axe. They interrogate the institutionalization of gender roles and power distributions that result from Klytemnestra's defeat, and, in the most radical cases, suggest that such role divisions can be undermined and rejected.

These late-twentieth-century Klytemnestra texts offer no easy solutions or glorious triumphs. Rather they provide a multivalent and complex Klytemnestra who is torn by her many conflicting attitudes and qualities; she is a thoroughly dialogized character as the last millennium ended. She no longer has the glorious scope of tragic action of her ancient counterpart, but she has a broader psychological arena and every bit as much involvement in the balancing of gender relationships in Western culture. These modern revisions undercut any essentialist view of women as being exclusively nurturing, loving beings, although they also demand the right of women to retain this role as part of their selves. The late-twentieth-century revisions of Klytemnestra insist that we acknowledge a more complicated figure who cannot be forced into a simple mold or easily condemned. Matriarch and mariticide, Klytemnestra rocks the cradle, wields the axe, and reflects on the meaning of both. She helps us to reexamine the very concept of gender and the female.

Some of these female revisionists take us beyond the rhetoric of female frustration and outrage, beyond the constant trap of victimhood in Klytemnestra's story. These authors compel us to rethink a good many cultural values—including the Western construction of gender roles, the ways in which violence can be used to reinforce that construction or to deconstruct it, and even concepts such as "cultural values" themselves. Productively disturbing, these late-twentieth-century revisions of Klytemnestra exemplify women rejecting the limits of gender prescriptions and exploring the varied potentials of female identity—both maternal and mariticidal.

Notes

1. In "Her Body, Himself," Clover discusses the phenomenon of the slasher film's heroine, "Final Girl." In *Men, Women, and Chain Saws,* Clover predicts that the female heroine of these films will lead to a more active and violent female figure in future films (as has already been the case in such films as *Alien* and *Aliens*). Clover's discussion of the gender confusions and crossovers in the slasher films is particularly insightful. In many ways, Klytemnestra, too, occupies both female and male roles; she is both female victim and male hero. But her effect on the audience diverges from that described by Clover. The phallic knife may be Klytemnestra's weapon, but she also drowns Agamemnon in the female fluids of the bath. Both Bogen and Brückner insist on this point. Brückner's Klytämnestra, for example, claims to drown Agamemnon in water—which Brückner depicts as a distinctly female symbol—which also figures her female powers. She murders the reigning male not in order to replace him as surrogate male, but to free a repressed female power that has been usurped by the male for his own purposes. Perhaps this is why male audiences of classical tragedy—unlike the audiences of Clover's slasher films—do not seem to exhibit the tendency to identify with Klytemnestra as a victim-hero.

2. The concept is discussed by Laura S. Brown, in "Not Outside the Range: One Feminist Perspective on Psychic Trauma," 107, who bases her discussion on the work of Maria Root, including her 1989 paper "A Model for Understanding Variations in the Experience of Traumata and Their Sequelae" and "Reconstructing the Impact of Trauma on Personality."

3. Lanser is particularly informative in generating a "feminist poetics of narrative voice." See also DuPlessis.

4. Wolf's Klytaimnestra has virtually no voice of her own in the text. She and Kassandra communicate by looks and mutual understanding. Although Kassandra conveys Klytaimnestra's thoughts, her psychology and actions are remarkably close to that of the other

Klytemnestras depicted by the women revisionists. Perhaps Kassandra and Klytaimnestra share a common voice to form a multiple female self, what Kassandra would call a "we."

5. There is, perhaps, a male writer's response to this question—but it is hardly encouraging. In 1989, Stefan Schütz wrote a play entitled *Orestesobsession,* first produced in 1991 at the Kapuziner Theater in Luxembourg, with its German premier in 1993 at the Freie Kammerspiele in Magdeburg; the English translation by Jonathan Kalb appeared in *TheatreForum,* 1993, with a commentary by Kalb entitled "The Obsessions of Stefan Schütz." In Schütz's version, Orestes rejects both his father and his mother but refuses to kill either. Instead, he strangles Electra and dismembers himself in a dream sequence. While this gives neither the feminine nor the masculine the upper hand, it makes clear that everyone loses—in Troy, Nazi Germany, and Germany of the 1990s.

6. On the performativity of gender as constitutive of identity, see Butler, *Gender Trouble,* particularly 134–41.

7. My quoted phrases here are from Holquist and Emerson and their definition of what constitutes the dialogic in Bakhtin, *The Dialogic Imagination,* 427.

8. News reports from 1999 recorded a similar cycle as abused and traumatized ethnic Albanians of Kosovo returned to pillage the homes of their Serbian abusers and to rape and kill in turn. Vengeance seems never to be far away in modern culture. Posters from the 1960s reading "Give Peace a Chance" are covered by bumper stickers in the late 1990s reading "Give War a Chance." The spiral of violence—ethnic, racial, national, sexual—seemed to begin again as the millennium ended.

Appendix

Genealogies of the House of Atreus

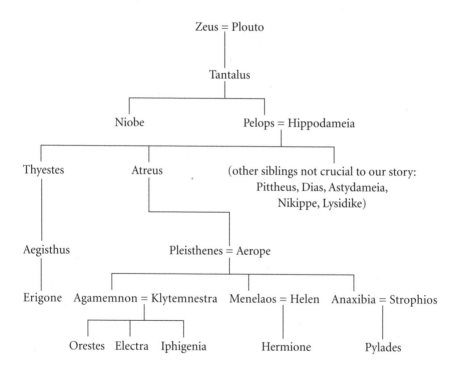

Alternate Version of House of Atreus

In this version, Thyestes rapes his daughter Pelopia to engender Aegisthus. Atreus later marries Pelopia thinking her another king's daughter. When Aegisthus is born, she commits suicide and tries to expose him. He is saved by Atreus, who thinks Aegisthus to be his own son. Atreus sends him to slay Thyestes, who identifies himself as Aegisthus's father. Aegisthus then slays Atreus.

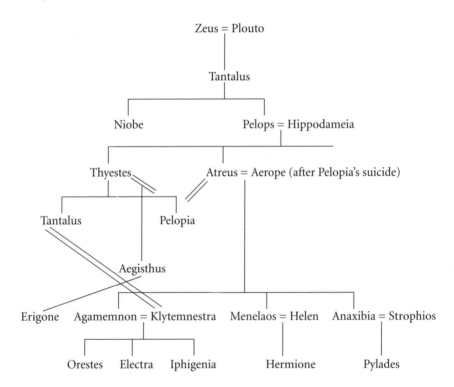

Genealogy of Klytemnestra

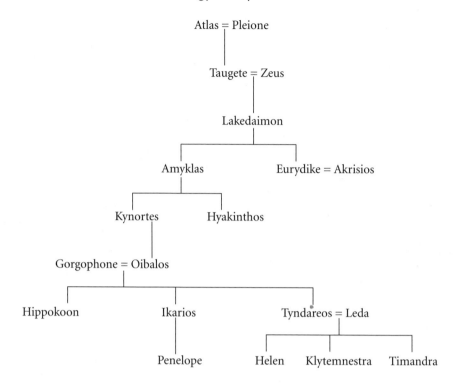

Atlas = Pleione

Taugete = Zeus

Lakedaimon

Amyklas   Eurydike = Akrisios

Kynortes   Hyakinthos

Gorgophone = Oibalos

Hippokoon   Ikarios   Tyndareos = Leda

Penelope   Helen   Klytemnestra   Timandra

Alternate Genealogy for Klytemnestra

In this version, Leda also mates with Zeus. Klytemnestra is always held to be Tyndareos's daughter, Helen to be Zeus's. The twin brothers Kastor and Pollux (the Dioskuri) are sometimes both mortal sons of Tyndareos, sometimes both immortal sons of Zeus, but most often Kastor is the mortal son of Tyndareos and Pollux the immortal son of Zeus.

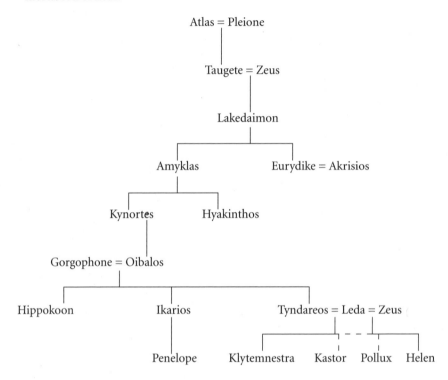

Bibliography

Abba, Luisa, Gabriella Ferri, Giorgio Lazzarello, Elena Medi, and Silvia Motta. *La coscienza di sfruttata*. Milan: Mazzotta, 1972.

Adams, Marion. "Christa Wolf: Marxismus und Patriarchat." In *Frauenliteratur: Autorinnen—Perspektiven—Konzepte*. Ed. Manfred Jurgensen. Bern: Lang, 1983. 123–37.

Aeschylus. *The Oresteia*. Trans. Robert Fagles. New York: Bantam, 1977.

Alabau, Magaly. *Electra, Clitemnestra*. New York: Libros del Maitén, 1986.

Amann, Jürg. *Iphigenie oder Operation Meereswind*. Düsseldorf: Verlag Eremiten-Presse, 1998.

Anderlini, Serena. "Dacia Maraini: Prolegomena for a Feminist Dramaturgy of the Feminine." *Diacritics* 21.2–3 (1991): 148–60.

Aristotle. *Generation of Animals*. Trans. A. L. Peck. Loeb Classical Library. Cambridge, Mass.: Harvard University Press, 1963.

———. *Poetics*. Trans. H. Rackham. Loeb Classical Library. Cambridge, Mass.: Harvard University Press, 1977.

Auerbach, Erich. *Mimesis: The Representation of Reality in Western Literature*. Trans. Willard R. Trask. Princeton: Princeton University Press, 1953. Originally published as *Mimesis: Dargestellte Wirklichkeit in der abendländischen Literatur*. Bern: A. Francke, 1946.

Auffret, Séverine. *Des couteaux contre des femmes*. Paris: Des Femmes, 1982.

———. *Mélanippe la philosophe*. Paris: Des Femmes, 1988.

———. *Nous, Clytemnestre: Du tragique et des masques*. Paris: Des Femmes, 1984.

———, contrib. *Conceptualización de lo feminino en la filosofía antigua*. Ed. Celia Amorós. Madrid: Siglo Veintiuno de España Editores, 1994.

———, ed. *Du célibat volontaire, ou, La vie sans engagement, 1700*, by Gabrielle Suchon. Paris: Indigo and Côte-femmes Editions, 1994.

———, ed. *Traité de la morale et de la politique, 1693: La liberté*, by Gabrielle Suchon. Paris: Des Femmes, 1988.

Austin, Norman. *Helen of Troy and Her Shameless Phantom*. Ithaca: Cornell University Press, 1994.

Bachofen, Johann Jakob. *Myth, Religion, and Mother Right*. Trans. Ralph Manheim. Princeton: Princeton University Press, 1967. Originally published as *Das Mutterrecht: Eine Untersuchung über die Gynaikokratie der alten Welt nach ihrer religiösen und rechtlichen Natur*. Stuttgart: Krais and Hoffman, 1861.

Bakhtin, Mikhail. *The Dialogic Imagination: Four Essays by M. M. Bakhtin*. Trans. Michael Holquist and Caryl Emerson. Ed. Michael Holquist. Austin: University of Texas Press, 1981.

———. *Esthétique et théorie du roman*. Paris: Gallimard, 1978.

———. *Problems of Dostoevsky's Poetics*. Trans. and ed. Caryl Emerson. Minneapolis: University of Minnesota Press, 1984.

———. *Rabelais and His World*. Trans. Helene Iswolsky. Cambridge, Mass.: MIT Press, 1965.

Balbo, Laura. *Stato di famiglia*. Milan: Etas Libri, 1976.

Bamberger, Joan. "The Myth of Matriarchy." In *Woman, Culture, and Society*. Ed. Michelle Zimbalist Rosaldo and Louise Lamphere. Stanford: Stanford University Press, 1974. 263–80.

Bammer, Angelika. "Testing the Limits: Christa Reinig's Radical Vision." *Women in German Yearbook 2*. Ed. Marianne Burkhard and Edith Waldstein. Lanham, Md.: University Press of America, 1986. 107–27.

Barthes, Roland. 1957. *Mythologies*. Trans. Annette Lavers. New York: Hill and Wang, 1972.

Bassi, Tina Lagostena. "Violence against Women and the Response of Italian Institutions." Trans. David Fairservice. In *Visions and Revisions: Women in Italian Culture*. Ed. Mirna Cicioni and Nicole Prunster. Oxford: Berg, 1993. 199–212.

Bauschinger, Sigrid. "Christine Brückner: Das Werk und seine Leser." In *Über Christine Brückner: Aufsätze, Rezensionen, Interviews*. Ed. Gunther Tietz. Frankfurt: Ullstein, 1989. 225–301.

Baym, Nina. "Melodramas of Beset Manhood: How Theories of American Fiction Exclude Women Authors." In *The New Feminist Criticism: Essays on Women, Literature, and Theory*. Ed. Elaine Showalter. New York: Pantheon Books, 1985. 63–80.

Beauvoir, Simone de. *The Second Sex*. Trans. H. M. Parshley. 1953. New York: Vintage Books, 1974. Originally published as *Le deuxieme sexe*. Paris: Librairie Gallimard, 1949.

Beer, Michael. *Klytemnestra: Trauerspiel in vier Abtheilungen*. Leipzig: Brockhaus, 1823.

Benoît de Sainte-Maure. *Le roman de Troie*. Paris: Firmin-Didot et cie, 1904–12.

Bethe, Erich. "Klytaimestra." In *Paulys Realencyclopädie der classischen Altertumswissenschaft*. Ed. August Friedrich von Pauly and George Wissowa. Rev. ed. Stuttgart: J. B. Metzler, 1914–95. 11, part 1:890–93.

Beye, Charles. "Male and Female in the Homeric Poems." *Ramus: Critical Studies in Greek and Roman Literature* 3.2 (1974): 87–101.

Biener, Joachim. "Die Fontane-Rezeption in erzählerischen Schaffen Christine Brückners." In *Über Christine Brückner: Aufsätze, Rezensionen, Interviews*. Ed. Gunther Tietz. Frankfurt: Ullstein, 1989. 33–50.

Blundell, Sue. *Women in Ancient Greece*. Cambridge, Mass.: Harvard University Press, 1995.

Bogen, Nancy. *Bobe Mayse: A Tale of Washington Square*. New York: Twickenham Press, 1993.

———. *How to Write Poetry*. 3d ed. New York: Macmillan, 1998.

———. *Klytaimnestra Who Stayed at Home*. New York: Twickenham Press, 1980.

———, ed. *William Blake: Book of Thel*. Providence: Brown University Press, 1971.

Bovenschen, Sylvia. *Die imaginierte Weiblichkeit: Exemplarische Untersuchungen zu kulturgeschichtlichen und literarischen Präsentationsformen des Weiblichen.* Frankfurt: Suhrkamp, 1979.

Bradley, Marion Zimmer. *The Firebrand.* New York: Pocket Books, 1987.

Briffault, Robert. *The Mothers: A Study of the Origins of Sentiments and Institutions.* New York: Macmillan, 1927.

Brooke-Rose, Christine. *Amalgamemnon.* Manchester: Carcanet, 1984.

Brown, Laura S. "Not outside the Range: One Feminist Perspective on Psychic Trauma." In *Trauma: Explorations in Memory.* Ed. Cathy Caruth. Baltimore: Johns Hopkins University Press, 1995. 100–112.

Brückner, Christine. "Bist du nun glücklich, toter Agamemnon?" In *Mein schwarzes Sofa.* Frankfurt: Ullstein, 1981. Rpt. in *Wenn du geredet hättest, Desdemona: Ungehaltene Reden ungehaltener Frauen.* Frankfurt: Ullstein, 1988. 155–68.

———. *Die Burgerinnen von Calais.* Berlin: Ullstein, 1997.

———. *Desdemona, If Only You Had Spoken!: Eleven Uncensored Speeches of Eleven Incensed Women.* Trans. Eleanor Bron. London: Virago, 1992.

———. *Ehe die Spuren verwehen.* Gutersloh, Germany: C. Bertelsmann, 1954.

———. *Gillyflower Kid.* Trans. Ruth Hein. New York: Fromm International, 1982. Originally published as *Jauche und Levkojen.* Berlin: Ullstein, 1975.

———. *Der Kokon.* Berlin: Ullstein, 1966.

Brügmann, Margret. *Amazonen der Literatur: Studien zur deutschsprachigen Frauenliteratur der 70er Jahre.* Amsterdam: Rodopi, 1986.

Bulwer-Lytton, Edward. *Clytemnestra, The Earl's Return, and Other Poems.* London: Chapman and Hall, 1855.

The Burning Bed. Dir. Robert Greenwald. Prod. Carol Schreder. Tisch/Avnet Productions, 1984.

Butler, Judith. *Antigone's Claim: Kinship between Life and Death.* New York: Columbia University Press, 2000.

———. *Gender Trouble: Feminism and the Subversion of Identity.* New York: Routledge, 1990.

Cacoyannis, Michael, dir. *Iphigenie.* Burbank, Calif.: Columbia Picture Home Entertainment, 1982. Videocassette.

Cairns, Lucille. "Passion and Paranoia: Power Structures and the Representation of Men in the Writings of Marie Cardinal." *French Studies* 46.3 (1992): 280–95.

———. "Roots and Alienation in Marie Cardinal's *Au Pays de mes Racines.*" *Forum* 29.4 (1993): 346–58.

Cameron, Averil, and Amelie Kuhrt. *Images of Women in Antiquity.* Detroit: Wayne State University Press, 1983.

Cancik, Hubert, and Helmut Schneider, eds. *Der neue Pauly: Enzyklopädie der Antike.* Stuttgart: J. B. Metzler, 1999.

Cardinal, Marie. *La clé sur la porte.* Paris: Grasset, 1972.

———. *La Médée d'Euripide.* Paris: Grasset, 1987.

———. *Le passé empiété.* Paris: Grasset, 1983.

———. *The Words to Say It.* Trans. Pat Goodheart. Cambridge: Van Vactor and Goodheart, 1983. Originally published as *Les mots pour le dire.* Paris: Grasset, 1975.

Cardinal, Marie, and Gisèle Halimi. *The Right to Choose.* Trans. Rosemary Morgan. St. Lucia: University of Queensland Press, 1977. Originally published as *La cause des femmes: Propos recueillis par Marie Cardinal.* Paris: Grasset, 1973.

Cardinal, Marie, and Annie Leclerc. *In Other Words.* Trans. Amy Cooper. Bloomington: Indiana University Press, 1995. Originally published as *Autrement Dit.* Paris: Grasset, 1977.

Cargill, Linda. *To Follow the Goddess.* Charlottesville, Va.: Cheops Books, 1991.

Carpenter, Rhys. *Folktale, Fiction, and Saga in the Homeric Epics.* Berkeley: University of California Press, 1946.

Caruth, Cathy. *Unclaimed Experience: Trauma, Narrative, and History.* Baltimore: Johns Hopkins University Press, 1996.

———, ed. *Trauma: Explorations in Memory.* Baltimore: Johns Hopkins University Press, 1995.

Case, Sue-Ellen. *Feminism and Theater.* London: Macmillan, 1988.

———, ed. *Performing Feminisms: Feminist Critical Theory and Theater.* Baltimore: Johns Hopkins University Press, 1990.

Cavallaro, Daniela. "Clytemnestra, Phaedra, and Medea in Contemporary Women's Theatre in Italy and Spain: Greek Characters in Search of a Female Author." Ph.D. diss., Northwestern University, 1994.

Ceccatty, René de, and Ryôji Nakamura. "La nuit de Tampaku-Ryô: Entretien avec Dacia Maraini." *Europe: Revue littéraire mensuelle* 64.693–94 (1987): 140–54.

Chaucer, Geoffrey. *The Works of Geoffrey Chaucer.* Boston: Houghton Mifflin, 1961.

Chesler, Phyllis. *Women and Madness.* Garden City, N.Y.: Doubleday, 1972.

Childbirth by Choice Trust. *Abortion in Law, History, and Religion.* Toronto: Childbirth by Choice Trust, 1995.

Chodorow, Nancy. *The Reproduction of Mothering: Psychoanalysis and the Sociology of Gender.* Berkeley: University of California Press, 1978.

Cixous, Hélène. "The Laugh of the Medusa." Trans. Keith Cohen and Paula Cohen. *Signs* 1.4 (Summer 1976): 875–93. Originally published as "Le rire de la méduse." In *L'arc.* N.p., 1975. 39–54.

Cixous, Hélène, and Catherine Clément. *The Newly Born Woman.* Trans. Betsy Wing. Minneapolis: University of Minnesota Press, 1986. Originally published as *La jeune née.* Paris: Union général d'éditions, 1975.

Clampitt, Amy. *Archaic Figure.* New York: Alfred A. Knopf, 1987.

Clover, Carol J. "Her Body, Himself: Gender in the Slasher Film." *Representations* 20 (Autumn 1987): 187–228.

———. *Men, Women, and Chain Saws: Gender in the Modern Horror Film.* Princeton: Princeton University Press, 1992.

Concannon, Diana M. *Helen's Passage.* Redondo Beach, Calif.: Cavatica, 1998.

Copioli, Rosita. "Elena." Ms. 1994.

Cramer, Sibylle. "Eine unendliche Geschichte des Widerstands: Zu Christa Wolfs Erzählungen *Kein Ort: Nirgends* und *Kassandra.*" In *Christa Wolf Materialienbuch.* Ed. Klaus Sauer. Rev. ed. Darmstadt: Luchterhand, 1983. 121–42.

Dagnino, Pauline. "*Fra madre e marito:* The Mother/Daughter Relationship in Dacia Maraini's *Lettre a Marina.*" In *Visions and Revisions: Women in Italian Culture.* Ed. Mirna Cicioni and Nicole Prunster. Oxford: Berg, 1993. 183–97.

D'Arms, Edward, and Karl Hulley. "The Oresteia Story in the *Odyssey.*" *TAPA* 77 (1946): 212–22.

Dassanowsky-Harris, Robert von. "Finding Words: Literary-Historical Revisionism in Christine Brückner's *Wenn du geredet hättest, Desdemona.*" *Seminar* 31.4 (1995): 331–44.

Davies, Malcolm. "Aeschylus' Clytemnestra: Sword or Axe?" *Classical Quarterly* 37.1 (1987): 65–75.

Davis, Natalie Zermon. "Women on Top." *Society and Culture in Early Modern France.* Stanford: Stanford University Press, 1975. 124–51.

Davreux, Juliette. *La légende de la prophetesse Cassandre d'après les textes et les monuments.* Paris: Bibliothèque de la Faculté de Philosophie et Lettres de l'Université de Liège, 1942.

Dexter, Miriam Robbins. *Whence the Goddesses: A Source Book.* New York: Pergamon Press, 1990.

DiBattista, Maria. "Memorializing Motherhood: *Literary Women* and Modernity." *Signs* 24.3 (1999): 763–70.

———. "The Triumph of Clytemnestra: The Charades in *Vanity Fair.*" *PMLA* 95.5 (1980): 827–37.

DuBois, Page. *Sappho Is Burning.* Chicago: University of Chicago Press, 1995.

DuPlessis, Rachel Blau. *Writing beyond the Ending: Narrative Strategies of Twentieth-Century Women Writers.* Bloomington: Indiana University Press, 1985.

Durham, Carolyn A. *The Contexture of Feminism: Marie Cardinal and Multicultural Literacy.* Urbana: University of Illinois Press, 1992.

———. "Patterns of Influence: Simone de Beauvoir and Marie Cardinal." *French Review* 60.3 (1987): 341–48.

Eigler, Friederike. "Feminist Criticism and Bakhtin's Dialogic Principles: Making the Transition from Theory to Textual Analysis." In *Women in German Yearbook 11.* Ed. Sara Friedrichsmeyer and Patricia Herminghouse. Lincoln: University of Nebraska Press, 1995. 189–203.

Electra.com. <http://electra.com> (March 20, 1999).

Eliot, T. S. "*Ulysses,* Order, and Myth." In *Criticism: The Foundations of Modern Literary Judgement.* Ed. Mark Schorer, Josephine Miles, and Gordon McKenzie. Rev. ed. New York: Harcourt, Brace, and World, 1958. 269–71.

Elliot, Patricia. "In the Eye of Abjection: Marie Cardinal's *The Words to Say It.*" *Mosaic* 20.4 (1987): 71–81.

Elstun, Esther. "Christa Reinig's *Emasculation:* Male Chauvinism as Science Fiction." In *Women Worldwalkers: New Dimensions of Science Fiction and Fantasy.* Ed. Jane B. Weedman. Lubbock: Texas Tech Press, 1985. 125–38.

Emmerich, Wolfgang. "Identität und Geschlechtertausch: Notizen zur Selbstdarstellung der Frau in der neueren DDR-Literatur." *Basis* 8 (1978): 127–54, 245–58.

Ester, Hans. Review of *Entmannung,* by Christa Reinig. *Deutsche Bücher* 8 (1978): 112–14.

Euripides. *Euripides 2: "The Cyclops," "Heracles," "Iphigenia in Tauris," "Helen."* Trans. William Arrowsmith, Witter Bynner, and Richmond Lattimore. Chicago: University of Chicago Press, 1969.

———. *Euripides 3: "Hecuba," "Andromache," "The Trojan Women," "Ion."* Trans. William Arrowsmith, John Frederick Nims, Richmond Lattimore, and R. F. Willetts. Chicago: University of Chicago Press, 1958.

————. *Euripides 4: "Rhesus," "The Suppliant Women," "Orestes," and "Iphigenia in Au-lis."* Trans. William Arrowsmith, Frank William Jones, Richmond Lattimore, and Charles R. Walker. 1958. Chicago: University of Chicago Press, 1968.

————. *Euripides: Ten Plays.* Trans. Moses Hadas and John McLean. New York: Bantam Press, 1960.

Fagles, Robert, and W. B. Stanford. Introduction to *The Oresteia,* by Aeschylus. Trans. Robert Fagles. New York: Bantam, 1977. 1–99.

Fallaci, Oriana. *Penelope alla guerra.* Milano: Rizzoli, 1962.

Fehervary, Helen. "Autorschaft, Geschlechtsbewußtsein, und Öffentlichkeit: Versuch über Heiner Müllers *Die Hamletmaschine* und Christa Wolf's *Kein Ort: Nirgends.*" In *Ent-würfe von Frauen in der Literatur des 20. Jahrhunderts.* Ed. Irmela von der Lühe. Berlin: Argument, 1982. 132–53.

Fetterley, Judith. *The Resisting Reader: A Feminist Approach to American Fiction.* Blooming-ton: Indiana University Press, 1978.

Foley, Helene, ed. *Reflections of Women in Antiquity.* London: Gordon and Breach, 1981.

Frabotta, Biancamaria, ed. *Femminismo e lotta di classe in Italia, 1970–1973.* Rome: Savel-li, 1973.

Fraenkel, Eduard, ed. *Aeschylus: "Agamemnon."* Oxford: Clarendon Press, 1950.

Freiert, William K. "Martha Graham's 'Clytemnestra.'" In *Views of Clytemnestra Ancient and Modern.* Ed. Sally MacEwen. Lewiston, N.Y.: Edwin Mellen Press, 1990. 84–90.

Froula, Christine. "When Eve Reads Milton: Undoing the Canonical Economy." In *Can-ons.* Ed. Robert von Hallbert. Chicago: University of Chicago Press, 1983. 149–75.

Galt, John. *The Tragedies of Maddalen, Agamemnon, Lady Macbeth, Antonia, and Clytem-nestra.* London: Cadell and Davies, 1812.

Gantz, Timothy. *Early Greek Myth: A Guide to Literary and Artistic Sources.* 2 vols. Balti-more: Johns Hopkins University Press, 1993–96.

Gilbert, Sandra M., and Susan Gubar. *The Madwoman in the Attic: The Woman Writer and the Nineteenth-Century Literary Imagination.* New Haven: Yale University Press, 1979.

Gilpin, Heidi. "*Cassandra:* Creating a Female Voice." In *Responses to Christa Wolf.* Ed. Marilyn Sibley Fries. Detroit: Wayne State University Press, 1989. 349–66.

Gimbutas, Marija. *The Goddesses and Gods of Old Europe, 6500–3500 B.C.: Myths and Cult Images.* 1974. Rev. ed. Berkeley: University of California Press, 1982.

————. *The Language of the Goddess: Unearthing the Hidden Symbols of Western Civili-zation.* San Francisco: Harper and Row, 1989.

Giraudoux, Jean. *Electre.* 1937. Paris: Gallimard, 1991.

Glenn, Cheryl. *Rhetoric Retold: Regendering the Tradition from Antiquity through the Re-naissance.* Carbondale: Southern Illinois University Press, 1997.

Gluck, Christoph Willibald. *Iphigénie en Aulide.* Braunschweig: H. Litolff, 1867.

Goethe, Johann Wolfang von. *Faust Parts 1 and 2 (German and English).* Trans. Walter Kaufmann. Garden City, N.Y.: Doubleday. 1961.

————. *Iphigenia.* Trans. Charles E. Passage. New York: F. Ungar, 1963.

————. *Iphigenie auf Tauris.* Freiburg: P. Siebeck, 1883.

Goldhill, Simon. *Language, Sexuality, Narrative: The "Oresteia."* Cambridge: Cambridge University Press, 1984.

Gordon, Linda. *Woman's Body, Woman's Right: A Social History of Birth Control in Amer-ica.* New York: Grossman, 1976.

Graham, Martha. *Blood Memory.* New York: Doubleday, 1991.

———. *The Notebooks of Martha Graham.* New York: Harcourt Brace Jovanovich, 1973.

Grahn, Judy. *The Queen of Swords.* Boston: Beacon, 1987.

———. *The Queen of Wands.* Trumansburg, N.Y.: Crossing Press, 1982.

Graves, Robert. *Mammon and the Black Goddess.* London: Cassell, 1965.

———. *The White Goddess: A Historical Grammar of Poetic Myth.* New York: Farrar, Straus, and Giroux, 1948.

Grene, David. "Introduction to the *Electra.*" In *Sophocles 2: "Ajax," "The Women of Trachis," "Electra," and "Philoctetes."* 1957. Chicago: University of Chicago Press, 1969. 122–24.

Gubar, Susan. "Mother, Maiden, and the Marriage of Death: Women Writers and an Ancient Myth." *Women's Studies* 6.3 (1979): 301–15.

Hadas, Pamela White. "A Penny for Her Thoughts." In *Designing Women.* New York: Alfred A. Knopf, 1979. 60–61.

Haigh, Samantha. "Between Irigaray and Cardinal: Reinventing Maternal Genealogies." *Modern Language Review* 89 (part 1) (1994): 61–70.

Hall, Colette. "L'Écriture féminine and the Search for the Mother in the Works of Violette Leduc and Marie Cardinal." In *Women in French Literature.* Ed. Michel Guggenheim. *Stanford French and Italian Studies* 58 (1988): 231–38.

———. *Marie Cardinal.* Amsterdam: Rodopi, 1994.

———. "'*She* Is More than *I*': Writing and the Search for Identity in the Works of Marie Cardinal." In *Redefining Autobiography in Twentieth Century Women's Fiction.* Ed. Janice Morgan and Colette Hall. New York: Garland Press, 1991. 57–71.

Harder, Ruth E. "Klytaimestra." In *Der neue Pauly: Enzyklopädie der Antike.* Ed. Hubert Cancik and Helmut Schneider. Stuttgart: J. B. Metzler, 1999. 6:611–12.

Hartsock, Nancy C. M. *Money, Sex, and Power: Toward a Feminist Historical Materialism.* New York: Longman, 1983.

Hauptmann, Gerhart. *Die Atriden-Tetralogie.* Berlin: Suhrkamp, 1949.

H. D. *Helen in Egypt.* New York: New Directions, 1961.

Herman, Judith. *Trauma and Recovery: The Aftermath of Violence—from Domestic Abuse to Political Terror.* New York: Basic Books, 1992.

Herrmann, Anne. *The Dialogic and Difference: "An/Other Woman" in Virginia Woolf and Christa Wolf.* New York: Columbia University Press, 1989.

Hilzinger, Sonja. *Christa Wolf.* Stuttgart: J. B. Metzler, 1986.

———. *Kassandra: Über Christa Wolf.* Frankfurt: Haag und Herchen, 1982.

Hirsch, Marianne. *The Mother/Daughter Plot: Narrative, Psychoanalysis, Feminism.* Bloomington: University of Indiana Press, 1989.

Hogan, Judy. *Cassandra Speaking.* Berkeley, Calif.: Thorp Spring Press, 1977.

Hofmannsthal, Hugo von. *Elektra: A Tragedy in One Act.* Trans. Arthur Symons. New York: Brentano's, 1912. Originally published as *Elektra.* Frankfurt: S. Fischer, 1904.

Hofmannsthal, Hugo von, and Richard Strauss. *Elektra: Tragedy in One Act: Opus 58.* London: Boosey and Hawke, c. 1943.

Homans, Margaret. "The Woman in the Cave: Recent Feminist Fictions and the Classical Underworld." *Contemporary Literature* 29.3 (1988): 396–402.

Homer. *The Iliad.* Trans. Richmond Lattimore. Chicago: University of Chicago Press, 1951.

———. *The Odyssey.* Trans. Robert Fagles. New York: Viking Penguin, 1996.

Horn, Peter. "Christa Reinig und 'Das weibliche Ich.'" In *Frauenliteratur: Autorinnen—Perspektiven—Konzepte.* Ed. Manfred Jurgensen. Bern: Lang, 1983. 101–22.

Hostert, Anna Camaiti. "Intervista con Dacia Maraini." *Forum Italicum* 28.1 (1994): 111–15.

Huet, Marie-Hélène. *Monstrous Imagination.* Cambridge, Mass.: Harvard University Press, 1993.

International Planned Parenthood Federation (European Region). "Abortion Laws in Europe." Rev. ed. London: Planned Parenthood in Europe, 1993.

Irigaray, Luce. *Le corps-à-corps avec la mère.* Montreal: Les Éditions de la Pleine Lune, 1981.

———. *Ce sexe qui n'en est pas un.* Paris: Minuit, 1977. Selections translated in *New French Feminism.* Ed. Elaine Marks and Isabelle de Courtivron. Amherst: University of Massachusetts Press, 1980. 99–110.

Jacobus, Mary. "Reading Woman (Reading)." In *Reading Women: Essays in Feminist Criticism.* Ed. Mary Jacobus. New York: Columbia University Press, 1986. 3–24.

Jadwin, Lisa. "Clytemnestra Rewarded: The Double Conclusion of *Vanity Fair.*" In *Famous Last Words.* Ed. Alison Booth. Charlottesville: University Press of Virginia, 1993. 35–61.

Jarratt, Susan C. *Rereading the Sophists: Classical Rhetoric Refigured.* Carbondale: University of Southern Illinois Press, 1991.

Jehlen, Myra. "Archimedes and the Paradox of Feminist Criticism." In *The Signs Reader: Women, Gender, and Scholarship.* Ed. Elizabeth Abel and Emily K. Abel. Chicago: University of Chicago Press, 1983. 69–96.

Jens, Walter. "Freudenhaus statt Totenhaus." In *Über Christine Brückner: Aufsätze, Rezensionen, Interviews.* Ed. Gunther Tietz. Frankfurt: Ullstein, 1989. 164–68.

Jentgens, Stephanie. *Kassandra: Spielarten einer literarischen Figur.* Zurich: Olms-Weidmann, 1995.

Jurgensen, Manfred. *Deutsche Frauenautoren der Gegenwart: Bachmann, Reinig, Wolf, Wohmann, Struck, Leutenegger, Schwaiger.* Bern: Francke, 1983. 65–79.

———, ed. *Frauenliteratur: Autorinnen—Perspektiven—Konzepte.* Bern: Lang, 1983.

Kaplan, Cora. "Pandora's Box: Subjectivity, Class, and Sexuality in Socialist Feminist Criticism." In *Making a Difference: Feminist Literary Criticism.* Ed. Gayle Greene and Coppélia Kahn. London: Methuen, 1985. 146–76.

Karapanou, Margarita. *Kassandra and the Wolf.* Trans. N. C. Germanacos. New York: Harcourt Brace Jovanovich, 1976. Originally published as *He Kassandra Kai Ho Lykos.* Athens: Hermes, 1974.

Kennelly, Laura. "Clytemnestra Junior in Detroit." In *A Measured Response.* Ed. H. Palmer Hall. San Antonio: Pecan Grove Press, 1993. 90–92.

———. *The Passage of Mrs. Jung.* San Francisco: Norton Coker Press, 1990.

———, ed. *A Certain Attitude: Poems by Seven Texas Women.* San Antonio: Pecan Grove Press, 1995.

Keuls, Eva C. *The Reign of the Phallus: Sexual Politics in Ancient Athens.* New York: Harper and Row, 1985.

King, Katherine Callen. *Achilles: Paradigms of the War Hero from Homer to the Middle Ages.* Berkeley: University of California Press, 1987.

Köhlmeier, Michael. *Kalypso.* Munich: Piper, 1997.

———. *Telemach*. Munich: Piper, 1995.

Kolodny, Annette. "Dancing through the Minefield: Some Observations on the Theory, Practice, and Politics of Feminist Literary Criticism." In *The New Feminist Criticism: Essays on Women, Literature, and Theory*. Ed. Elaine Showalter. New York: Pantheon Books, 1985. 144–67.

———. "A Map for Rereading; or, Gender and the Interpretation of Literary Texts." *New Literary History* 2.3 (Spring 1980): 451–67.

Komar, Kathleen L. "The Communal Self: Re-Membering Female Identity in the Works of Christa Wolf and Monique Wittig." *Comparative Literature* 44.1 (1992): 42–58.

———. "The Hand That Rocks the Cradle Wields the Axe—Clytemnestra: Matriarch or Mariticide?" *Thamyris* 1.1 (1994): 81–103.

———. "Kassandra as a Rebel against War: The Theme of Heroism in Christa Wolf's Re-Vision of the Trojan War." In *Themes and Structures: Studies in German Literature from Goethe to the Present*. Ed. Alexander Stephan. Columbia, S.C.: Camden House, 1997. 234–53.

———. "Klytemnestra in Germany: Re-Visions of a Female Archetype by Christa Reinig and Christine Brückner." *Germanic Review* 49.1 (1994): 20–27.

———. "Paradigm Change: The Female Paradigm in Brecht's *Mutter Courage und ihre Kinder* and Christa Wolf's *Kassandra*." *Euphorion* 82.1 (1988): 116–26.

———. "Visions and Re-Visions: Contemporary Women Writers Re-Present Helen and Clytemnestra." In *Visions in History: Visions of the Other*. Ed. Margaret R. Higonnet and Sumie Jones. Tokyo: International Comparative Literature Association/University of Tokyo Press, 1995. 593–600.

Kristeva, Julia. "From One Identity to an Other." Trans. Thomas Gora, Alice Jardine, and Leon S. Roudiez. In *Desire in Language: A Semiotic Approach to Literature and Art*. Ed. Leon S. Roudiez. New York: Columbia University Press, 1980. 124–47. Originally published as "D'une identité à l'autre." *Tel Quel* 62 (Summer 1975): 10–27.

———. "Stabat Mater." In *The Kristeva Reader*. Trans. León S. Roudiez. Ed. Toril Moi. New York: Columbia University Press, 1986. 160–86. Originally published as "Hérethique de l'amour." *Tel Quel* 74 (Winter 1977): 30–49. Rpt. as "Stabat Mater." In *Histoires d'amour*. Paris: Denoël, 1983.

———. "Word, Dialogue, and Novel." Trans. Thomas Gora, Alice Jardine, and Leon S. Roudiez. In *Desire in Language: A Semiotic Approach to Literature and Art*. Ed. Leon S. Roudiez. New York: Columbia University Press, 1980. 64–91. Originally published as "Le mot, le dialogue et le roman." In *Séméiotiké: Recherches pour une sémanalyse*. Paris: Seuil, 1969.

Kuhn, Anna. *Christa Wolf's Utopian Vision: From Marxism to Feminism*. Cambridge: Cambridge University Press, 1988.

———. "Rewriting GDR History: The Christa Wolf Controversy." *GDR Bulletin* 17.1 (1991): 7–11.

Langner, Ilse. *Dramen*. 2 vols. Würzburg: Bergstadtverlag Korn, 1983–91.

Lanser, Susan Sniader. *Fictions of Authority: Women Writers and Narrative Voice*. Ithaca: Cornell University Press, 1992.

Laqueur, Thomas. *Making Sex: Body and Gender from the Greeks to Freud*. Cambridge, Mass.: Harvard University Press, 1990.

Lattimore, Richmond, trans. *Greek Lyrics.* Chicago: University of Chicago Press, 1949.

Lauter, Estella, and Carol Schreier Rupprecht, eds. *Feminist Archetypal Theory: Interdisciplinary Re-Visions of Jungian Thought.* Knoxville: University of Tennessee Press, 1985.

Lazzaro-Weis, Carlo. "Gender and Genre in Italian Feminist Literature in the Seventies." *Italica* 65.4 (1988): 293–307.

Lebeck, Anne. *The "Oresteia": A Study in Language and Structure.* Cambridge, Mass.: Harvard University Press, 1971.

Le Clézio, Marguerite. "Mother and Motherland: The Daughter's Quest for Origins." *Stanford French Review* 5.3 (1981): 381–89.

Lefèvre, Raoul. *The Recuyell of the Historyes of Troye.* Trans. William Caxton. London: D. Nutt, 1894.

Lefkowitz, Mary. *Women in Greek Myth.* Baltimore: Johns Hopkins University Press, 1986.

Lennox, Sara. "'Der Versuch, man selbst zu sein': Christa Wolf und der Feminismus." In *Die Frau als Heldin und Autorin: Neue kritische Ansätze zur deutschen Literatur.* Ed. Wolfgang Paulsen. Bern: Francke, 1979. 217–22.

Lionnet, Françoise. *Autobiographical Voices: Race, Gender, and Self-Portraiture.* Ithaca: Cornell University Press, 1989.

Lister, Henry B. *Clytemnestra.* San Francisco: La Boheme Club, 1923.

Loraux, Nicole. *The Children of Athena: Athenian Ideas about Citizenship and the Division between the Sexes.* Trans. Caroline Levine. Princeton: Princeton University Press, 1993.

———. *The Experiences of Tiresias: The Feminine and the Greek Man.* Trans. Paula Wissing. Princeton: Princeton University Press, 1995.

Lord, Albert. *The Singer of Tales.* Cambridge, Mass.: Harvard University Press, 1960.

Love, Myra. "Christa Wolf and Feminism: Breaking the Patriarchal Connection." *New German Critique* 16 (Winter 1979): 31–53.

MacEwen, Gwendolyn. *The Trojan Women.* Toronto: Playwrights Canada, 1979.

MacEwen, Sally, ed. *Views of Clytemnestra, Ancient and Modern.* Lewiston, N.Y.: Edwin Mellen Press, 1990.

Mactoux, Marie. *Penelope: Légènde et mythe.* Paris: Belles Lettres, 1975.

Malloy, Judy. *Its Name Was Penelope.* Watertown: Eastgate Systems, 1992.

Maraini, Dacia. *The Age of Discontent.* Trans. Frances Frenaye. London: Weidenfeld and Nicolson, 1963. Originally published as *L'eta del malessere.* Turin: Einaudi, 1963.

———. *Il bambino Alberto.* Milano: Bompiani, 1986.

———. "Dacia Maraini: Prolegomena for a Feminist Dramaturgy of the Feminine." *Diacritics: A Review of Contemporary Criticism* 21.2–3 (1991): 148–60.

———. *Dreams of Clytemnestra.* Trans. Tim Vode. In *Only Prostitutes Marry in May.* Ed. Rhoda Helfman Kaufman. New York: Guernica, 1994. 177–315. Originally published as *I sogni di Clitennestra e altre commedie.* Milan: Tascabili Bompiani, 1981.

———. *Letters to Marina.* Trans. Elspeth Spottiswood. London: Camden, 1987. Originally published as *Lettere a Marina.* Milan: Bompiani, 1981

———. *La lunga vita di Marianna Ucria.* Milano: Rizolli, 1990.

———. *Memories of a Lady Thief.* Trans. Nino Rootes. London: Abelard-Schuman, 1973. Originally published as *Memoria di una ladra.* Milan: Bompiani, 1972.

———. *Women at War.* Trans. Mora Benetti and Elspeth Spottiswood. London: Lighthouse Books, 1984. Originally published as *Donna in guerra.* Turin: Einaudi, 1975.

Margraff, Ruth. *The Elektra Fugues.* Commissioned by Tiny Mythic Theater Company. New York, 1996.

Marks, Elaine, and Isabelle de Courtivron, eds. *New French Feminisms.* Amherst: University of Massachusetts Press, 1980.

Marquardt, Patricia A. "Clytemnestra: A Felicitous Spelling in the *Odyssey.*" *Arethusa* 25 (Spring 1992): 241–54.

Marshall, Catherine. "Ilse Langner's *Klytämnestra:* A Feminist Response to the Rhetoric of War." In *Women in German Yearbook 14.* Ed. Sara Friedrichsmeyer and Patricia Herminghouse. Lincoln: University of Nebraska Press, 1999. 183–99.

Martha Graham Dance Company. Prod. Emile Ardolino. Dir. Merrill Brockway. New York: Nonesuch, 1998. Videocassette. Originally recorded February 1976 in Nashville, Tennessee.

Matthieu, Pierre. *Clytemnestre: De la vengeance des injures perdurable à la postérité des offencez, et des malheureuses fins de la volupté.* Ed. Gilles Ernst. Geneva: Libr. Droz, 1984.

Mauser, Wolfram. "Das 'dunkle Tier' und die Seherin: Zu Christa Wolfs *Kassandra*-Phantasie." *Freiburger literatur-psychologische Gespräche* 4 (1985): 139–57.

McAlister-Hermann, Judith. "Literary Emasculation: Household Imagery in Christa Reinig's *Entmannung.*" In *Beyond the Eternal Feminine: Critical Essays on Women and German Literature.* Ed. Susan L. Cocalis and Kay Goodman. Stuttgarter Arbeiten zur Germanistik 98. Stuttgart: Heinz, 1982. 401–19.

McDonald, Marianne. "Suzuki's 'Clytemnestra': Social Crisis and a Son's Nightmare." In *Views of Clytemnestra Ancient and Modern.* Ed. Sally MacEwen. Lewiston, N.Y.: Edwin Mellen Press, 1990. 65–83.

McLaughlin, Ellen. "Electra." Ms. Commissioned by the Actors Gang of Los Angeles. Los Angeles, 1992.

———. *Iphigenia and Other Daughters.* New York, 1995.

———. "Notes on playbill for *Iphigenia and Other Daughters.*" Copy sent to Kathleen L. Komar, Mar. 1999.

McPherson, Karin. "Ist der Schriftsteller an sein Geschlecht gebunden?: Zu Christa Wolfs Prosa seit Beginn der 70er Jahre." *Die Horen* 28.4 (1983): 68–75.

Meagher, Robert Emmet. *Helen: Myth, Legend, and the Culture of Misogyny.* New York: Continuum, 1995.

Merkel, Inge. *Eine ganz gewöhnliche Ehe: Odysseus und Penelope.* Salzburg: Residenz, 1987.

Merwin, W. S., and George E. Dimock Jr., trans. *Euripides' Iphigenia in Aulis.* New York: Oxford University Press, 1978.

Meyer-Gosau, Frauke. "Unsere Christa." *Emma* 6 (1984): 44–46.

Miller, Nancy K. "Arachnologies: The Woman, the Text, and the Critic." In *The Poetics of Gender.* Ed. Nancy K. Miller. New York: Columbia University Press, 1986. 270–96.

———. "Emphasis Added: Plots and Plausibilities in Women's Fiction." In *Subject to Change: Reading Feminist Writing.* Ed. Nancy K. Miller. New York: Columbia University Press, 1988. 25–46.

Millett, Kate. *Sexual Politics.* Garden City, N.Y.: Doubleday, 1970.

Mills, Linda G. "Justice Still Eludes Battered Women." *UCLA Today* 25 May 1999: 7.

Minh-ha, Trinh T. "L'innécriture: Féminisme et littérature." *French Forum* 8.1 (1983): 45–63.

———. *Woman, Native, Other: Writing Postcoloniality and Feminism.* Bloomington: Indiana University Press, 1989.

Mittman, Elizabeth. "Locating a Public Sphere: Some Reflections on Writers and *Öffentlichkeit* in the GDR." In *Women in German Yearbook 10.* Ed. Jeanette Clausen and Sara Friedrichsmeyer. Lincoln: University of Nebraska Press, 1995. 19–38.

Moi, Toril. *Sexual/Textual Politics.* 1985. New York: Routledge, 1991.

Molinaro, Ursule. *The Autobiography of Cassandra, Princess and Prophetess of Troy.* Danbury, Conn.: Archer Editions Press, 1979.

Montefiore, Jan. *Feminism and Poetry: Language, Experience, Identity in Women's Writing.* London: Pandora, 1987.

Neely, Carol Thomas. "Feminist Criticism in Motion." In *For Alma Mater: Theory and Practice in Feminist Scholarship.* Ed. Paula A. Treichler, Cheris Kramarae, and Beth Stafford. Urbana: University of Illinois Press, 1985. 69–90.

Neumann, Erich. *The Great Mother: An Analysis of the Archetype.* Trans. Ralph Manheim. Princeton: Princeton University Press, 1955.

Nochlin, Linda. "Why Have There Been No Great Women Artists?" *Art News* Jan. 1971: 22–39, 67–71.

Nord, Deborah Epstein. "Commemorating *Literary Women:* Ellen Moers and Feminist Criticism after Twenty Years." *Signs* 24.3 (1999): 734–47.

———. "The 'Epic Age': Realism and Rebellion in Ellen Moers's *Literary Women.*" *Signs* 24.3 (1999): 749–55.

O'Brien, Sharon. "'I Can Dare to Generalize': Celebrating *Literary Women.*" *Signs* 24:3 (1999): 757–61.

O'Neill, Eugene. *Mourning Becomes Electra: A Trilogy.* New York: H. Liveright, 1931.

Orenstein, Gloria Feman. *The Reflowering of the Goddess.* New York: Pergamon Press, 1990.

Ostriker, Alicia. "The Thieves of Language: Women Poets and Revisionist Mythmaking." In *The New Feminist Criticism: Essays on Women, Literature, and Theory.* Ed. Elaine Showalter. New York: Pantheon Books, 1985. 314–38.

Pallotta, Augustus. "Dacia Maraini: From Alienation to Feminism." *World Literature Today* 58.3 (1984): 359–62.

Passerini, Luisa. "The Women's Movement in Italy and the Events of 1968." Trans. David Fairservice. In *Visions and Revisions: Women in Italian Culture.* Ed. Mirna Cicioni and Nicole Prunster. Oxford: Berg, 1993. 167–82.

Patterson, Cynthia B. *The Family in Greek History.* Cambridge, Mass.: Harvard University Press, 1998.

Pauly, August Friedrich von. *Paulys Realencyclopädie der classischen Altertumswissenschaft.* Updated by Georg Wissowa, Wilhelm Kroll, and Kurt Witte. Stuttgart: J. B. Metzler, 1914–95.

Pearson, Carol Lynn. *Mother Wove the Morning.* Walnut Creek, Calif.: Pearson, 1992.

"People versus Clytemnestra." <http://www.members.tripod.com/NWO_2/index.html>.

Peradotto, John, and J. P. Sullivan, eds. *Women in the Ancient World: The Arethusa Papers.* Albany: State University of New York Press, 1984.

Pickering-Iazzi, Robin. "Designing Mothers: Images of Motherhood in Novels by Aleramo, Morante, Maraini, and Fallaci." *Annali D'Italianistica* 7 (1989): 325–40.

Pickle, Linda Schelbitzki. "Christa Wolf's *Cassandra:* Parallels to Feminism in the West." *Critique* 28 (Spring 1987): 149–58.

————. "'Scratching away the Male Tradition': Christa Wolf's *Kassandra*." *Contemporary Literature* 27.1 (1986): 32–47.

Pindar. *The Odes of Pindar*. Trans. C. M. Bowra. New York: Penguin Books, 1969.

Piper, Judith. "(Re)Dressing the Canon: Collage in Performance." Ms. 1990.

Piper, Judith, and Nancy Tuana. *The Fabulous Furies reVue*. Dallas: Judith Piper, 1988.

Pomeroy, Sarah. *Goddesses, Whores, Wives, and Slaves: Women in Classical Antiquity*. New York: Schocken, 1975.

————. *Women in Hellenistic Egypt: From Alexander to Cleopatra*. New York: Schocken, 1984.

Porter, David H. "A Note on Aeschylus *Agamemnon* 332." *Classical Philology* 83.4 (1988): 307–8.

Porter, James I. "Resisting Aesthetics: The Cassandra Motif in Christa Wolf and Aeschylus." In *Responses to Christa Wolf*. Ed. Marilyn Sibley Fries. Detroit: Wayne State University Press, 1989. 378–94.

Powrie, Phil. "A Womb of One's Own: The Metaphor of the Womb-Room as a Reading-Effect in Texts by Contemporary French Women Writers." *Paragraph* 12.3 (1989): 197–213.

Rabinowitz, Nancy. "From Force to Persuasion: Aeschylus's *Oresteia* as Cosmogenic Myth." *Ramus* 10.2 (1981): 159–91.

Rabinowitz, Nancy, and Amy Richlin, eds. *Feminist Theory and the Classics*. New York: Routledge, 1993.

Racine, Jean. *Iphigénie*. Paris: Compagnie des Libraires, 1743.

Ragué i Arias, Maria-Josep. *Clitemnestra*. Barcelona: Millà, 1987.

Ransmayr, Christoph. *Die letzte Welt*. Nördlingen: F. Greno, 1988.

Reinig, Christa. *Die Ballade vom blutigen Bomme*. Düsseldorf: Eremiten-Presse, 1972.

————. *Entmannung: Die Geschichte Ottos und seiner vier Frauen erzählt von Christa Reinig*. 1976. Darmstadt: Hermann Luchterhand Verlag, 1977.

————. *Erkennen, was die Rettung ist: Christa Reinig im Gespräch mit Marie-Luise Gansberg und Mechthild Beerlage*. Munich: Frauenoffensive, 1986.

————. *Die Frau im Brunnen*. Munich: Frauenoffensive, 1984.

————. *Die himmlische und die irdische Geometrie*. Düsseldorf: Eremiten-Presse, 1975.

————. *Mädchen ohne Uniform*. Düsseldorf: Eremiten-Presse, 1981.

————. *Mein Herz ist eine gelbe Blume: Christa Reinig im Gespräch mit Ekkehart Rudolph*. Düsseldorf: Eremiten-Presse, 1978.

————. *Sämtliche Gedichte*. Düsseldorf: Eremiten-Presse, 1984.

————. *Der Wolf und die Witwen*. Düsseldorf: Eremiten-Presse, 1980.

Rich, Adrienne. "When We Dead Awaken: Writing as Re-Vision." In *On Lies, Secrets, and Silence: Selected Prose, 1966–78*. New York: Norton, 1979. 33–49.

Riding, Laura. *A Trojan Ending*. 1937. Manchester: Carcanet Press, 1984.

Riviello, Tonia Caterina. "The Motif of Entrapment in Elsa Morante's *L'Isola di Arturo* and Dacia Maraini's *L'Età del Malessere*." *Rivista di Studi Italiani* 8.1–2 (1990): 70–87.

Robertson, Charles Martin, and Herbert Jenning Rose. "Clytemnestra." In *The Oxford Classical Dictionary*. Ed. N. G. L. Hammond and H. H. Scullard. 2d ed. Oxford: Clarendon Press, 1970. 256–57.

Robinson, Lillian S. "Canon Fathers and Myth Universe." *New Literary History* 19.1 (1987): 23–35.

———. "Treason Our Text: Feminist Challenges to the Literary Canon." In *The New Feminist Criticism: Essays on Women, Literature, and Theory.* Ed. Elaine Showalter. New York: Pantheon Books, 1985. 105–21.

Roch, Anne Donedey. "Répétition, maternité, et transgression dans trios œuvres de Marie Cardinal." *French Review* 65.4 (1992): 567–77.

Root, Maria. "A Model for Understanding Variations in the Experience of Traumata and Their Sequelae." Paper delivered at the Eighth Advanced Feminist Institute, Banff, Alberta, 1989.

———. "Reconstructing the Impact of Trauma on Personality." In *Personality and Psychopathology: Feminist Reappraisals.* Ed. Laura S. Brown and Mary Ballou. New York: Guilford, 1992. 229–65.

Rubin, Gayle. "The Traffic in Women: Notes on the 'Political Economy' of Sex." In *Toward an Anthropology of Women.* Ed. Rayna Rapp Reiter. New York: Monthly Review Press, 1975. 157–210.

Rutherford, Megan. "Women Run the World." *Time* 28 June 1999: 74G.

Sampaio, Alice. *Penelope, a infanta.* Lisbon: n.p., 1977.

Sartre, Jean-Paul. *Huis clos; suivi de, Les mouches.* Paris: Gallimard, 1947.

Sauer, Klaus, ed. *Christa Wolf Materialienbuch.* Rev. ed. Darmstadt, Germany: Luchterhand, 1983.

Schnell, Veronika. "Blutrünstiges und Monströses in *Entmannung:* Einige Überlegungen zur literarischen Aufarbeitung geschlechtsspezifischer Gewaltverhältnisse bei Christa Reinig." In *Der Widerspenstigen Zähmung: Studien zur bezwungenen Weiblichkeit in der Literatur vom Mittelalter bis zur Gegenwart.* Ed. Sylvia Wallinger and Monika Jones. Innsbrucker Beiträge zur Kulturwissenschaft, Germanistische Reihe 31. Innsbruck: Inst. für Germanistik, Universität Innsbruck, 1986. 311–34.

Schondorff, Joachim, ed. *Elektra: Sophokles, Euripides, Hofmannsthal, O'Neill, Giraudoux, Hauptmann.* Munich: Langen Müller, 1965.

Schrott, Raoul. *Finis terrae.* Innsbruck: Haymon, 1995.

Schubert, Werner. "'Quid dolet haec?': Zur Sappho-Gestalt in Ovids *Heroiden* und Christine Brückners *Ungehaltene Reden ungehaltener Frauen.*" *Antike und Abendland* 31.1 (1985): 76–96.

Schütz, Stefan. 1989. *Orestesobsession.* Trans. Jonathan Kalb. *TheatreForum* 3 (Spring 1993): 41–53.

Schweickart, Patrocinio. "Reading Ourselves: Toward a Feminist Theory of Reading." In *Speaking of Gender.* Ed. Elaine Showalter. New York: Routledge, 1989. 17–44.

Seneca. *Agamemnon.* In *Seneca: 9 Tragedies 2.* Trans. Frank Justus Miller. Loeb Classical Library. Cambridge, Mass.: Harvard University Press, 1968.

Serra, Bianca Guidetti. "Donne, violenza politica, armi: Un'esperienza giudiziaria." *Rivista di storia contemporanea* 17.2 (April 1988): 218–45.

Seyffert, Oskar. *Dictionary of Classical Antiquities.* Rev. and ed. Henry Nettleship and J. E. Sandys. New York: Meridian Books, 1956.

Seymour, Miranda. *The Goddess.* New York: Coward, McCann, and Geoghegan, 1979.

Showalter, Elaine. *The Female Malady: Women, Madness, and English Culture, 1830–1980.* New York: Pantheon Books, 1985.

———. "Feminist Criticism in the Wilderness." In *The New Feminist Criticism: Essays* on Women, Literature, and Theory. Ed. Elaine Showalter. New York: Pantheon, 1985. 243–70.

————. *A Literature of Their Own: British Women Novelists from Brontë to Lessing.* Princeton: Princeton University Press, 1977.

Siegel, Janice. *Oresteia.* "A photo from Dr. J's Illustrated Aeschylus' *Oresteia.*" <http://nimbus.temple.edu/-jsiegel/texts/oresteia/0017.htm>.

Smith, Barbara. "The Truth That Never Hurts: Black Lesbians in Fiction in the 1980s." In *Wild Women in the Whirlwind: Afra-American Culture and the Contemporary Literary Renaissance.* Ed. Joanne Braxton and Andreé Nicola McLaughlin. New Brunswick: Rutgers University Press, 1990.

Smith, Stevie. "I Had a Dream . . ." In *The Frog Prince.* London: Longmans, 1966. 17–19.

Solanas, Valerie. 1967. *SCUM Manifesto.* San Francisco: AK Press, 1996.

Sommerstein, Alan H. "Again Klytaimestra's Weapon." *Classical Quarterly* 39.2 (1989): 296–301.

Sophocles. *Sophocles 2: "Ajax," "The Women of Trachis," "Electra," and "Philoctetes."* Trans. John Moore, Michael Jameson, and David Grene. Chicago: University of Chicago Press, 1969.

Spacks, Patricia Ann Meyer. *The Female Imagination.* New York: Knopf, 1975.

Sprigath, Gabriele. "Frauen und Männer und die Wirklichkeit der Kunst." *Kürbiskern* 4 (1983): 147–54.

Stephan, Alexander. "Christa Wolf." In *Neue Literatur der Frauen: Deutschsprachige Autorinnen der Gegenwart.* Ed. Heinz Puknus. Munich: Beck, 1980. 149–58, 238–42.

————. *Christa Wolf.* Expanded ed. Munich: Beck, 1991.

Stephan, Inge, and Sigrid Weigel, eds. *Feministische Literaturwissenschaft.* Berlin: Argument-Verlag, 1984.

————, eds. *Die verborgene Frau.* Berlin: Argument-Verlag, 1983.

Stesichorus. "Helen and Klytaimestra." In *Greek Lyrics.* Trans. Richmond Lattimore. Chicago: University of Chicago Press, 1949. 23.

Stone, Merlin. *Ancient Mirrors of Womanhood: A Treasury of Goddesses and Heroine Lore from around the World.* Boston: Beacon Press, 1984.

————. *When God Was a Woman.* New York: Dial Press, 1976.

Strauss, Richard. *Elektra: Opus 58.* Libretto by Hugo von Hofmannsthal. Music by Richard Strauss. London: Boosey and Hawkes, 1943.

Sumeli Weinberg, Maria Grazia. "An Interview with Dacia Maraini." *Tydskrif vir letterkunde* 27.3 (August 1989): 64–72.

Suzuki, Mihoko. *Metamorphoses of Helen: Authority, Difference, and the Epic.* Ithaca: Cornell University Press, 1989.

Terry, Walter. *Frontiers of Dance: The Life of Martha Graham.* New York: Thomas Y. Crowell, 1975.

Thackeray, William Makepeace. *Vanity Fair.* London: Bradbury and Evans, 1848.

Tietze, Christopher. *Induced Abortion: A World Review.* New York: Alan Guttmacher Institute, 1986.

Tripp, Edward. *The Meridian Handbook of Classical Mythology.* New York: New American Library, 1970.

Vogelsang, Laurie Melissa. "Killa's Tertium: Christa Wolf and Cassandra." In *Responses to Christa Wolf.* Ed. Marilyn Sibley Fries. Detroit: Wayne State University Press, 1989. 367–77.

Wagner, Rudolf G. "On Christa Wolf's *Cassandra.*" In *History: Another Text.* Ed. Marianna D. Birnbaum and R. Trager-Verchovsky. Ann Arbor: University of Michigan Press, 1988.

Walker, Barbara G. *The Woman's Encyclopedia of Myths and Secrets.* San Francisco: Harper and Row, 1983.

Warner, Marina. *Six Myths of Our Time.* New York: Vintage Books, 1995.

Weedman, Jane B., ed. *Women Worldwalkers: New Dimensions of Science Fiction and Fantasy.* Lubbock: Texas Tech Press, 1985.

Wehr, Demaris S. "Religious and Social Dimensions of Jung's Concept of Archetype: A Feminist Perspective." In *Feminist Archetypal Theory: Interdisciplinary Re-Visions of Jungian Thought.* Ed. Estella Lauter and Carol Schreier Rupprecht. Knoxville: University of Tennessee Press, 1985. 23–45.

Weigel, Sigrid. "Double Focus: On the History of Women's Writing." Trans. Harriet Anderson. In *Feminist Aesthetics.* Ed. Gisela Ecker. Boston: Beacon Press, 1985. 59–80. Originally published as "Der schielende Blick: Thesen zur Geschichte weiblicher Schreibpraxis." In *Die verborgene Frau: Sechs Beiträge zur einer feministischen Literaturwissenschaft.* Berlin: Argument-Verlag, 1983. 83–137.

———. "Vom Sehen zur Seherin: Christa Wolfs Umdeutung des Mythos und die Spur der Bachmann-Rezeption in ihrer Literatur." *Text und Kritik* 46 (3d expanded ed.) (1985): 67–92.

Whitmont, Edward C. *Return of the Goddess.* New York: Crossroad Publishing, 1982.

Winnett, Susan. "Coming Unstrung: Women, Men, Narrative, and Principles of Pleasure." *PMLA* 105.3 (1990): 505–18.

Winnington-Ingram, R. P. *Studies in Aeschylus.* Cambridge: Cambridge University Press, 1983.

Wittig, Monique. *Les guérillères.* Trans. David Levay. London: P. Owen, 1971. Originally published as *Les guérillères.* Paris: Éditions de Minuit, 1969.

Wolf, Christa. *Accident: A Day's News.* Trans. Heike Schwarzbauer and Rick Takvorian. New York: Farrar, Straus, and Giroux, 1989. Originally published as *Störfall: Nachrichten eines Tages.* Berlin: Aufbau-Verlag, 1987.

———. *Cassandra: A Novel and Four Essays.* Trans. Jan van Heurck. New York: Farrar, Straus, and Giroux, 1984. Originally published as *Kassandra.* Darmstadt: Luchterhand, 1983; and *Voraussetzungen einer Erzählung: Kassandra.* Darmstadt: Luchterhand, 1983.

———. "Documentation: Christa Wolf." *German Quarterly* 57.1 (1984): 91–115.

———. *Medea: A Modern Retelling.* Trans. John Cullen. New York: Nan A. Talese, 1998. Originally published as *Medea: Stimmen.* Darmstadt: Luchterhand, 1996.

———. *A Model Childhood.* Trans. Ursule Molinaro and Hedwig Rappolt. New York: Farrar, Straus, and Giroux, 1980. Rpt. as *Patterns of Childhood,* 1984. Originally published as *Kindheitsmuster.* Berlin: Aufbau-Verlag, 1976.

———. *The Quest for Christa T.* Trans. Christopher Middleton. New York: Farrar, Straus, and Giroux, 1970. Originally published as *Nachdenken über Christa T.* Halle, Germany: Mitteldeutscher Verlag, 1968.

———. *What Remains and Other Stories.* Trans. Heike Schwarzbauer and Rick Takvorian. New York: Farrar, Straus, and Giroux, 1993. Originally published as *Was bleibt: Erzählung.* Berlin: Aufbau-Verlag, 1990.

Women's Global Network for Reproductive Rights. "Defending the Law in Italy." *Women's Global Network for Reproductive Rights Newsletter* 31 (October–December 1989): 28.

Yaeger, Patricia. "'Because Fire Was in My Head': Eudora Welty and the Dialogic Imagination." *PMLA* 99.5 (1984): 995–1073.

Yalom, Marilyn. *Maternity, Mortality, and the Literature of Madness.* University Park: Pennsylvania State University Press, 1985.

Yourcenar, Marguerite. *Fires.* Trans. Dori Katz in collaboration with the author. Chicago: University of Chicago Press, 1994. Originally published as *Feux.* Paris: Librairie Plon, 1936. Reissued, Paris: Gallimard, 1974.

Zabuzhko, Oksana. "Clytemnestra." *A Hundred Years of Youth: A Bilingual Anthology of Twentieth Century Ukrainian Poetry.* Ed. Olha Luchuk and Michael M. Naydan. L'viv, Ukraine: Litopys, 2000. Originally published as *Avtostop.* Kiev: Ukrains'kyi pysmennyk, 1994.

Zei, Alki. *Achilles Fiancée.* Athens: Kedros, 1987.

Zeitlin, Froma I. "The Dynamics of Misogyny: Myth and Mythmaking in the *Oresteia.*" *Arethusa* 11.1–2 (Spring/Fall 1978): 149–84.

Zeller, Konradin. "Christa Reinig." In *Neue Literatur der Frauen: Deutschsprachige Autorinnen der Gegenwart.* Ed. Heinz Puknus. Beck'sche Schwarze Reihe 227. Munich: Beck, 1980. 200–208.

Ziolkowski, Theodore. *The Mirror of Justice: Literary Reflections of Legal Crises.* Princeton: Princeton University Press, 1997.

Index

Main entries for characters use classicist spellings. Characters' names in subentries are spelled as they appear in the revisionist work being cited.

Wolf's borrowings from, 109–10, 151n13; Wolf's critique of, 110–12

Orestes (Klytemnestra's son), 25–26; acquittal of, as rationalization, 110–11; capitalist success of, 84; Clytemnestra's reconciliation with, 63, 64–65, 96–97, 98; eponymous billing of, 30; in Euripides' *Orestes*, 54n36; incest/misogyny of, 85–86; matricidal motivations of, 35–36; nonblood killing by, 37, 38–39, 53n25; in *Odyssey*, 29; realigned gender attitudes of, 47–48; in Schütz's play, 189n5; social guilt of, 140, 153n39; in Sophocles' *Electra*, 42–43; as trauma survivor, 46–47, 54n35; and Web site culture, 166; Web site named for, 156–57

Orestes (Euripides), 54n36, 156

Orestesobsession (Schütz), 189n5

Orgasm, mature versus immature, 87; joint male/female (Cardinal), 122–23

Origins: of Athenian citizenship, 9–10, 27–28; of *labrys*, 25; of legal system, 26–27, 30, 38, 52–53n20, 53n21; revisionist challenge to, 14–15

Ostriker, Alicia, 7

Pandora (first female), 9

Papas, Irene, 56

Le passé empiété (Backstitch; or, The Past Reappropriated; Cardinal), 5; child sacrifice in, 119, 120, 146; classical/modern dialogue of, 123, 124–27, 174–75; double vision of, 173; economic castration in, 120, 147; embroidery/creativity in, 79, 119–20, 152n28; embroidery/revision in, 126–30; father figure of, 128–29; female voice of, 150, 183; gender dialogic of, 185, 186, 187; gender fusions in, 118, 121–23, 149; as hybrid text, 148; isolation solution of, 174–75; marriage options in, 130, 146; title of, 105n30, 126–27; trauma recast in, 129–30, 149–50, 168, 179; violence concern in, 148. *See also* Cardinal, Marie

Passerini, Luisa, 106n39

Patriarchy: Athena's appropriation by, 8–11, 20n11, 21n16; cultural persistence of, 168–69, 171; dreams of, in Maraini, 89; Electra's loyalty to, 36, 49; Freudian plot of, 88–89, 175; insanity response to, 84, 105n33; Kassandra's visions of, 109, 110, 151n13; of literary tradition, 3–4, 7–8, 17, 117; marriage ploy of, 39, 45–46, 80–81, 139, 145; motherhood's fusion with, 128; motherhood's threat to, 37–39, 44, 48–49,

53n25; origins of, 26–28, 30, 39–40, 51n7, 51n8, 52–53n20, 53n21, 53–54n28; popular culture experience of, 141–43; religion's restoration of, 85; reversal of, in *The Fabulous Furies reVue*, 144, 147; reversal of, in Reinig, 71, 72–73; submissive/receptive female of, 70–71, 73, 86–87, 97; suffering into knowledge strategy of, 111; traumatic effects of, 178–79; on Web site, 166–67; women's complicity with, 8–9, 84, 175–76. *See also* Literary tradition; Myths; Western culture

Patterson, Cynthia B., 53–54n28

Pearson, Carol Lynn, 111, 151n14, 173

Pelops (Tantalus's son), 31

Penelope (Odysseus's wife), 28, 52n15, 80, 152n28

Penelope, a infanta (Sampaio), 5

Penelope: Légènde et mythe (Mactoux), 5

Penelope alla guerra (Fallaci), 5

Penis: as death symbol, 94; as male dominance symbol, 78, 88, 97; and penis envy, 53n25, 86

"A Penny for Her Thoughts" (Hadas), 5

"The People vs. Clytemnestra" (Web site): feminist perspective on, 165–66; gender assumptions of, 166–67; home page of, 161–62; trial testimony of, 164–65, 169n6

"A Photo from Dr. J's Illustrated Aeschylus's *Oresteia*" (Web screen), 167–68, 170n9

Pindar, 54n32

Piper, Judith, 5–6, 14, 141. *See also The Fabulous Furies reVue*

Plath, Sylvia, 20n7

"Poetik-Vorlesungen" (Wolf), 116–17

Pomeroy, Sarah, 20n8

Priam (Kassandra's father), 109, 115, 145

Princess and Prophetess of Troy (Molinaro), 5

Problems of Dostoevsky's Poetics (Bakhtin), 16

Pythia, the, 37–38

The Queen of Swords (Grahn), 5

The Queen of Wands (Grahn), 5

Rabelais and His World (Bakhtin), 16

Rabinowitz, Nancy, 20n8, 60

Ragué i Arias, Maria-Josep, 5, 103n5, 153–54n40

Rape, 76, 78

Reagan, Ronald, 57, 58

Recuyell of the Historyes of Troye (Lefèvre), 55

KATHLEEN L. KOMAR is a professor of comparative literature and German at the University of California at Los Angeles, where she has also served as the associate dean of the Graduate Division. She is the author of *Transcending Angels: Rainer Maria Rilke's "Duino Elegies"* and *Pattern and Chaos: Multilinear Novels by Dos Passos, Faulkner, Döblin, and Koeppen,* and the coeditor (with Ross Shideler) of *Lyrical Symbols and Narrative Transformations.*

The University of Illinois Press
is a founding member of the
Association of American University Presses.

Composed in 10.5/13 Adobe Minion
by Jim Proefrock
at the University of Illinois Press
Manufactured by Thomson-Shore, Inc.

University of Illinois Press
1325 South Oak Street
Champaign, IL 61820-6903
www.press.uillinois.edu